BODACIOUS HUMAN CAPITAL

The Tiara of KNOWLEDGE MANAGEMENT

BODACIOUS HUMAN CAPITAL

The Tiara of KNOWLEDGE MANAGEMENT

Krishna Nath Pandey & Chhaya Yadav

ZORBA BOOKS

ZORBA BOOKS

Publishing Services by Zorba Books, November 2020

Website: www.zorbabooks.com
Email: info@zorbabooks.com
Contact: 0124-4259579 / 8800509579

Print Book ISBN: 978-93-90011-68-1
Ebook ISBN: 978-93-90011-69-8

Zorba Books Pvt. Ltd. (opc)
Sushant Arcade,
Next to Courtyard Marriot,
Sushant Lok 1, Gurgaon – 122009, India

Dedicated To
Dr Picheswar Gadde, Chancellor, Lingaya's Vidyapeeth,
the doyen of higher education in the global domain

Acknowledgement

I would like to express my deep and sincere gratitude to Dr Picheswar Gadde, Chancellor, Lingaya's University and Dr Anil Roy Dubey, Vice-Chancellor, Lingaya's University for their inspiring the author to pen this book. Three great individuals- My eldest brother Late Sankata Pandey, Mr B.K Banerjee my mentor in NTPC and POWERGRID and Late Ram Naresh Tiwari my father-in-law for shaping me what I am today. I am indebted to these three great minds for initiating me in the field of Knowledge Management.

Ananya Ganesh, my grand-daughter is an internal source of my happiness Thank you Pranu. The three persons - my wife Mrs. Mala Pandey, daughters Neha Pandey and Medha Pandey - sacrificed their precious time for enabling me to concentrate on this book. A huge thank you to the trio. Thanks are also due to my son-in-law Ganesh Krishna Murthy for supporting me through thick and thin of my intellectual dangling.

Last but not the least my brothers N.M Pandey and V.M Pandey and sisters-in-law Malati, Satyabhama superimposed by Raghumati deserve my sincere gratitude. Thanks to my foster mother Kamla Sahani, Chandan Chaudhari, IPS and her husband Govind Jaiswal, IAS in Itanagar were making me to feel very young, without which this book could not have seen the light of the day Thanks Folks.

- Krishna Nath Pandey

First and foremost, praises and thanks to my guru, Nityanand Swamiji for his shower blessings throughout my research work and this book. I am overwhelmed in all humbleness and gratefulness to acknowledge my depth to my parents - Mrs. Sonia Yadav and Mr. Sanjay Yadav, who helped me alot in gathering different information, date and guiding me time to time in writing down this book. My heartiest thanks to my loving brother Bharat Yadav, who always helped me to put these ideas, well above the level of simplicity and into something concrete. And lastly, my uncle Rajiv Yadav who provided all the support needed for penning down this book, my reverence to him!

- Chhaya Yadav

Preface

This book provides an overview of the authors' thoughts and perspective on Human Capital. Human Capital may be defined as the sum total of attitude and skills required for accomplishing a task that comes into existence because of education, exposure and experience. The Human Capital is part of Intellectual which is the most important part of the three components of Intellectual Capital and the rest two are known as Structural or Organizational and Social Capital. The management of Human Capital is dependent on, and; is an integral part of the Knowledge Management coupled with emerging field of Wisdom Management.

This book is an endeavor to trace the interrelatedness of the Human Capital as a part of Knowledge Management (KM) as depicted in Rigveda ('Ved' means Knowledge) and is in consonance with the latest trend of KM as on date. Though the Indian i.e. oriental thought, as envisaged in Rigveda has delineated the KM under *Shruti Tradition* depicting the mantra of KM which is described in 1.81.1. In a way, knowledge was recorded during C. 1500-1200 BCE which is known as Rigveda; but the same was relegated to the oblivion till Ralph T.H. Griffith translated Rigveda into English in 1912 subsequent to its earlier translation into German in 1845 by Max Muller. The usefulness of this ancient KM into the modern KM as propounded by IT Companies in 1996 onwards led by the successful implementation of KM in Microsoft, and it started; a chain of KM as an effective tool for optimization for C - Suite executives in corporate world across the globe. This new form of KM has been implemented by almost all the modern organizations.This book is an attempt to pinpoint the ways, tools, drivers,in addition to; the skills required by the managers in implementing KM in an organization in 21st Century besides underlining the prominence of Human Capital as an eternal source for remaining at the pinnacle.

Contents

CHAPTER 1

INTRODUCTION

1.1 INTRODUCTION

Today, in the global scenario, Knowledge Management is accorded critical importance because it is the key for global economic transformation, innovation and sustainable competitive advantage. Knowledge Management has emerged as an important factor of economic growth of countries in the global economy as it is the basis of innovation within organizations. It is also posited as an important source of wealth and competitiveness within the organization as it proffers new capabilities, innovativeness and performance leading to enhanced customer value. In this context, several eminent researchers have drawn upon and defined Knowledge Management in varied ways as the capability to manage knowledge, such as gathering internal or external knowledge of organizations; converting them to new ideas or strategy and applying them and guarding them (Gold et al., 2001).

It is a systematic, explicit and application of knowledge that will help the organizations to maximize the knowledge-related effectiveness and returns from the knowledge assets (Lytras et al., 2002). "Knowledge Management is also defined as a process of capturing, storing, sharing and using knowledge (Chang & Lin, 2015)." It had been emphasized earlier also by scholars (Leidner et. al. 2006).

Thus, in essence, it can be stated that Knowledge Management comprises of the processes related to the creation, acquisition, collation, sharing, use, reuse and capitalization of knowledge in an organization (Audretsch, et. al; 2020).

Besides, it can also be defined as a systematic process for gathering, organizing and communicating both tacit and explicit knowledge of employees which can be used in their works (Schultze & Leidner, 2002; Alavi et al., 2005; Massey & Montoya-Weiss, 2006). There are four main elements and processes in Knowledge Management (Kayworth & Leidner, 2003; Zaim, 2006; Fong & Choi, 2009; Turner et al., 2012), as delineated below-

1. Knowledge Creation and Knowledge Acquisition,
2. Knowledge Storage,
3. Knowledge Dissemination and Knowledge Transfer,
4. Knowledge Application.

Organizations are able to gain, maintain and leverage their knowledge resources by turning to Knowledge Management initiatives and technologies (Kankanhalli et al., 2005; Greiner et al., 2007). Thus, the main goal of Knowledge Management is to enable the organizations to be aware of their knowledge and update the requisite knowledge entailing the processes of storing and archiving the knowledge, so that they can effectively and efficiently use knowledge (Newell et al., 2004; Alavi et al., 2005). Griffith et al. (2003) Pawlowski and Bick (2012) asserted that the scientific understanding of knowledge in organizations is still in the nascent stage; artificial intelligence enabled development of cognitive skills could be possible to optimize Knowledge and its related assets in consonance with Knowledge Management.

Nevertheless, the importance of Knowledge Management has been recognized by researchers, who opined that it will effectuate positive outcomes of the organizations' innovation, product improvement as well as the skill sets of the employees could also be honed. (Kiesling, et. all 2011); has provided a framework to make decisions fructifying in a strategic competitive advantages for organizations which was earlier propagated by the scholars (Marques & Simon, 2006; Rahimli, 2012; Nawaz et al., 2014; Loureiro et al., 2015). Scholars had also underlined that KM leads to sustainable competitive advantage (Lee & Lan, 2011; Liu & Deng, 2015; Fierro et al., 2011; Suresh, 2012)while paving the way to create new business processes to enhance the organizations' performance simultaneously (Wu & Chen, 2014; Rasula et al., 2012; Ahmed et al., 2015).

The role and importance of Knowledge Management has been established by researchers to enhance the effectiveness and efficiency of organization's manpower (Bhatti & Qureshi, 2007; Dahiya et al., 2012; Byukusenge et. al., 2016)facilitating and enhancing organizational performance by reducing the lead time, product-to-market time, design cycle time as well as improving the product quality (Rodriguez and Edwards, 2010; Jelenic, 2011); resulting in improved customer services performance (Bueren et al., 2005; Guchait et al., 2011; Pension et al., 2013) and innovation management (Canongia et al., 2004; Dickel & Moura, 2016; Storck and Hill, 2000; Jones & Linderman, 2014).

Taking cognizance of these positive outcomes leads to the strategic alignment of modern organizations to adopt Knowledge Management practices as its core function for gaining sustainable competitive advantage. However, Knowledge Management has to be examined.

Intricately for its evolution by deciphering its origin for implementation by organizations in a comprehensive way apropos the culture of that organization. For the successful implementation and optimal utilization of Knowledge Management, the organizations must have a clear understanding on how knowledge has been organized, disseminated and applied within organizations (Ipe, 2003; Hooff & Huysman, 2009). Knowledge acquired from inside and outside of the organizations needs to be assimilated strategically and imbibed through the practices and cultural domain in response to the environmental forces acting upon it.

The Knowledge Management implementation theorists have elaborated various phases and generations of Knowledge Management. Phases include 'assembly of a realization team, analysis of the initial state, and creation of a knowledge strategy and realization of Knowledge Management activities' (Bures, 2009). There are three generations of Knowledge Management- the first generation, which focused on timely information provisions for decision support and business process re-engineering, i.e. driven by 'IT'; the second generation initiated with the 'SECI model of Nonaka' with impetus on organizational learning and knowledge creation; and the third generation which is trying to focus on the sheer challenges in 'content management'.

In all, the manifestations of Knowledge Management whether it is Information and Communication Technology or in Artificial Intelligence; it is essentially the indispensable 'human asset' that is the main thrust in all factors in Knowledge Management through all the phases, stages and generations. So, this study primarily concentrates on the people perspective issues related with Knowledge Management implementation with special reference to POSOCO (Power System Operation Corporation Limited). Power System Operators are the backbone for management of the power supply for the benefit of the country. At present, POSOCO faces many challenges as the Indian Power Sector is undergoing a significant change which is redefining the very outlook of the industry itself. The thrust of the Government of India has come to ensure 'quality power' through optimizing the performance of assets. Knowledge Management is the only tool and the Driver of the intrinsic motivation of personnel that can enable us face these challenges. So, it is imperative to understand the Knowledge Management implementation as perceived by the internal employees for its effectiveness and viability at present and in the times to come.

1.2 THEORITICAL BACKGROUND

Knowledge Management has pervaded organizations globally and the Indian Power Sector is no exception to this. So, here we discuss the theoretical background that pertains to i) Definitions of Knowledge Management, ii) Models of Knowledge Management, iii) Processes involved in Knowledge Management; and iv) Organizational aspects of Knowledge Management. These are depicted below to provide the backdrop of the conceptual and process related evolution for Knowledge Management in its present avtar.

1.2.1 Definitions of Knowledge Management

In the first place, it is pertinent to define Knowledge Management to gain insight into its meaning, process, components and scope for implementation in organizations. The prominent definitions of Knowledge Management are delineated ahead. Bukowitz, W.R. & Williams, R.L.(1999) elaborated that "Knowledge Management is the process by which the organization generates wealth from its intellectual or knowledge-based assets" Alavi, M & Leidner, D.E. (2002) added that "Knowledge Management, refers to a systemic and organizationally specific process for acquiring, organizing and communicating both tacit and explicit knowledge of employees so that other employees may make use of it to be more effective and productive in their work".

Conway, S. & Sligar, C. (2002) propounded that "Knowledge Management is not a new term. Over the past decade it has become a generic phrase used to refer to many types of information exchange between people however, Knowledge Management has a specific meaning: the process of revealing and mapping the work activities, behaviors and knowledge sources within an organization". O' Dell, C. (2004) elaborated Knowledge Management as a "Systematic approaches to help information and knowledge flow to the right people at the right time so they can act more efficiently and effectively. Find, understand, share and use knowledge to create value".

Brelade, S. & Harman, C. (2006) were of the opinion that "Common to the various definitions were the two dimensions of people and information. Knowledge Management lies in the relationship of these two dimensions, mediated by systems and processes. It is generally seen as a holistic approach which recognizes the inter-dependency for the organizational effectiveness of people, the technology they use and the systems and processes within which they use it".

Hawryszkiewycz, I. (2010) added that "Knowledge, however; is more difficult to define - one is to see it as using information to make decisions. Knowledge is more on knowing how to interpret information and providing new insights to some problems at hand. It is often using previous experience to interpret the information and use the interpretation to initiate some action it is also the ability to transfer knowledge and experience from one context to another". Desouza, K.C. & Paquette, S. (2011) "Knowledge Management is about increasing an organization's effectiveness through application of its Knowledge assets. It is important to note that Knowledge Management is not exclusive to any particular type of organization. Organizations of all types must manage their Knowledge if they are to adequately perform in their environments. No matter what their missions, all organizations have Knowledge assets that need to be leveraged".

Durmusoglu, S. et.al. (2014) elaborated that, "The growing use of knowledge in business contributed to the emergence of the theory of Knowledge Management. Knowledge Management activities can be conceptualized as actuators stimulating the development of new knowledge for the purpose of achieving objectives through identifying, capturing, reusing and leveraging pertinent knowledge. The purpose of Knowledge Management activities in organizations is to ensure growth and continuity of performance by protecting critical knowledge at all levels, applying existing knowledge in all circumstances, combining knowledge in synergistic ways, acquiring relevant knowledge continuously and developing new knowledge through continuous learning".

Pandey, K.N. (2016) in his research clarified and elaborated the inter-relatedness of various interchangeable terms and provided the crystal clear definition. He stated that, "By looking at the semantic and professional points, it can be concluded that data has got universal value, but it remains meaningless until it is put to some context. Once the data gets contextualized, it attains meaning and metamorphoses itself into information which can be used. The apt and appropriate use of information at the right moment may be termed as knowledge. These inferences are strictly deduced apropos managerial repertoire. With this perspective, wisdom can be seen as that faculty of mind which ensures maximum returns from the probabilities". Johnsen, M. (2020) provided the evolved definition of KM as "Overall, Knowledge Management is an activity restraint that promotes a shared and integrative move toward the establishment, capture, organization, admission and use of information resources, including the inferred, un-captured knowledge of people. It is the course of action of converting information and rational assets into long-term significance. In an organizational setting that would mean a methodical move toward getting a business to make the best possible use of knowledge in implementing its undertaking, roughly viewed as either sustainable competitive improvement or lasting high routine"

To summarize the above definitions abounding Knowledge Management, it is seen that there is no one common universally accepted definition of Knowledge Management. However, most of these definitions assert the reuse of individual and organizational knowledge by the people who need them in time. The main crux lies in unraveling the complexity involved in the aspects of Knowledge Management in an organization i.e. creation, acquisition, collation, updation, dissemination, use, reuse, sharing and capitalization of knowledge assets.

1.2.2 Knowledge Management Models

A Knowledge Management (KM) model is a structured way to look at the process of Knowledge Management used by an organization in order to investigate its properties and tailoring it to the organization's specific needs. There are many models, the important ones are explained below:-

1.2.2.1 Socialisation, Externalisation, Combination and Internalisation Model

This model was proposed by Nonaka and Takeuchi (1995) which is recognized as a key model for explaining knowledge creation and knowledge transfer theory. As per this, there are four ways that knowledge types can be combined and converted in an organization. The model is based on the two types of knowledge only i.e. tacit and explicit.

The model states the Four Modes of Knowledge Conversion, as:-

- Socialization (tacit to tacit),
- Externalization (tacit to explicit),
- Combination (explicit to explicit), and
- Internalization (explicit to tacit).

The SECI model is the acclaimed model of KM describing how explicit and tacit knowledge is generated, transferred, and recreated in organizations. The knowledge creation process takes place continuously and pervades all levels in the organization.

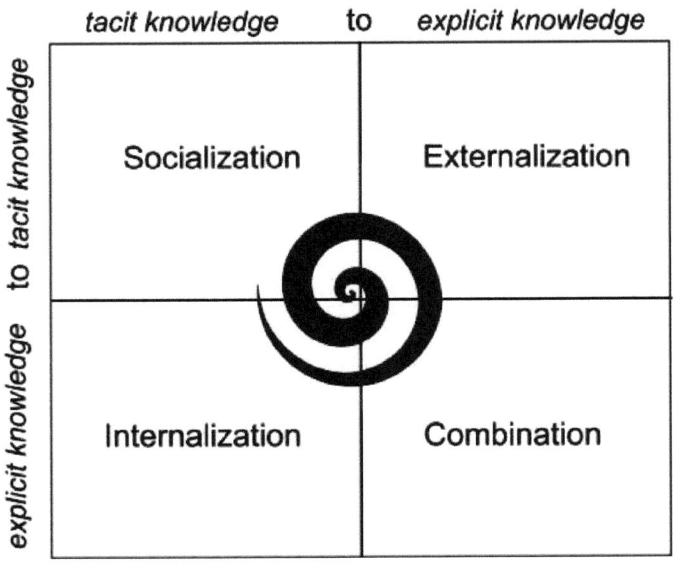

Figure 1.1: SECI model

1.2.2.2 Hierarchical Model

Prat (2006) proposed the Hierarchical model for KM that majorly assimilated the preexisting KM models of (Alavi & Leidner, 2001; Davenport and Prusak, 1998; Grover & Davenport, 2001; Nissen, *2002).* He states that "the existing KM models are often descriptive, abstract, semantic models that are frameworks." This model comprises i) Knowledge types ii) KM processes, and; iii) KM context which exhibits a hierarchy. This is better represented in the Figure 1.2.

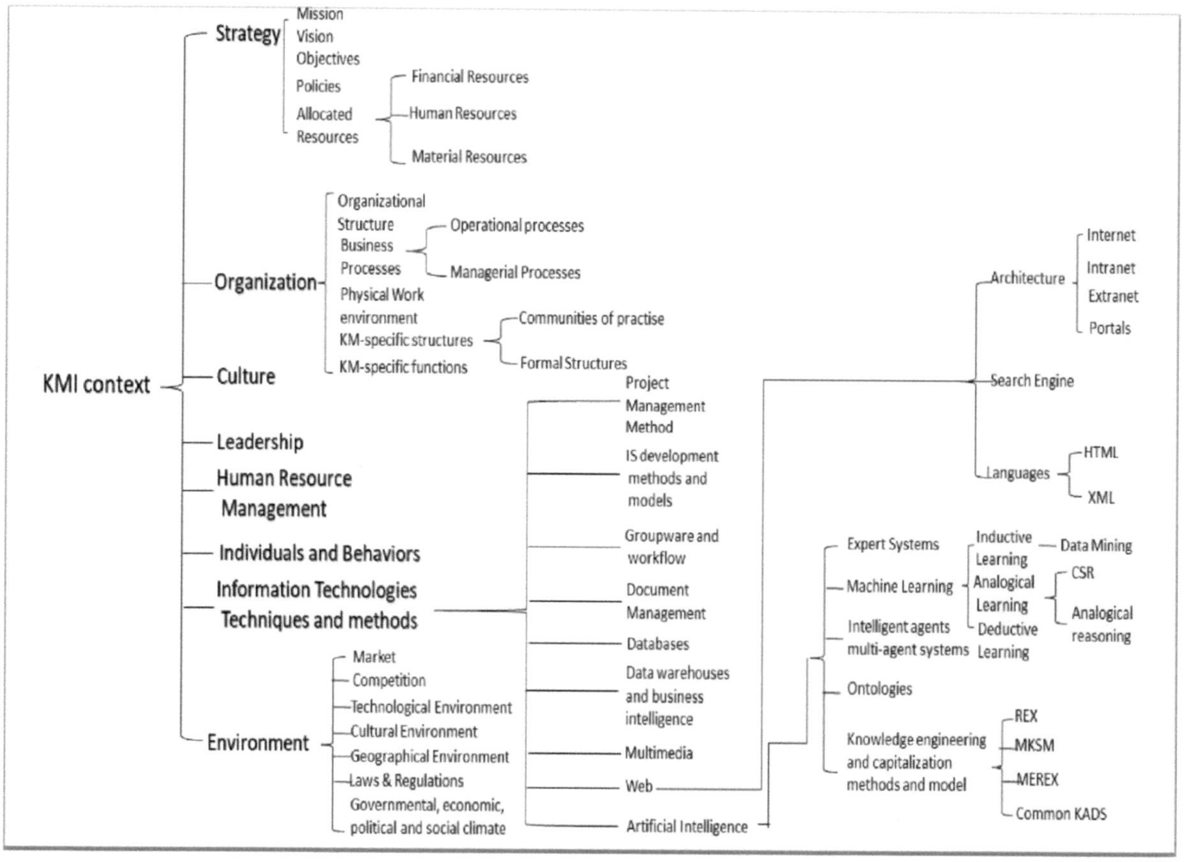

Figure 1.2: Hierarchical Model

This model introduced the quantitative assessment for the first time in the KM literature.

1.2.2.3 Process Model

In the realm of Knowledge Management, experts have emphasized the existence of knowledge as process itself. There are two representative process models under this realm which are explained and enumerated in the following paragraphs:-

a) *Process Model of Establishing KM*

Kjaergaard and Kautz (2006) through their empirical study posited the 'Process Model of KM' which "explained how the organizational members make sense of the action and behavior of management and how this understanding influences their own perceptions and actions in the process of establishing Knowledge Management. This led to the establishment of KM as an autonomous venturing process".

This model focuses on the process of conducting KM through employee's actions at organizational level. Thus, there is a 'process of establishing KM as a member-driven start up process, which emerges and develops outside the scope of the current corporate strategy'. They termed it as 'KM venturing', comprising of the 'creating process' 'process of negotiating' and 'formalizing process'. The same is depicted below:

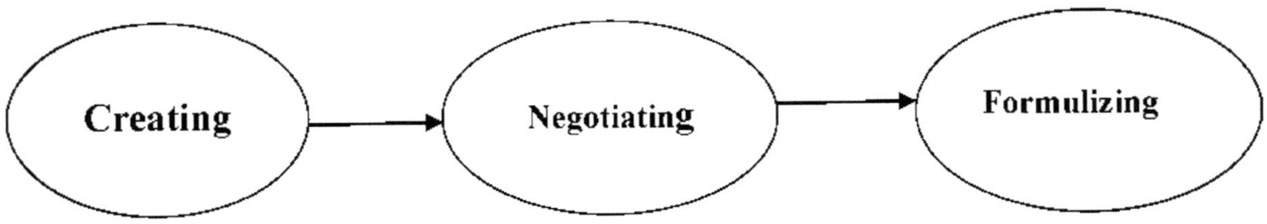

Figure 1.3: Process Model

This model is different from other process models in four ways, as explained below:-

- First, it is a process study as opposed to a variance study which emphasizes on how events, organizational members and context interact and unfold with time rather than on the relationship between dependent and independent variables and their subsequent results.
- Second, it entails a bottom up, employees driven process, contrary to the top-down management driven process.
- Third, it emphasizes the interrelationship between meaning and action rather than on action alone.
- Last but not the least, it explains an organization's identity and culture which impacts the process of KM.

b) *Process-centered KM with respect to Enterprise Development Perspective*

The enterprise perspective for process centered KM is classified into two types:- Process knowledge and Task support knowledge. Han & Park (2009) advocated 'process centered model and enterprise ontology for the development of KM system' according to which "all domain concepts are related to the process, concept", both directly and indirectly. According to them, "in order to survive in today's competitive environment, most enterprises recognize the importance of knowledge assets for attaining enterprise performance goals. However, when knowledge is separated from the context of the business process; it cannot contribute to performance goals, because knowledge is utilized and created during the execution of business processes".

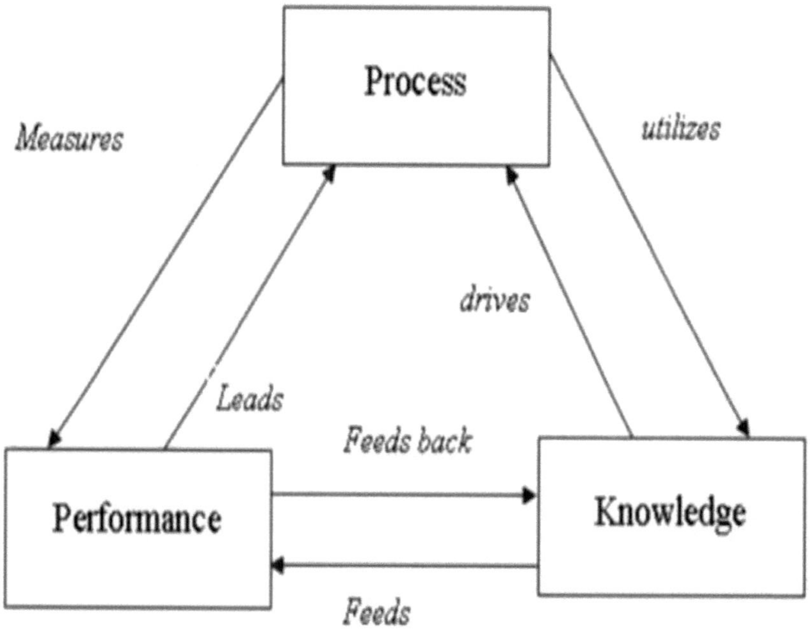

Figure 1.4: Process-Centered Perspective on Enterprise

So, "An agile and flexible structure process is a core element of business operations. Therefore, business process execution knowledge feeds performance for higher achievement, and performance leads a process to attain business goals. In turn, a business process measures performance through metrics; performance feeds back knowledge for the later use of that knowledge, and knowledge drives the process to improve day-to-day operations"

Han and Park (2009) also advocated an additional model related to the structure of the process-centered knowledge model. They have stated that "Process Knowledge is acquired and refined during and after process execution, and provides guidelines and tools for task execution". In this connection their model as depicted below reifies their ideas.

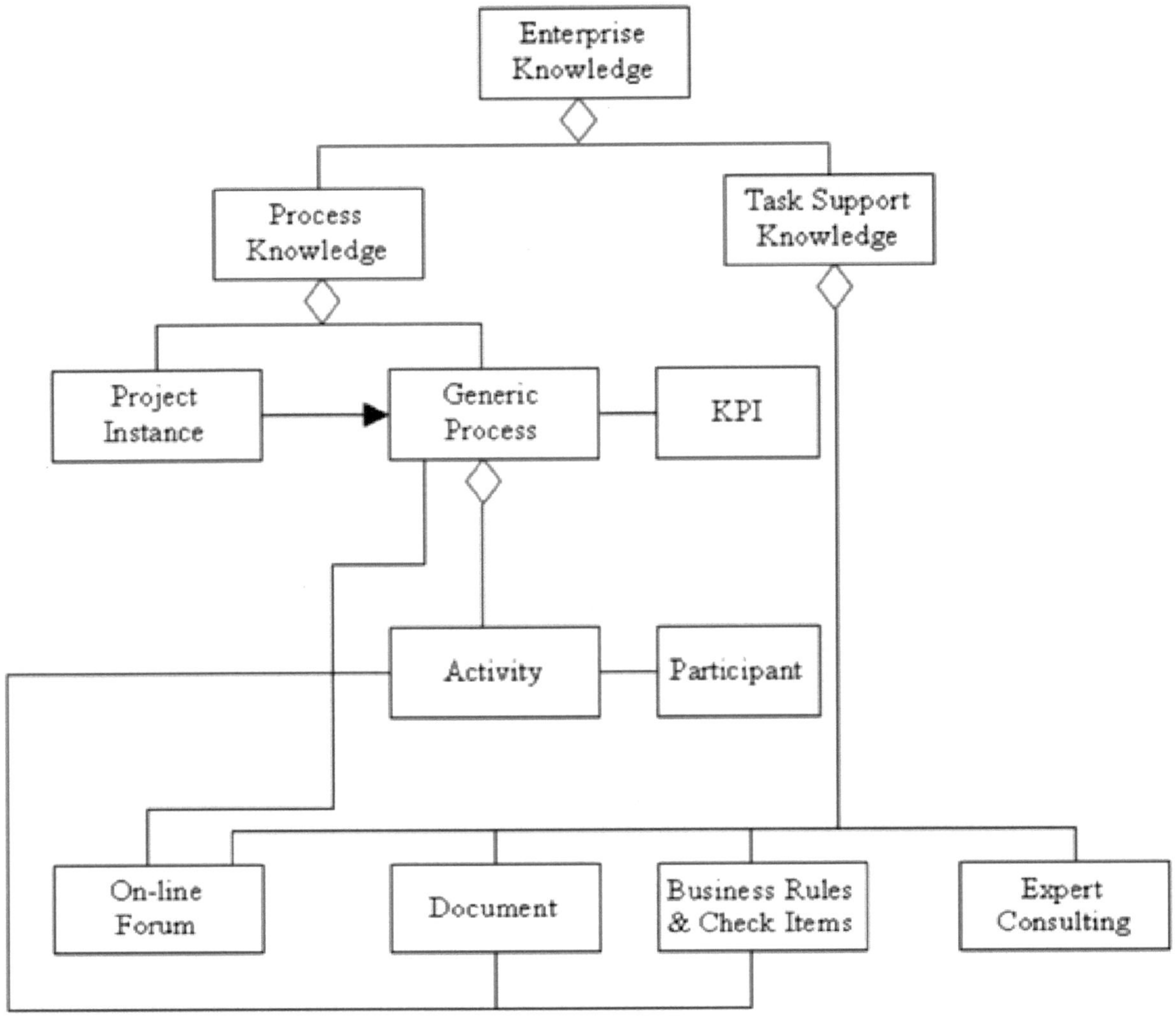

Figure 1.5: Structure of Process-Centered Knowledge Model

Process Knowledge has a KPI (Key Performance Indicator) in order to measure performance and consists of one or more activities whereas task support knowledge is required in order to make the decisions for target performance during process execution. The scholars (Han and Park, 2009) lastly proposed process-centered enterprise ontology as delineated in the following model.

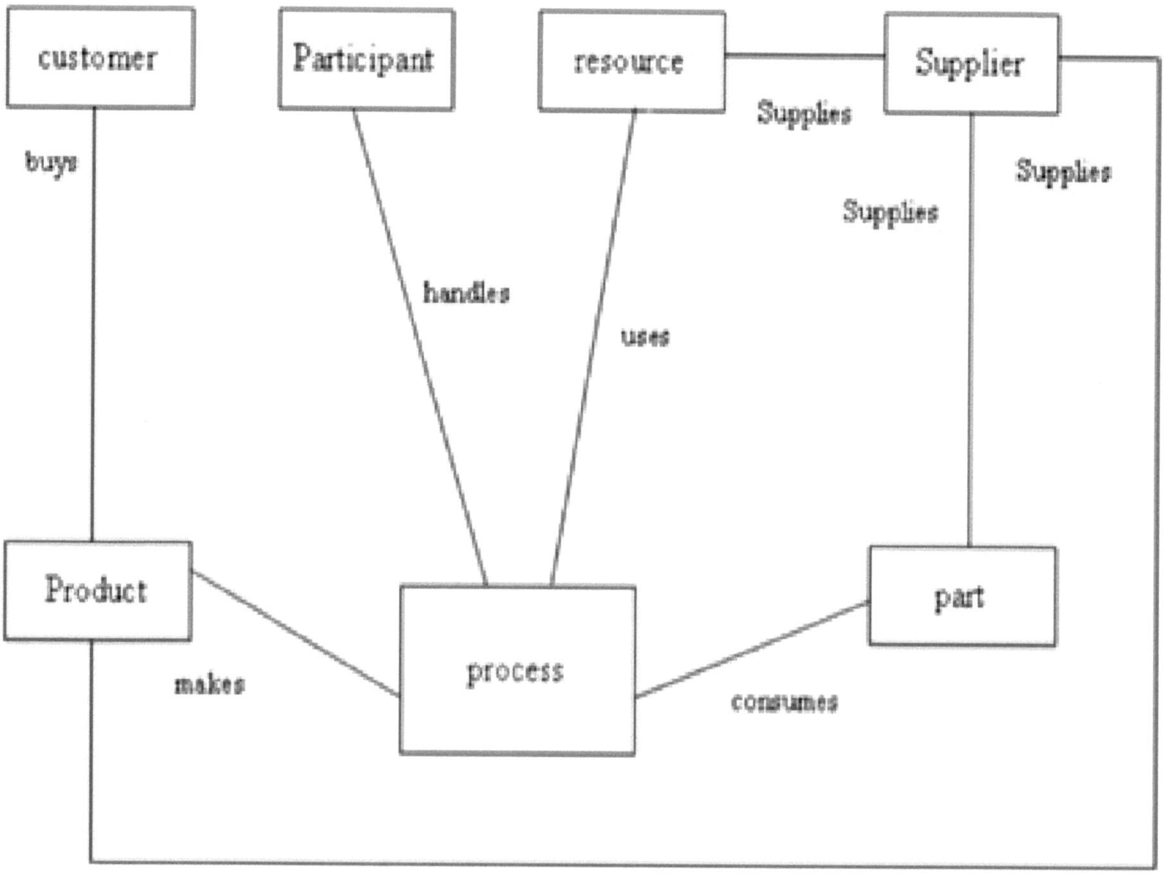

Figure 1.6: Process-Centered Enterprise Ontology

Figure 1.6 shows the proposed process-centered enterprise ontology, which represents major enterprise concepts and the relationships between them in a process-centered way. Since the 'process' concept is the element of the process-centered enterprise structure, all domain concepts are related to the 'process' concept directly or indirectly (Han and Park 2009).

1.2.3 Processes Involved in Knowledge Management

As any entity or society advances towards a knowledge economy, they make their 'living from knowledge creation and knowledge application' (Gottschalk, 2007). This entails the usage of knowledge in various forms, stages, situations and purposes. Thus, the KM process comprises of the following aspects:-

1.2.3.1 Knowledge Creation and Knowledge Acquisition

Business transactions and activities create a huge amount of data and information. In order to create value and remain in a competitive advantageous position, the firms have to create Knowledge. 'Creating knowledge requires the existence of a person or group of people who come up with new ideas, new concepts, innovative products or processes etc. (Captureanu & Captureanu, 2010). 'Thus, Knowledge creation involves a people dimension, technology dimension and the processes that link the people and technology (Wickramasinghe, 2006). Geisler and Wickramansighe (2009) summarized this aspect when they narrated that 'two conceptual streams of thought have emerged that describe knowledge creation either as a people or technology centric process'. They further report that 'Nonaka's people centric knowledge spiral is the most widely used framework for knowledge creation through socialization, combination, externalization and internalization'. By looking at various people centric models and approaches, we may infer that different organizations require different models and no single model can be quoted 'to fit all' kinds of firms. In addition to people centric approach some researchers have concluded that technology centric approach may also be used by way of mechanistic method which enables knowledge discovery in databases through data mining tools.

Knowledge Acquisition is an activity which explores the possibility of finding expertise which should be acquired from outside through 'relationship with customers, suppliers, competitors and partners in co-operative ventures' (Probst et. al., 2002). It means it is the prerequisite of Knowledge Acquisition 'to identify the required knowledge domains in alignment with the Knowledge Management strategy, locate the source of this knowledge and acquire the required knowledge' (Shukla & Srinivasan, 2002). Of late, firms have been increasingly interested in inter firm relations and want to develop proximity with the outside world. Martinez-Canas et.al. (2012) have reported that 'the resource based view of the firm posits that intangible resources that are valuable, rare, imperfectly imitable and not substitutable in the long term provide a competitive advantage for organization'. They further state that the 'knowledge based view of the firm also asserts that more innovative firms must leverage their acquisition capabilities to update their knowledge capital constantly to match new environmental conditions'. With this in view, firms should have their requisite skills and ability through repeated interaction to 'recognize and evaluate' the pertinent external knowledge.

1.2.3.2 Knowledge Storage

Once knowledge has been created, acquired or collated it is to be stored in repositories so that individuals, groups and organizations can have access to it. "Empirical studies have shown that while organizations create knowledge and learn, they also forget (i.e. do not remember or lose track of the required knowledge). Thus the storage, organization and retrieval of organizational knowledge, also referred to as organizational memory; constitute an important aspect of effective organizational Knowledge Management' (Gottschalk 2007). Knowledge Storage may be done in hard copy form and electronically enabled tools or in both. The documents in hard copy form may include 'memos, reports, presentations, articles and so forth and put it into a repository where it can be easily stored and retrieved' (Davenport and Prusak, 2002).

From storage and retrieval perspective, the repositories may be classified into three main categories - i) external knowledge, ii) structured internal knowledge, and, iii) informal internal knowledge (Davenport and Prusak, 2002). Documented repository becomes handy in this regard because it is a computer based application for storing and retrieving documents in an organized way. It is generally equipped with a search engine that uses keyword matching and similar techniques to locate and retrieve documents of potential interest to users. The greater aim of Knowledge Storage is, in fact; its use in organization by personnel who require knowledge and want it at the right time and at the right place. Now-a- days most of the 'knowledge' in form of information, transaction and data are stored in Cloud also.

1.2.3.3 Knowledge Dissemination

Knowledge Dissemination has been known by various terms such as knowledge translation, knowledge transfer and knowledge exchange. It has been defined as the 'transfer of conceptually (as learning, enlightenment, or acquisition of new perspectives or attitude) or instrumentally, (in the form of modified or new) practices'. There are, however, those who see dissemination as having other legitimate outcomes.

1.2.3.4 Knowledge Application

Knowledge Application happen when the Knowledge is available is used by the organization or people to make decision and performance task which enable the organization to move ahead. In this process, the individual process the knowledge to achieve tangible goal. Some of the outcome of Knowledge Dissemination includes (1) increased awareness; (2) ability to make informed choices among alternatives; and (3) the exchange of information; materials or perspectives' (McKibbon & Lokker, 2012). Dissemination is delivering and receiving of knowledge by engaging an individual in the process of transfer of best practices, lessons learned, innovations made or improved processes etc. within the context of an organization.

1.2.4 Organizational Aspects of Knowledge Management

It has been rightly conceived by Peter F. Drucker who advocated the role of 'knowledge worker' and 'knowledge as resource' (Drucker, 2002); since then several eminent researchers (Soliman & Spooner, 2000; Mello, 2001); affirmed that Knowledge Management activities should result in improving productivity, enhancing the business environment and increasing levels of innovation. Marrewijk & Timmers (2003) also asserted that 'The HRM function assigns itself a strategically important position as a sounding board for Top management, and facilitator and change agent in the restructuring and transformation process'. Therefore, the study of HR aspects of Knowledge Management is of utmost importance especially in addressing culture, change-management, leadership, communication, motivation, training and development, reward and recognition, etc.

1.2.4.1 Culture

'Organizational Culture' refers to a system of shared meaning held by members that distinguishes the organization from other organizations. Thus, 'culture influences the way we think, what we do, how we work, and what is acceptable in the company environment'. This manifests itself in beliefs, stories and experiences of personnel; goals, norms and history of the firm; and symbols, rituals and values of the company.

In accordance with Frunham & Barrie (1993) twelve types of culture are prevalent. However, only two types of culture namely; the humanistic-helpful, affiliated culture; and approval and perfectionist culture have gained proper attention in the realm of Knowledge Management.

As per Janz and Prasaruphanich (2003) "Organizational Culture is believed to be the most significant input to effective KM and organizational learning in that corporate culture that determines values, beliefs and work systems which could encourage or impede knowledge creation and sharing". Out of the determinants of values, belief and work systems 'values are more visible'. Value orientations such as trust and collaboration, will lead to greater willingness among members to share insights and expertise with each other. To the contrary, value systems that emphasize individual power and competition among members will lead to knowledge hoarding behaviors (Alavi, and Leidner, 2002).

It is also stated that the aggressive, conciliated approaches to change do not meet the requirements of KM because they lead to 'crisis of change' and come back to 'status quo' respectively. However, corrosive and indoctrinated types which usher in 'high participation' and 'socializing' are conducive to KM. Hence, the ethical and trusting culture dimension is common to all firms for effective creation, conversion and sharing of knowledge

1.2.4.2 Structure

Structure stands for variables such as size, 'degree of specialization' in the tasks assigned to the employees and their jurisdiction and dependence on each other. It also has to take care of 'workflow' in an organization-design, work process redesign, and workplace design (Ulrich & Brockbank, 2005). As per Hendricks (2006), there is a strong 'link between knowledge and organization structure' Losey, Meisinger and Ulrich (2005) also reported that organizations flourish and performance abounds in organizations that embody winning practices. Thus, structure becomes central in KM by providing proper structure to the organization.

There are three types of organization structures which have been said to be knowledge-friendly basic structures - 'team based organization, the network structure and the hypertext organization'. The main advantage of a team based structure is that it can integrate various knowledge nuggets in a cohesive unit. Network structure allows maximum freedom to knowledge workers whereas Hypertext organization facilitates amalgamation of flexibility in a 'traditional function structure'. The 'nonhierarchical, self-organizing organizational structures' have also been said to 'encourage sharing and collaboration across boundaries within the organization' (Gold, Malhotra & Segars, 2001).

If the existing structure does not support the Knowledge Management efforts, it could be changed. Also, it has been reported that, "redesigning the company's departmental structure, coordination, span of control, reporting relationships, tasks or decision-making procedures [are] relatively quick and direct way to change an organization" (Dessler, 2003). The latest research has brought out an entirely new form of structure to deal with knowledge intensity, namely, 'knowledge-intensive organizations (KIOS)' which delineate that "Workers have high cognitive skills; workers use novel knowledge to solve complex problems; worker is held highly accountable for decisions; organization produces and sells knowledge; and organization is accredited by a self-regulated body" (Makani & Marche, 2012).

1.2.4.3 Strategy

Strategy entails planning for achieving a particular 'long term aim'. Planning per se is done by 'senior management to define a direction or the future state they wish to achieve' (Desouza & Paquette, 2011). In fact, while strategizing for Knowledge Management the continuous assessment of existing knowledge is required for its suitability for future needs which involves strategic planning. It underlines 'applying creativity to a scientifically rigorous process' which involves framing a choice, generating possibilities, specifying conditions, identifying barriers, designing tests, conducting tests and making choices. This can be taken in both the realms of formulation and implementation. In order to leverage and transform the knowledge into competitive advantages, the strategy plays a very important and critical role.

1.2.4.4 Reward, Incentives and Recognition

Compensation 'includes both monetary compensations (wages and salaries) and nonmonetary compensations (appreciation and benefits like flexible hours, homeworking, housing, insurance, sick leave, medical care, vacation, holidays, leisure activities training etc.)' The reward system should aim at rewarding 'individuals for their skills, knowledge and competencies relative to their external market value' and 'it should be individualized to fit the characteristics of individuals' (Mello, 2001).

Rewards and recognition are based on quality (Pfeffer & Sutton, 2000). 'Thus, performance management of knowledge workers is quite non- traditional. Similarly, knowledge workers require and expect immediate and frequent rewards in recognition of their good work' (Thite, 2004). Rewards, incentives and recognition should be aligned by organizations to procure the human capital of knowledge workers. Holsapple & Wu (2008) reported their research where they mentioned that "the reward of Knowledge Management would influence the performance of knowledge workers positively and if the enterprises could timely encourage staff to share knowledge and relate the contribution of sharing knowledge with performance assessment, then better outcome of knowledge sharing would be obtained for sure".

1.2.4.5 Training

Training has been seen as one of the four major, basic, fundamental activities of the functions of Human Resource Management besides sourcing of manpower, their maintenance and separation. "Training consists of planned programs designed to improve performance at the individual, group and/or organizational levels. Improved performance, in turn; implies that there have been measurable changes in knowledge, skills, attitudes, and/or social behavior" (Cascio & Nambudiri, 2010). Training and Development help to ensure that organizational members have the knowledge and skills needed to perform jobs effectively, take on new responsibilities and adapt to changing conditions' (Jones & George, 2011).

In the context of KM, Training and Development is aimed at encouraging information sharing, countering the resistance to disseminate knowledge and information, recognizing individual contribution, providing security and status for those individual contributors. It must ensure the updating of knowledge, its use, reuse and capitalization. Like any other tool, training with reference to Knowledge Management is for 'improving competence, in turning what you know into what you do. It pinpoints that training imparted should be evaluated. ' Stone (2011) has rightly concluded that, "when an evaluation is carried out, a systematic and credible process must be used to collect and analyze data and report findings, conclusions and recommendations." In this context it has been proved through research that "practitioners are keen to strengthen our understanding of challenges related to investment in knowledge and technology internally" (Brown, 2020).

With this in view, this effort has been made by the researcher; being a practitioner, to trace the trajectory of Knowledge Management in POSOCO to find out as how the implementation Knowledge Management has taken place.

1.3 CASE SELECTION AND ITS RATIONALE AND ITS RATIONALE FOR STUDY

Today, the power setup is changing faster than ever before. The achievement of a reliable and secure grid requires new rules, new technologies, and new ways of operating the power system. Closer cooperation among all players, be it generators power exchanges, power suppliers or technology providers are key factors essential optimization of the overall system. So, it is multifaceted, driven by closely knit relationships between knowledge workers and many departments that must be integrated for effective functioning. All this calls for the effective implementation of Knowledge Management in POSOCO. This may provide the tools, Drivers and motivational factors for Knowledge Management.

Power System Operation Corporation Limited (POSOCO), is an independent government company, which started operating the NLDC (National Load Dispatch Centre) and RLDCs (Regional Load Dispatch Centers) with effect from the 3rd January, 2017 in accordance with Ministry of Power (MoP) Gazette notification dated 19th December, 2016.

In POSOCO, the focus is on security & reliability. POSOCO strives to manage weather impacts and perfect generation dispatch for one of the largest power systems in the world, operating at a single frequency. Sustained growth of the Power Sector is a key parameter to drive economic development. As an impartial grid operator, POSOCO has no financial interest in any market segment. POSOCO ensures that diverse resources have equal access to the transmission network and ensure load generation balance at all times. The assets of the POSOCO mainly comprise human resources and Supervisory Control and Data Acquisition - Energy Management System (SCADA-EMS) along with software tools for all functions related to System Operation and Market Operation installed in the Control Centers of the NLDC (National Load Dispatch Centre) and RLDCs (Regional Load Dispatch Centers). This necessitates for the effective implementation of KM in POSOCO, the objectives for which are mentioned below.

1.4 OBJECTIVES OF THE STUDY

The main aim of the study is to analyze the Knowledge Management implementation in POSOCO. To achieve this, the following specific objectives are in focus in this study:

1. To examine the various 'Drivers of Knowledge Management' impacting organizational processes and structural make up for Knowledge Management orientation in POSOCO.
2. To validate the 'Drivers of Knowledge Management' in order to help in the theory- building effort of Knowledge Management Implementation.
3. To identify the relationship between the 'Drivers of Knowledge Management' and the overall 'effectiveness of KM implementation' in POSOCO.
4. To ascertain the relationship of the Drivers of KM and the overall effectiveness of KM implementation across the demographic variables.
5. To provide a Technology Acceptance Model for man-machine amelioration in the domain of Knowledge Management.

1.5 HYPOTHESIS

In this study, various KM Drivers were postulated to be related to the overall effective implementation of KM in POSOCO. So each of the Drivers, (as extracted from the results emanating through factor analysis), were taken up to constitute the corresponding hypotheses to explain.

First, was the relationship between Drivers and effective implementation of KM in POSOCO. Second, was the relationship of the Driver with the effectiveness of KM implementation across the demographic variables.

Accordingly, several hypotheses and their sub-hypotheses were articulated to present the results in a systematic manner. All the hypotheses testing in this study was conducted at 95% confidence level. The Hypotheses are presented below.

Table 1.1: Relationship between KM Drivers and effectiveness in KM implementation (Hypotheses)

S. No.	Hypothesis
1	H1a: There is a relationship between Structures and overall effectiveness of KM implementation
2	H1b: There is a relationship between Knowledge Assets and overall effectiveness of KM implementation

Table 1.1: Continue

S. No.	Hypothesis
3	H1c: There is a relationship between Processes and overall effectiveness of KM implementation
4	H1d: There is a relationship between Culture and overall effectiveness of KM implementation
5	H1e: There is a relationship between Technology and overall effectiveness of KM implementation
6	H1f: There is a relationship between Strategy and overall effectiveness of KM implementation
7	H1g: There is a relationship between Deterrents and overall effectiveness of KM implementation
8	H1h: There is a relationship between Incentives and overall effectiveness of KM implementation
9	H1i: There is a relationship between Enablers and overall effectiveness of KM implementation
10	H1j: There is a relationship between Training and overall effectiveness of KM implementation

Table 1.2: Relationship between KM Drivers and overall effectiveness of KM implementation across Genders (Hypotheses)

S. No.	Hypothesis
1	H2a: There is a relationship between Structures and overall effectiveness of KM implementation across Genders
2	H2b: There is a relationship between Assets and overall effectiveness of KM implementation across Genders
3	H2c: There is a relationship between Processes and overall effectiveness of KM implementation across Genders
4	H2d: There is a relationship between Culture and overall effectiveness of KM implementation across Genders
5	H2e: There is a relationship between Technology and overall effectiveness of KM implementation across Genders
6	H2f: There is a relationship between Strategy and overall effectiveness of KM implementation across Genders

Table 1.2: Continue

S. No.	Hypothesis
7	H2g: There is a relationship between Deterrents and overall effectiveness of KM implementation across Genders
8	H2h: There is a relationship between Incentives and overall effectiveness of KM implementation across Genders
9	H2i: There is a relationship between Enablers and overall effectiveness of KM implementation across Genders
10	H2j: There is a relationship between Training and overall effectiveness of KM implementation across Genders

Table 1.3: Relationship between KM Drivers and overall effectiveness of KM implementation across various Age Groups (Hypotheses)

S. No.	Hypothesis
1	H3a: There is a relationship between Structures and overall effectiveness of KM implementation across various Age Groups
2	H3b: There is a relationship between Assets and overall effectiveness of KM implementation across various Age Groups
3	H3c: There is a relationship between Processes and overall effectiveness of KM implementation across various Age Groups
4	H3d: There is a relationship between Culture and overall effectiveness of KM implementation across various Age Groups
5	H3e: There is a relationship between Technology and overall effectiveness of KM implementation across various Age Groups
6	H3f: There is a relationship between Strategy and overall effectiveness of KM implementation across various Age Groups
7	H3g: There is a relationship between Deterrents and overall effectiveness of KM implementation across various Age Groups
8	H3h: There is a relationship between Incentives and overall effectiveness of KM implementation across various Age Groups
9	H3i: There is a relationship between Enablers and overall effectiveness of KM implementation across various Age Groups
10	H3j: There is a relationship between Training and overall effectiveness of KM implementation across various Age Groups

Table 1.4: Relationship between KM Drivers and overall effectiveness of KM implementation across the levels of Education (Hypotheses)

S. No.	Hypothesis
1	H4a: There is a relationship between Structures and overall effectiveness of KM implementation across the levels of Education
2	H4b: There is a relationship between Assets and overall effectiveness of KM implementation across the levels of Education
3	H4c: There is a relationship between Processes and overall effectiveness of KM implementation across the levels of Education
4	H4d: There is a relationship between Culture and overall effectiveness of KM implementation across the levels of Education
5	H4e: There is a relationship between Technology and overall effectiveness of KM implementation across the levels of Education
6	H4f: There is a relationship between Strategy and overall effectiveness of KM implementation across the levels of Education
7	H4g: There is a relationship between Deterrents and overall effectiveness of KM implementation across the levels of Education
8	H4h: There is a relationship between Incentives and overall effectiveness of KM implementation across the levels of Education
9	H4i: There is a relationship between Enablers and overall effectiveness of KM implementation across the levels of Education
10	H4j: There is a relationship between Training and overall effectiveness of KM implementation across the levels of Education

H5: There is a relationship between KM Drivers and overall effectiveness of KM implementation across Levels of Hierarchy in the organization. Levels of Hierarchy are in terms of pay scales, with E-1 being the lowest Executive level of employee designated as Assistant Officer and E-9 being the level just below the Board of Directors. E-9 level of Executives are designated as Executive Directors.

Table 1.5: Relationship between KM Drivers and overall effectiveness of KM implementation across Levels of Hierarchy (Hypotheses)

S. No.	Hypothesis
1	H5a: There is a relationship between Structures and overall effectiveness of KM implementation across Levels of Hierarchy
2	H5b: There is a relationship between Assets and overall effectiveness of KM implementation across Levels of Hierarchy

Table 1.5: Continue

S. No.	Hypothesis
3	H5c: There is a relationship between Processes and overall effectiveness of KM implementation across Levels of Hierarchy
4	H5d: There is a relationship between Culture and overall effectiveness of KM implementation across Levels of Hierarchy
5	H5e: There is a relationship between Technology and overall effectiveness of KM implementation across Levels of Hierarchy
6	H5f: There is a relationship between Strategy and overall effectiveness of KM implementation across Levels of Hierarchy
7	H5g: There is a relationship between Deterrents and overall effectiveness of KM implementation across Levels of Hierarchy
8	H5h: There is a relationship between Incentives and overall effectiveness of KM implementation across Levels of Hierarchy
9	H5i: There is a relationship between Enablers and overall effectiveness of KM implementation across Levels of Hierarchy
10	H5j: There is a relationship between Training and overall effectiveness of KM implementation across Levels of Hierarchy

Table 1.6: Relationship between KM Drivers and overall effectiveness of KM implementation across number of years of Experience (Hypotheses)

S. No.	Hypothesis
1	H6a: There is a relationship between Structures and overall effectiveness of KM implementation across number of years of Experience
2	H6b: There is a relationship between Assets and overall effectiveness of KM implementation across number of years of Experience
3	H6c: There is a relationship between Processes and overall effectiveness of KM implementation across number of years of Experience
4	H6d: There is a relationship between Culture and overall effectiveness of KM implementation across number of years of Experience
5	H6e: There is a relationship between Technology and overall effectiveness of KM implementation across number of years of Experience
6	H6f: There is a relationship between Strategy and overall effectiveness of KM implementation across number of years of Experience

Table 1.6: Continue

S. No.	Hypothesis
7	H6g: There is a relationship between Deterrents and overall effectiveness of KM implementation across number of years of Experience
8	H6h: There is a relationship between Incentives and overall effectiveness of KM implementation across number of years of Experience
9	H6i: There is a relationship between Enablers and overall effectiveness of KM implementation across number of years of Experience
10	H6j: There is a relationship between Training and overall effectiveness of KM implementation across number of years of Experience

1.6 OVERVIEW OF RESEARCH METHODOLOGY

In this study, an Exploratory-cum-Descriptive research design is used to understand the research problem leading to identification of variables and formulation of hypotheses. It uses the technique of exploratory research to gain familiarity with the research problem. Descriptive analysis is used to describe the KM Drivers-- Culture, Structure, Assets, Technology, Strategy, Deterrents, Enablers, Training, Processes, Incentives related to KM implementation in POSOCO. The quantitative data is collected mainly through the quantitative survey instrument using structured close-ended Questionnaire. It was distributed randomly among 432 executives covering all the Departments viz. System Operation, Market Operation, Decision Support Systems, Human Resource Management, Finance and Accounts, Infrastructure Services, Contracts & Materials, Legal & Regulatory Affairs, Information Technology, Renewable Energy Management Centers in POSOCO. Out of these 432 responses received, 403 responses were found valid which were taken up for this study. The data was then analyzed statistically using the SPSS AMOS 26 software for drawing the final conclusions. Qualitative data was collected by using Focus Group Discussion, In-depth Interview, Elite Interview and Observation.

1.7 SIGNIFICANCE OF STUDY

This study has significantly touched upon the most emerging issues in the domain of KM for organizational transformation in the context of POSOCO. This research tries to capture the Drivers of Knowledge Management Implementation with special reference to POSOCO. The outcome of this study would definitely help the company under study and other such companies which have real time interface in power industry to use the Knowledge Management Drivers for improving their overall performance and competitiveness.

1.8 SCHEME OF CHAPTERS

The Study of the Human Resource Aspects of Knowledge Management in POSOCO, has been presented in six interrelated chapters under.

The first chapter is the Introduction which introduces the concept of Knowledge Management at the national and international platforms. The conceptual and theoretical framework and models of Knowledge Management have been discussed in this chapter.

The second chapter is a Review of Literature and scholarly contributions to the concept of Knowledge Management.

The third chapter consists of the profiling of the case used in the study, i.e. the formation of POSOCO, its vision, mission and its role in Power Sector.

The fourth chapter is that of the Research Methodology which has been discussed in detail. The fifth chapter deals with the Analysis and Findings of the study. The sixth chapter comprises of the Conclusion and Recommendation.

References are enlisted after the sixth chapter.

Appendices follow the References.

CHAPTER 2

REVIEW OF LITERATURE

2.1 INTRODUCTION

This chapter presents the studies to delineate the conceptual underpinnings surrounding the Knowledge Management implementation from the perspectives of human resource as a discipline in different sectors worldwide. The main idea has been to study the different research themes abounding KM, KM adoption; factors influencing KM, KM implementation perspectives at organizational and people /employee level, and various dimensions of KM in organizational context, namely; work culture, structure, process, leadership, technology, etc that have been highlighted through salient studies from various sources. An attempt has also been made to go for an in-depth study and use of inverted pyramid to find out the research gaps. These form the basis for this study.

The review of literature is in reverse chronological order and same is presented to delineate the embellished literature on Knowledge Management. "Now the tyranny of the present is supreme. A lot of organizations have had no choice but to focus on surviving immediate threats (there are no futurists in foxholes). But many business and political discussions still demand farsightedness. The stakes and decisions that leaders make now may have ramifications for years-or even decades" (Scoblic 2020; p.40)

Games, D. and Rendi, R.P. (2019), had foreseen it earlier and they reported a research regarding the solution of the conundrum of the ramifications' in their work titled "The effects of Knowledge Management and risk taking on SME financial performance in creative industries in an emerging market: the mediating effect of innovation outcomes". In this research, it was attempted to examine the effects of Knowledge Management and risk taking on financial performance while considering negative innovation outcomes as mediator variable among 165 SMEs in creative industries in Indonesia. The findings revealed the importance of KM and risk taking in reducing negative innovation outcomes. The results also showed that negative innovation outcomes did not mediate the links between KM, risk taking, and SMEs financial performance.

In another study by Abdelwhabet. al (2019), titled "Key factors influencing knowledge sharing practices and its relationship with organizational performance within the oil and gas industry"; the researchers aimed at investigating the key elements influencing knowledge sharing practice and the relationship between knowledge sharing practice and organizational performance within the oil and gas (OG) industry. For this a sample of 203 responses were collected from the OG industry and analyzed using Structural Equations Modeling (SEM) to validate the model and test the hypotheses. The finding showed significant relationships among the model constructs and positive impact on organizational performance through cost reduction, organization growth and intangible benefits.

In a study by Shrafat, F. (2018), titled "Examining the factors influencing Knowledge Management System (KMS) adoption in small and medium enterprises SMEs", the researcher aimed at assessing factors influencing KMS adoption in SMEs on a sample of 247 respondents using SPLS- DA which is based on Partial Least Squares regression (PLS) for discrimination analysis to build, run and validate the process model. This Smart PLS is a key multivariate analysis which exhibits both the measurement model and the structural model. The results revealed that Knowledge Management capability, knowledge sharing, organizational learning capabilities and IT capabilities are significant factors influencing the KMS adoption.

In their study Abu-Shanab, E. and Shehabat, I. (2018), titled "The influence of Knowledge Management practices on e-government success: A proposed framework tested", the researchers attempted at examining the perceived influence of KM practices on the success of e-government initiatives on a sample of 181 civil servants. They proposed a framework depicting the interactions between the environment and KM practices and associated processes in the context of e-government using SEM. The conceptual framework included four major constituents: IT infrastructure, administrative issues, KM practices and e-government projects' success; completed a survey measuring the factors included in the research model. The findings revealed that IT infrastructure and administrative issues are significant predictors of e-government project's successes, wherein the relationship was mediated by KM practices.

Eugenie Byukusenge and John C. Munene (2017) conducted a study titled, "Knowledge Management and Business Performance: Does innovation matter? "on a sample of 250 SMEs in Rwanda using the bootstrap method to carry out mediation analysis. The purpose was examining the mediating effect of innovation on the relationship between KM and business performance. The findings revealed that innovation fully mediates in the relationship between KM and business performance of SMEs in the context of developing nations.

Pandey (2016) undertook a research to find out the 'human resource factors' in the implementation of Knowledge Management and reported that except information and communication technology, all other factors required for Knowledge Management are from HR and the same was validated by subsequently providing the Technology Acceptance Model in this context. Prior to his research, he had hypothecated a 'proposed model which is reproduced in Figure 2.1.

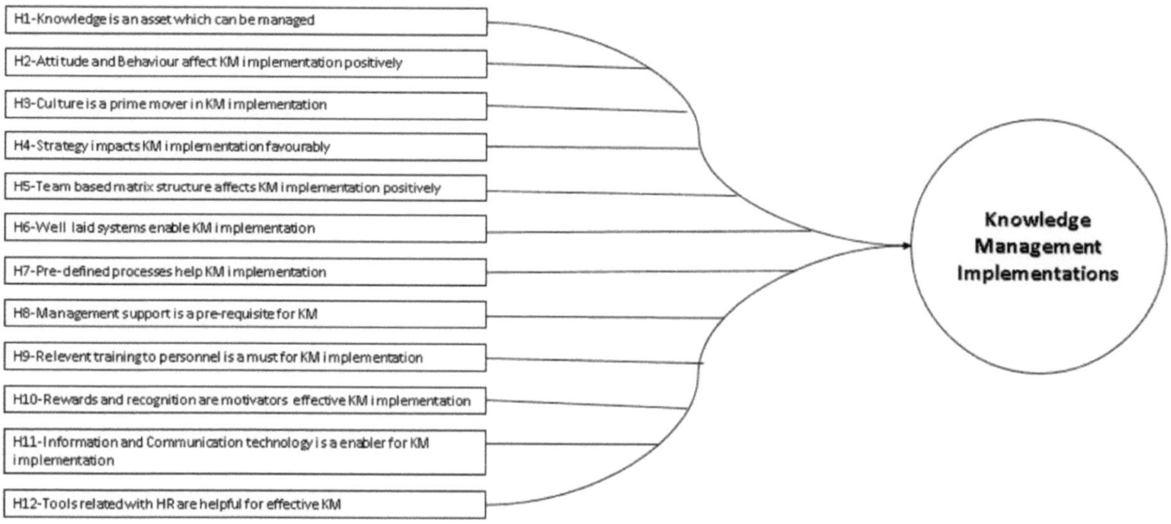

Figure 2.1: Hypothesized Research Model (Pandey, 2016)

The researcher had used both the qualitative and quantitative tools for his research and concluded that HR functions are of paramount importance in KM.

Vaishate Kulkarni (2016) conducted a study titled "Expectations of Indian B schools based on KM systems". The main aim was to understand the perception and implementation of KM in B-schools. For this, stratified sampling technique was used to identify the data from respondents from fifty B schools. The findings showed that 50% B schools had excellent storage structure but they lacked mentoring services. They also witnessed deterioration in the knowledge exchange and archiving process to a great extent.

L. G. Pee and A. Kankanhalli (2016) in their research study titled, "Interactions among Factors Influencing Knowledge Management in Public-Sector Organizations:

A Resource- Based View" attempted to identify the factors influencing KM and its relatedness to their interaction leading to impinging effects based on the resource based view. The aim was also to examine the impact of KM on organizational effectiveness. For this, the data was collected from 101 public organizations. The findings revealed that there was a strong positive relationship between KM capability and organizational effectiveness.

Liana, R., Kathrin, Kirchener & Pia N. (2016)in their study aimed to understand the factors driving employees' participation and the factors impeding their participation in enterprise social media. For this, a unified research model integrating demographic, individual, organizational and technological factors were taken into research to pinpoint the influence of motivation of employees to share the knowledge and the same was tested. The sample collected for this study was 114 respondents in Denmark. The findings of the study revealed that the significant Drivers that were helping others, monetary rewards, management support, change of knowledge sharing behavior and recognition. The significant identified barriers to knowledge sharing were: change of behavior, lack of trust and lack of time.

Sasmita Palo and Linu Charles (2015) conducted the study titled, "Investigating Factors Affecting Knowledge Sharing Intention of Salespeople" with the aim of examining the role of various economic, socio-psychological and sociological factors that influence a salesperson's intention to share knowledge with other salespersons. The research framework for this study was based on the TRA (Theory of Reasoned Action (Fishbein, M., & Ajzen, I., 1975). For this purpose data was generated from 164 respondents across the sectors. The technique of Partial Least Square (PLS) was used to measure validation and model testing. The study findings revealed that subjective norm (SN) followed by attitude towards Knowledge Sharing (KS) had the strongest influence on the intention of salespeople to share knowledge among themselves. Among factors that affect attitude towards Knowledge Sharing (KS), perceived reputation enhancement exerted the maximum impact, followed by other variables, such as, perceived loss of knowledge power, organizational commitment and anticipated reciprocal benefits. Besides, the study also found a negative and insignificant relationship that existed between perceived organizational incentives and attitude towards Knowledge Sharing (KS).

Girish, G P & Joseph, Dennis & Roy, Souvik & Raju, Amar (2015) conducted a study titled, "Factors influencing adoption of Knowledge Management Systems in India from a Micro, Small and Medium Enterprises (MSME)' Perspective' had aimed to investigate the factors influencing successful adoption of KM systems (KMS) in India; in micro, small and medium enterprises. The study was based on the Technology Acceptance Model (TAM) model, Trust Research Advisory (TRA) and Sluggish Cognitive Tempo (SCT). The findings of the study advocated several constructs which pointed out that the applicability of these models in KM adoption in Indian MSMEs is a reality.

In similar vein, Sangeetha Namdu Dhamdhere (2015) in her study titled "Importance of Knowledge Management in the Higher Educational Institute" attempted to assess KM applications in higher education institutions in Pune along with developing a model to manage the knowledge which is available in all its effectiveness. The findings of the study showed that although educational institutions are primarily knowledge driven, yet the staffs were not clear with the conceptual foundations of KM. The scholar suggested that awareness programs should be conducted. Most of the institutions were still at a nascent phase in KM implementation.

In their study, Vasudevan, Hari & Chawan, Anup. (2014) titled, "Demystifying Knowledge Management in Indian Manufacturing SMEs," the researchers aimed at understanding KM practices of Indian manufacturing in Small and Medium Scale Enterprises (SMEs). It also aimed at understanding various barriers to KM therein. The findings of the study revealed that in-depth study of market orientation, (which is one of the subsets of Knowledge Management) learning from consultants, attending conferences/workshops outside India, specifically on a particular topic and subtopic of manufacturing processes, extensive use of internet and frequent interactive sessions with employees were key driving factors of KM.

Ding et.al (2013) in their research on knowledge transfer strategies reported that "First, firms should choose their internal knowledge transfer strategies based on their knowledge storage forms. If firms mainly store knowledge using a systematization method, they should stress on a codification strategy and encourage workers to access knowledge embodied in firms' documents, IT systems and so on. On the other hand, if firms' knowledge is mainly stored in employees' brains, firms should stress on a rich-media strategy and encourage people to communicate and share this tacit knowledge. For example, firms should create culture promoting collaboration and develop places or facilities supporting workers contact".

Lopez and Esteves (2013) conducted a research and reported that "On the one hand, companies apply the *codification strategy,* where knowledge is carefully codified and stored in an appropriate repository; enabling easy access and use by anyone in the company. On the other hand, the *personalization strategy* should be applied where knowledge is closely tied to the person who has developed it and this is shared mainly through direct person-to-person contacts".

Handzic and Ozlen (2013) carried out research on clinical service environments from Knowledge Management success perspective and reported that the structures of "both private and public healthcare organizations are increasingly implementing

Knowledge Management solutions (KMS) to acquire, convert and provide access to relevant information and knowledge". In an exhaustive study on Knowledge Management, Hislop (2013) discussed the 'hypertext organization' and argued that this form of organization facilitates knowledge creation by synthesizing the efficiency achievable in hierarchical organizations with the adaptability of more flexible organizational structures. He also underscored the resilience as a pivotal factor in the realm of Knowledge Management.

Andries and Wastyn (2012) undertook a research in value enhancing and cost increasing effects of Knowledge Management and found out that the systems should include the tools and Drivers of a written policy regarding Knowledge Management; incentives for employees to share information within the company; specific resources to detect and acquire knowledge outside the company; a policy to involve external experts from universities, research institutes or other companies in projects if necessary; and regular updating of internal databases or manuals regarding common practices, lessons learned, or expert advice are required. To test the hypotheses the authors used structural equation modeling with manifest variables comprising of research and development, procurement of relevant software, obtaining licenses from external sources, investing in the training of personnel to operationalize the licenses, developing activities honed for introducing new products in the market and performing other activities for the implementation of new services and products to the market. The authors concluded that "firms increasingly adopt Knowledge Management techniques to spur the generation and acquisition of new knowledge by adopting the systems which can ensure a sustainable competitive advantage by putting tenable systems in place".

Mansoor Ezzati Jivan and Maryam Zarandi (2012), researched on the factors affecting Knowledge Management in Service-Oriented Organizations. They have prioritized the factors effective in implementing KM in service-oriented organizations, eliciting responses from top managers and analyzing them by using the technique of Analytic Hierarchy Process (AHP). The results showed that organizational culture and individual employee relations; jointly engaged in Knowledge Sharing and along with this the individual networking were reported as the first three priorities. The last two priorities include, creating the suitable infrastructures for Information Technology and encoding. In mansoor's view, these factors can affect Knowledge Management implementation in organizations.

Ram Shukla and Rohtak, C.(2012) in their study titled "Knowledge Management in higher education" referred to Knowledge Management (KM) as pillars of institutions' learning, leadership, organization and technology. The study investigated the practices and perceptions of KM in higher educational institutions and the challenges in its implementation, using structured interviews and a case study approach. The case examined the characteristics of the universities that impede or promote the implementation of the KM, and its perceptions among the staff in higher educational institutions.

Chen et.al. (2012) in their study titled, "Does Knowledge Management 'fit' matter to business performance?" examined the "fit" between the Business and Knowledge Management. Besides, the main theme is centered on the match between strategy and organization which is the key Driver in achieving organizational aim. The study focused on three types of strategies that are critical to firms in today's knowledge era. These are mainly Knowledge Management [Strategy], Information Technology (IT)[Strategy], and Human Resource Management (HRM) [Strategy]. A proper integration between these strategies is required for effective KM implementation in organizations.

Antonio Mihi Ramirez, Victor Jesus Garcia Morales and Rodrigo Martin Rojas (2011), in their research titled, "Knowledge Creation, Organizational Learning and their effects on Organizational Performance" aimed at analyzing the four basic modes of Knowledge Conversion Model as proposed in the 'Knowledge Creating Organization' by Nonaka &

Takeuchi, (1995). Their study reaffirmed the close relationship between these forms of knowledge conversion and the creation of knowledge. It also revealed that organizational learning (OL) permits firms to increase the quality and quantity of performance and facilitates in achieving a competitive advantage. The study also proved that the 'knowledge creation process' is critical because it indirectly influences the performance.

Mamta Bhusry and Jayanti Rajan (2011) conducted a study under the rubric of "Knowledge collaboration in higher education institutions in India: Designing a Knowledge Management solution". The basic purpose of the study was to examine the KM systems in higher educational institutions in India. For this purpose, the study had been conducted in Delhi by collecting 152 university respondents from B-schools and engineering schools. The findings of the study revealed that the major lacuna was due to inept research orientation, poor institutional planning, weak IT infrastructure and slow innovative learning process. The study also found that knowledge acquisition is high in these institutions with respect to knowledge transfer. But the dissemination of knowledge is a critical area that should be improved.

Andries. P. & Wastyn (2010), the creator of the Rubik Cube KM method, had identified the benefits of Knowledge Management to organizations. The study demonstrated the development, creation, and the implementation process of KM in organizations, particularly for both manufacturing and service sectors. The study advocated that organizations must employ knowledge mapping, user planning, set knowledge champions and have measurable indicators. The study uniquely contributes with the introduction and deployment of KM at local level and also points at the unique characteristics and methods dealing with the KM life cycle.

Abhilasha Singh and Ebrahim Soltani (2010), in their research study titled, "Knowledge Management Practices in Indian Information Technology Companies" had aimed at examining the level of awareness of KM principles and practices in the context of Indian IT firms. The findings of the study revealed that though people are aware of the importance of documentation, still a lot needs to be done here. It also showed through the KM index, that awareness of Intellectual Property in IT companies was rather low, but the same was high for IT. The findings indicated that employees were not duly rewarded for their contribution in the Knowledge sharing. So, the study recommended that KM should be given importance in the performance appraisal system so that benefits of Knowledge Management can be seen throughout the organization.

Garcia Muina, Fernando Enrique, Martin de Castro, Gregorio and Lopez Saez Pedro (2010) through their research with the title of "The Knowledge-Creation Process: A Critical Examination of the SECI Model" reported that they had advanced and developed a holistic model, EO-SECI, which provides a comprehensive and theoretical framework to understand the key processes to determine the actual sources of competitive advantage for diverse organizations in the present knowledge-based economy.

Deepak Chawla and Himanshu Joshi (2010), in their study titled, "Knowledge Management implementation in Indian manufacturing, IT and IT Enabled Services (ITES) and power generation and distribution companies" attempted to analyze the KM implementation in detail. The findings of the study provide inputs to firms in the IT and ITES and Power Sector for understanding and developing best KM practices for enhancing organizational performance.

Saleh et. al (2010) undertook a study of intellectual capital as a non-monetary asset. These researchers focused on the lessons learnt from Scandinavian countries from the perspective of quality. While suggesting the measures of ensuring the intellectual capital they recommended that the firms have to "retain and attract quality employees" and retaining the customers through "synergetic collaborations". Their study also covered the impact of the intellectual capital on society as it provides the implementational tools for ethical disclosures to the stakeholders. Throughout their study, the researchers used KM as an imperative for achieving the intellectual capital.

Pathak Deepti (2009) in the study titled, "Managing Knowledge Workers across different stages of employment", attempted to provide a framework for the efficient management of knowledge workers in the volatile economy. They also purported to understand the methodologies for optimum utilization of knowledge workers in innovation and affluent organizations. The findings of the study provide definitive explanations and reasons as to why Knowledge Workers should be managed using quality of work life concepts and organizational structures should enable employee branding and employee empowerment.

In his thesis Miikka Lehtonen (2009), titled, "Nonaka's Knowledge Creation Theory Revisited: A semiotic Analysis of Communicating Knowledge in a Geographically Dispersed Team" had been assessing the members of two different cultures and countries as to how they share and communicate knowledge in a multicultural project team. For this, the data was collected through semi-structured and focus group interviews in various locations of Finland and in India. It was posited that technical knowledge is controlled and is enhanced by the individual and therefore resides in the mind of the individual. Although knowledge is quite distinct in terms of social and technical repertoire, it should be treated as complementary to each other. Besides these facets, it also showed that knowledge creating and sharing is tightly embedded in everyday life.

In his study Dan Holsthouse (2009) namely, "The Future of Knowledge Workers", he had a purpose to highlight the role and importance of organizational strategies. Holsthouse iterates that it is critical to identify opportunities on the horizon as well as challenges before they become insurmountable. Dan Holsthouse conducted the research with the main objective of focusing on longer-term trends to determine how organizations will try to provide a compelling work environment that could attract, retain and leverage the best of the knowledge nuggets of Knowledge Workers and they may continue this process unabated.

In a review study, Keng-Boon Ooi (2009), reported his research on KM as "TQM and Knowledge Management", and emphasized that Total Quality Management (TQM) and Knowledge Management (KM) contribute significantly to the improvisation of performance of any organization. Keng-Boon has proposed a model which seeks to close the gap in the literature for the assessment of the multidimensionality of TQM and its association with organizational KM. The author states that the six dimensions of TQM are salubrious and bring the important attributes of Knowledge Management to the fore.

Vedpuriswar (2009) conducted a wholesome study known as, "Knowledge as a Competitive Edge", to explain the innovative knowledge that offers the firms in a given industry and examined whether it provides a competitive advantage over the others or not. The researcher also asserted that "knowledge based competitive advantage is sustainable because it has the potential to create a virtuous circle". He emphasized the need for KM as a critical factor in achieving success. Later on in

2009, Vedpuriswar brought out the Knowledge Management from the silo of 'higher ups' of both the corporate and higher education for 'common folks'.

In a study, Sanghani Parag(2008) published his research findings titled "Does Organization Size Matter for Starting a Knowledge Management Program?', he had attempted to empirically examine the relationship between KM awareness and the organization size. The results of the study suggest that there is no significant association between KM awareness and the organization size since the first one is implicit and the second one is an entity.

In a groundbreaking study, Lopes I. T. (2008), documented by using the rubric of "Towards an Electronic Knowledge Management Culture". The researcher aimed at exploring the typology of information effectively related to stakeholders of one hundred and forty four companies in Portugal. The study revealed that an Electronic Knowledge Management Culture (EKMC) is actually based on several capabilities enshrined throughout the company on its websites and also through the effective contribution and linkage between stakeholders and the respective companies. The findings revealed that size of the company and financial performance indicators contribute positively to both the quality and quantity of information disseminated. The metadata was collected by the researchers from the repositories maintained in the "curating pathways".

In one study by Singh Sanjay Kumar (2008), he reported his finding in "Managing Knowledge in Software Company-Role of Peoples Biographical Profiles", and provided a standardized psychometric instrument to assess KM processes. This research also undertook the onerous tasks of examining the relationships and contributions of an individual's biographical profile with KM processes in the organization. In order to achieve this aim, the Knowledge Management Assessment Tool (KMAT) of Maier and Mosley, (2003) was used to obtain scores of Explicit Knowledge Management Practices (EKMP) and Tacit Knowledge Management Practices (TKMP). The findings revealed that educational qualifications play a major role in comparison with the other factors such as age, gender, work experience and promotions of employees in predicting some amount of variance in total variances of KMP in the firm.

In the study, Chalard Chantarasombat and Rungthip Snigporn (2008), titled, "Developing A Knowledge Management Model for Educational Quality Assurance (QA) in the Faculty of Education", the researchers attempted to develop a KM model for quality assurance in education. For this, the researchers first ensured whether the KM agenda in the QA is intertwined with the work development activity plans or not. Second, they examined QA models for quality control along with activity for efficient work mechanisms, and finally examined the conditional factors of success in QA in the quality control of the Faculty of Education of a university in Thailand. The study proposed the conceptual structure and finally created a model for knowledge administration in the education system in the varsities in Thailand.

Mathew Vijuand Mary Kavitha (2008) brought a new avant-garde in Knowledge Management research in their work titled, "The Critical Knowledge Transfer in an Organization: Approaches". The researchers attempted to highlight the use of Knowledge at various levels and also enumerated the different types of Knowledge Transfer (KT) models which organizations can use for the transfer of both tacit and explicit knowledge.

Gumus M (2007) conducted a study titled, "The Effect of Communication on Knowledge Sharing in Organizations" with the purpose of investigating the effects of communication on Knowledge Sharing in organizations. The study statistically analyzed the relationships among communication satisfaction, communicator's style, knowledge donating, knowledge collecting and seven other demographic variables. The findings of the study showed that knowledge sharing is strongly related with the communication satisfaction and communication style. Knowledge dissemination was also shown to have a strong relationship with communication style. However, the implicit knowledge was left aside in this research.

Sung Chul Park (2007) conducted an exploratory study under the title, "The Comparison of Knowledge Management Practices between Public and Private Organizations: An Exploratory Study". The study was conducted with the aim of presenting a comparative analysis of Knowledge Management practices between public and private organizations. The author claimed that KM in public organizations is still undervalued, even though KM is so important for public organizations. The study is based on the *MIT90* 'sFramework (1991), i.e. the knowledge strategy includes coding and personalization, the knowledge structure includes vertical and horizontal structures and the coordination and knowledge processes their acquisition and creation, archiving and recovery, transfer and sharing and applications. The study found that in most KM practices, private organizations fare better than the public organizations.

Po-Ying Chu, Li-Chieh Chen and Wan-Li Wei (2007) conducted their research and reported it as, "A study on the effect of using a Knowledge Management system in design education "in order to build insight into the Design Knowledge Management System (DKMS) that is focused on the importance of peer learning in design education. The Design Knowledge Management System (DKMS) was built to facilitate peer-to-peer learning among students and it enabled a web-based platform for students to share their knowledge. The finding of the study revealed that there was a high level of learning and satisfaction among students under the DKMS.

A.F. McCarthy (2006) in his study titled, "Knowledge Management: Evaluation of the strategies and processes used in higher education" attempted to explore strategies to increase knowledge activities aligned with the objectives of the institutions. It also aimed to examine the applicability of KM process in the field of higher education. The findings of the study revealed that teaching and learning can be improved using KM and also when information is shared among all members while using KM. Furthermore, KM enforcement increased the effectiveness of the education system and it advocated the adoption of KM practices in educational settings.

In yet another study, Singh and Agarwal (2005) emphasized on collaborative networks as determinants of Knowledge Diffusion Patterns. Singh hypothesized that persons in an organization (from either the same region or same firm) have closer collaborative relations; thereby affecting higher probability of knowledge flows. The researcher also found that intra-regional and intra-firm knowledge flows exhibited stronger links affecting knowledge diffusion among individuals than outside the regional or firm boundaries.

A study by Manish Kumar, Souren Paul and Suresh Tadisina (2005) was conducted and reported under the title "Knowledge Management Practices in Indian Software Development Companies: Findings from an exploratory study'. The researchers attempted to understand the KM Practices of eight leading software companies in India. The findings of the study showed the importance of technological and cultural requirements on KM capability. It also pointed out that advancement in the current KMS provides several tangible benefits to organizations.

Arumugamand Mahalingam (2005) in their study titled, "Knowledge of Design Management System", found that the use of Information & Communication Technology (ICT) can increase the practice of Knowledge Sharing and thus will improve the learning process.

In a study, Sourav Mukherji (2005) brought to the fore an exploration titled "Knowledge Management and Innovation in Indian Software Firms", a tangible festschrift to conduct an extensive research on KM and organizational learning. The author discusses the growing importance of KM and robust systems to power innovation in Indian firms by leveraging their domain knowledge and expertise. He found that KM fosters an increasing innovation in Indian firms which also leverage their domain knowledge and creativity. It emphasized facilitating culture for promoting efficient use of its intellectual capital.

In another study, Tanriverdi (2005), attempted to find the relationship between KM and corporate performance. His model hypothesized that "KM capability creates and exploits cross-unit synergies of the product, customer and managerial knowledge resources of the firm. These synergies increase the financial performance of the firm. IT relatedness also indirectly influences corporate performance through the mediation of KM capability".

Tarun Narayan (2005) completed a study titled 'The Knowledge Edge', and he focused on KM Practices being adopted by Eureka Forbes for achieving competitive difference. The findings of the case study showed that Eureka Forbes is using KM as a motivational tool; one of them is the 'Euro SMS'. This initiative helped the company in triggering employees to improve their performance substantially.

Cummings (2004) conducted a slightly different KM study to understand the influence of structural diversity on work group performance in a global organizational context. He found that "when members of structurally diverse work groups share knowledge external to the group, their performance improves". Thus, it can be concluded that improvement stems from active exchange of knowledge through unique sources.

In their study, Levin and Cross (2004) attempted to understand the mediating role of trust in Knowledge transfer. The findings of the study revealed that - "(1) Competence and benevolence-based trust among individuals, in an organization influence the link between the strength of ties among two individuals and receipt of useful Knowledge. (2) The researchers find a benefit of weak ties (i.e. between dissimilar individuals who do not routinely interact) antecedent to Knowledge transfer".

In his master thesis, Mathi Kavindra (2004) provided a lucid reading under the title of 'Key Success Factors for Knowledge Management', and successfully tried to understand the critical factors affecting application of KM. The study hypothesized that the Key Success Factors (KSFs) depend upon the quality and quantity of the contributions from the employees. The study confirmed KSF as dependent on both internal and external knowledge sharing and interaction.

Lee and Choi (2003) attempted to examine the link between organizational performance [including KM satisfaction, return on assets, return on sales], and organizational effectiveness. Their model includes KM processes to focus on socialization, externalization, combination and internalization within the Knowledge Creation Process and KM enablers, to include culture, structure, people and information technology. The study provided an integrative KM research framework, in which enablers influence processes; processes influence intermediate outcomes; intermediate outcomes influence organizational performance.

Probert K Stephen (2003) analyzed the topic of Knowledge Creation from a philosophical perspective. The study of Probert K Stephen has reaffirmed Nonaka and Takeuchi's (1995) SECI model of Knowledge creation. It has also provided an apt commentary on the conviviality of knowledge of an individual and an entity.

Through their study, Davenport and Glaser (2002) established that knowledge-sharing programs often fail due to unforeseen hindrances making it harder for people to do their jobs. They suggested that successful implementation of KM depends on integrating specialized Knowledge reuse which is extremely ordained for accessibility and unavoidability.

Orlikowski (2002) in the study titled 'Knowing in Practice: Enacting a Collective Capability in Distributed Organizing', stated that global product development in any modern enterprise, requires both competent, collective and distributed knowledge, grounded in the everyday practices of individuals belonging to an organization.

In the study, Alavi, M. and D. Leidner (2001), emphasized on KM as a significant organizational resource. For this, they coined the term Knowledge Management Systems (KMS) as an integral part of KM. In an exceptional study, Becerra-Fernandez and R.S. Irma (2001) examined the link between Knowledge processes and the KM performance amongst KM users. The findings of the study revealed that the task characteristics moderate the relationship between the two variables i.e. Knowledge processes and KM performance with task orientation comprising of internalization, externalization, combination or socialization. In his study, Markus (2001) attempted to work on knowledge reuse, and its domain comprised of the situations and factors surrounding situations where knowledge reuse was being done. She found that there are different requirements for the design of a KM repository. Markus et. al.(2002) undertook further studies in KM and found that unique set of requirements are to be placed for new product development, strategic business planning and organizational design including Emerging Knowledge Processes-EKP's They linked organizational design with KM design system, and asserted that Emerging Knowledge Processes - EKP design is linked to organizational information systems.

In the research, Gold et al. (2001), had put across the four processes of acquisition, conversion, application, and protection in the KM infrastructure capabilities of an organization. The research found that KM infrastructure capabilities and knowledge processes significantly impact organizational effectiveness.

Ciborra C. and R Andreu (2001), in their study researched the use of knowledge and its management as a dependent one upon the organizational context. Cramton (2001) attempted to research the problems associated with maintaining mutual knowledge in the remote teams. The study found "five types of mutual knowledge failures; (a) Failure to communicate and retain contextual information.(b) Unevenly distributed information, (c) Difficulty communicating and understanding the salience of information, (d) Differences in speed of access to information and (e) Difficulty interpreting the meaning of silence (or noncontribution of information)". Cramton (2001) had already emphasized on the importance of mutual knowledge sharing as an important driver and facilitator for an organization in his work.

In a research, Argote and Ingram (2000), put forth the point of Knowledge transfer as a competitive advantage for companies. The researchers found that greater interactions amongst employees bring more knowledge transfer within firms and consequently bring competitive advantage. Newman B.D. and Kurt W.Conrad (2000), in their study titled 'A framework for Characterizing Knowledge Management Methods, Practices and Technologies', gave a framework of tools (methods, practices and technologies) for KM practitioners.

Choo, C. W. (2000) has brought to the fore the variables of organizational performance and assistance in providing knowledge in the context of Library Management. He reported in his research that for better performance, it is essential to define three categories of Organizational Knowledge: tacit knowledge, explicit knowledge, and cultural knowledge. This study brings out the point that there are many opportunities for information professionals in which they can contribute in managing KM.

KM, Dyer and Nobeoka (2000) undertook their seminal work and; pointed out the value of creating a high-performance "Knowledge-Sharing Network that motivates members to participate, prevents free riders and reduces the costs of getting knowledge. They emphasized on strong relationships amongst employees for dynamic learning. This study had given an in-depth articulation by the authors and the community of practice concept took further roots in the area of KM. In one of the studies, Hansen et al. (1999) attempted on the point to bring balance in automating KM and ability of the individuals to share knowledge through traditional ways. The authors highlighted that the strategy of the balance depends on the quantity of explicit and tacit knowledge.

Alavi and Leidner (1999), in their study, discuss that knowledge is personalized and it is in the brains of the individuals. This study suggested a framework for analysis of four tenets in KM i.e. knowledge creation, knowledge sharing, knowledge transfer and knowledge application. In the research, Costello, G. (1996) underlined the point that strategic alliances amongst the KM partners is of paramount importance to gain competitive advantage. Management of this process is termed as an Alliance Knowledge Management.

Ikujiro Nonaka and Hirotaka Takeuchi' (1995) in their pioneering study found that the most important purpose of the organization "is it's ability to adapt to the changing environment by creating new Knowledge, disseminating it effectively and embodying this knowledge into practice".

In his study Nonaka (1994) focused on the point that knowledge viewing is either an individual or a collective activity. He emphasized that the improvement in individual and organizational knowledge stems from the organizational code. The study by Carley (1992) used a model to investigate the relationship between organizational learning and employee turnover. She found that "institutionalized memory, embodied in the memories of distributed individuals and the relationships between individuals, determines the consequences in an organizational milieu for personnel turnover".

To sum up, organizations should imbibe the spirits of KM in such a way so that they can combine their structure, information, decision processes, and people in a unique way for achieving sustainable competitive advantage. This would create a unique organizational design equipped to match the complexity of an organization's structure with the complexity of its environment and technology and one where the human assets prove their mettle in all respect as knowledge nuggets, in reality; may be the assets of pragmatic and critically important assets.

Accordingly, the study has extensively covered the pertinent review of literature studies, as discussed above; and thereby posits the scope and flow of the review of literature in the figure given below:

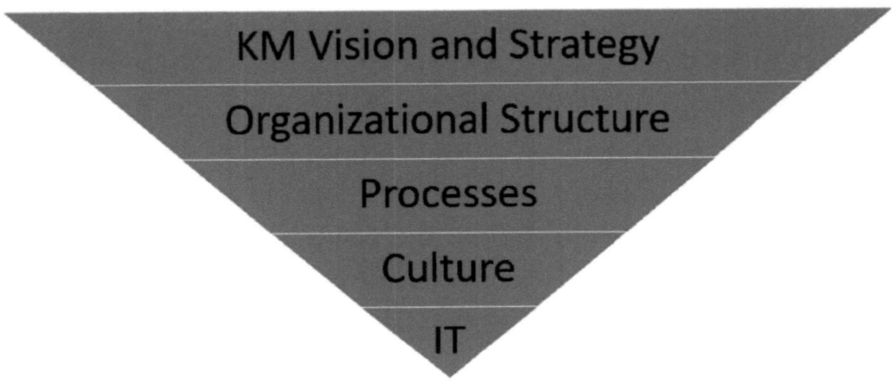

Figure 2.2: Scope and Flow of the Review of Literature

The figure 2.2 depicts that KM started initially by professionals of Information Technology leading to the culture of KM. Subsequently, it brought the relevant processes. However, in order to take the benefits of the KM; organizations had to change their structure followed by the KM vision and strategy by the top management.

2.2 RESEARCH GAPS

The extensive review of representative, epoch making and seminal components of literature in the Knowledge Management reveal that extant studies have focused on ways and the extent of Knowledge Management work practices and these practices need to be examined in totality from concept to commissioning to implement the KM practices in organizations. Some recent studies have linked Knowledge Management with organizational performance, organizational learning, and adoption of Knowledge Management for ushering in innovations and enhancing the firm's capability. But these are dealt with in a sporadic manner and to a very limited extent, especially in the case of organizations in Indian Power Sector. Many studies have been occidental in the western world that have discussed the key drivers of Knowledge Management but they have not linked it with the implementation of KM from employee's perspective. There is hardly any study in the Indian context with this perspective. So, the present study tried to fill this important gap. It studies various dimensions of Knowledge Management, and assesses its implementation in an organization in power industry from the immense contribution of employees through the case study method. This will require redesign and reinvent of HR strategies to spur its growth in today's knowledge driven economy. The case of POSOCO is an imperative in this context to trace the KM progression. POSOCO is a unique organization and a pivotal one in power industry, as it has got a unique place entailing the interfaces starting with generation of power and moving to transmission and finally ending in the consumption of power. With this in view POSOCO provides the microcosmic view of the entire power industry. It also brings out the latent commonalities in all the firms operating in the power industry in India.

2.3 CONCLUSION

This chapter presented the literature review of the study within larger areas of MSME and highly technical firms with less manpower from the perspective of Knowledge Management. It was imperative apropos the organization i.e. POSOCO which is studied from the lenses of Knowledge Management having 592 employees only. This is symmetrical from the totality of the consonance which was guided by the study's aim and objectives. The next chapter consists of the profiling of the case used in the study, i.e. the formation of POSOCO, its vision, mission and the role in Power Sector. The odyssey of KM has provided the congruity across the companies in Power Sector in India, in particular; and world over; in general.

CHAPTER 3

The CASE FOR STUDY: POWER SYSTEM OPERATION CORPORATION LIMITED (POSOCO)

3.0 INTRODUCTION

Indian Power Industry was obfuscated because the optimization of power was not taking place as a litany of organizations was given the responsibility of various verticals which was manifesting in the 'priority job'. An organization, namely, Power Grid Corporation of India Limited was allotted three functions. First, asset creation and asset management of 'high tension' power lines from 440 KV to the 'pinnacle point of 1200 KV'; that made it the "only company in the world" aiming to transmit power at a capacity of 1200 KV. Second, the function of Grid Management, and third; is 'Central Transmission Utility' which entails the control over the generation, transmission and distribution of power.

3.1 ADVENT OF POSOCO

'Transmission' and 'Grid Management' are essential functions for smooth evacuation of power from generating stations to the consumers. System Operator is to ensure, every moment, the power balance in the interconnected power system; in a secure and reliable manner. Grid management involves taking care of the overall reliability, security, economy and efficiency of the power system.

The Grid Management in India is being carried out on a regional basis. The country is electrically demarcated into five regions namely, Northern Region, Western Region, Southern Region, Eastern Region and North Eastern Region. As per the Indian Electricity Act, 2003 (herein after, 'the Act'), each of the five regions has a Regional Load Dispatch Centre (RLDC), which is the apex body to ensure integrated operation of the power system in the concerned region. The RLDCs for Northern, Western, Southern, Eastern, and NorthEastern regions are located in Delhi, Mumbai, Bengaluru, Kolkata and Shillong respectively. At national level, National Load Dispatch Centre (NLDC) has been established for optimum scheduling and dispatch of electricity among the regions. NLDC has been designated as an apex body to ensure integrated operation of national power system, by Ministry of Power (MoP), through notification dated 02nd March, 2005. The NLDC is based in Delhi.

The RLDCs, in conjunction with State Load Dispatch Centers (SLDCs); are responsible for monitoring the real time operation along with dispatch of electricity within the region through secure and economic operation of the regional grid. All activities are undertaken in accordance with the Grid Standards stipulated by the Central Electricity Authority (CEA) and the Grid Code and other Regulations notified by the Central Electricity Regulatory Commission (CERC). POSOCO, consisting of RLDCs and NLDC is performing mission critical tasks of national importance and discharging the statutory functions in a fair, transparent and neutral manner assigned under the Act and Rules notified by MoP.

3.2 FORMATION OF POSOCO

Central Electricity Authority (CEA) was entrusted with operations of Regional Electricity Boards (REBs) after their establishment in 1964. Power Grid Corporation of India Ltd. (POWERGRID) was formed in 1989. The erstwhile REBs i.e. RLDCs were transferred to POWERGRID during the period 1994 to 1996, in a phased manner. Subsequently, the RLDCs were strengthened / modernized with state-of-the-art technology and System Operation was being looked after by POWERGRID.

Section 5.3.7 of the National Electricity Policy, 2005 clearly mentioned that the spirit of the provisions of the Act was to ensure independent system operation through NLDC, RLDCs and SLDCs. These Dispatch Centers, as per the provisions of the Act; were to be operated by a Government company or authority as notified by the appropriate Government. However, till such time these agencies/authorities were established through the Act were mandated that the Central Transmission Utility (CTU) or State Transmission Utility (STU), as the case may be; would operate the RLDCs or SLDCs.

There was a directive from MoP to POWERGRID in, July 2008, to set up POSOCO as a wholly owned subsidiary. The functions of POSOCO, included; inter-alia, supervision and control of all aspects of operations of NLDC and RLDCs, to act as an apex organization for manpower requirement of NLDC and RLDCs, to ensure planning and implementation of infrastructure required for smooth operation and development of NLDC and RLDCs as well as to advise and assist the SLDCs in different ways, including specialized training, etc.

In line with MoP directives, Power System Operation Corporation Limited (POSOCO) was, incorporated as a wholly owned subsidiary of POWERGRID. POSOCO was registered on 20th March 2009 to oversee the grid management function of the five RLDCs and NLDC. MoP vide notification dated 27th September, 2010, notified that POSOCO shall operate the five RLDCs and NLDC w.e.f. 1st October, 2010. POSOCO has since been discharging the statutory function of power system operation, under the Act.

With the manifold expansion of Indian transmission network, the security and reliability in operation of the power system has attained paramount importance. On 31st December 2013, the Southern Grid was synchronized with the national grid, making the Indian Power System a very large grid with associated complexities. The Enquiry Committee, set up to analyze the Grid disturbances that occurred in July, 2012, had recommended, inter-alia; setting up of an Independent System Operator. Further, CERC has vide its order in Petition No. 167/Suo- Moto/2012 dated 22.2.2014, mentioned the need to expedite establishment of POSOCO as an independent company.

After inter-ministerial consultations, the proposal for independent system operator was considered by Empowered Finance Committee (EFC), Ministry of Finance in the meeting held on 5th May 2014. EFC recommended that approval of the Union Cabinet may be sought for establishment of POSOCO as an Independent Government company.

Union Cabinet approval was sought by MoP for setting up of POSOCO which would be as an Independent Government Company. The Union Cabinet, in its meeting held on 10th December, 2014, approved the proposal of MoP.

The communication from MoP, dated 25th March, 2015, conveyed the sanction of the Hon'ble President of India for setting up of Power System Operation Corporation (POSOCO) as a wholly owned Government Company to ensure independent system operation and for providing the level playing field to all stakeholders. Power System Operation Corporation Limited (POSOCO), as an independent government company, started operating the NLDC and RLDCs with effect from the 3rd January, 2017 in accordance with Ministry of Power Gazette notification dated 19th December, 2016.

In POSOCO, the focus is on security & reliability. "We strive to manage weather impacts and perfect generation dispatch for one of the largest power systems in the world, operating at a single frequency" (POSOCO, www.posoco.in, 2020). Sustained growth of the Power Sector is a key parameter to drive economic development. As an impartial grid operator, POSOCO has no financial interest in any market segment. POSOCO ensures that diverse entities have equal access to the transmission network and ensure load generation balance at all times. The assets of the POSOCO mainly comprise of Human Resources and Supervisory Control and Data Acquisition - Energy Management System (SCADA-EMS) along with software tools for all functions related to System Operation and Market Operation installed in the Control Centers of the RLDCs and NLDC.

POSOCO is committed towards Integrated Operation of Regional Power System and National Power System including the systems of Bhutan and Nepal so as to facilitate transfer of electric power within and across the regions and trans-national exchange of power with Reliability, Security and Economy. It strives for independent system operation and provides the level playing field to all stakeholders.

Vision of POSOCO

"To be a global institution of excellence for reliable & resilient power systems, fostering efficient electricity markets, promoting economy and sustainability." (www.posoco.in)

Mission of POSOCO

- *"Ensure Integrated Operation of the Indian Power System to facilitate transfer of electric power within and across the regions and trans-national exchange of power with Reliability, Economy and Sustainability.*
- *Facilitate competitive and efficient wholesale electricity markets and administer settlement systems.*
- *Promote innovation and adoption of latest technology with cyber security.*
- *Nurturing human & intellectual capital."* (www.posoco.in)

3.3 OBJECTIVES OF POSOCO

POSOCO has the onerous responsibility of operating the All India synchronous grid, one of the largest and most complex in the world, ensuring reliability and security. It manages the inter-state transmission of power to utilities across India ultimately reaching to over 1.3 billion consumers. POSOCO also operates India's electricity market through coordination with thousands of entities every day for balancing demand and generation every 15 minutes.

The Corporation has set the following objectives in line with its Mission for integrated operation of regional and national power system through "National Load Dispatch Center and Regional Load Dispatch Centers" to discharge the following statutory functions assigned in the Indian Electricity Act, 2003:

3.3.1 Functions of POSOCO as per directives of Ministry of Power issued from time to time:

- *"To supervise and control all aspect concerning operations and manpower requirement of RLDCs and NLDC.*
- *To act as the apex organization for human resources requirement of NLDC and RLDCs.*
- *To ensure planning and implementation of infrastructure required for smooth operation and development of NLDC and RLDCs.*
- *To coordinate the functioning of NLDC and all the RLDCs.*
- *To advise and assist state level Load Dispatch Centers, including specialized training etc.*
- *To perform any other function entrusted to it by the Ministry of Power."*

3.3.2 Functions of NLDC (Ministry of Power notification dated 2nd March, 2005):

- *"Supervision over the Regional Load Dispatch Centers;*
- *Scheduling and dispatch of electricity over inter-regional links in accordance with grid standards specified by the Authority and grid code specified by Central Commission in coordination with Regional Load Dispatch Centers;*
- *Coordination with Regional Load Dispatch Centers for achieving maximum economy and efficiency in the operation of National Grid;*
- *Monitoring of operations and grid security of the National Grid;*
- *Supervision and control over the inter-regional links as may be required for ensuring stability of the power system under its control;*
- *Coordination with Regional Power Committees for regional outage schedule in the national perspective to ensure optimal utilization ofpower resources;*
- *Coordination with Regional Load Dispatch Centers for the energy accounting of interregional exchange of power;*
- *Coordination for restoration of synchronous operation of national grid with Regional Load Dispatch Centers;*
- *Coordination for trans-national exchange ofpower;*
- *Providing operational feedback for national grid planning to the Authority and the Central Transmission Utility;*
- *Levy and collection of such fee and charges from the generating companies or licensees involved in the power system, as may be specified by the Central Commission.*

- *Dissemination of information relating to operations of transmission system in accordance with directions or regulations issued by Central Electricity Regulatory Commission and the Central Government from time to time."*

3.3.3 Functions of RLDC (Section 28 of Indian Electricity Act, 2003):

- *"Be responsible for optimum scheduling and dispatch of electricity within the region, in accordance with the contracts entered into with the licensees or the generating companies operating in the region;*
- *Monitor grid operations;*
- *Keep accounts of quantity of electricity transmitted through the regional grid;*
- *Exercise supervision and control over the inter-State transmission system; and*
- *Be responsible for carrying out real time operations for grid control and dispatchof electricity within the region through secure and economic operation of the regional grid in accordance with the Grid Standards and the Grid Code.*
- *To levy and collect such fees & charges from the generating companies or licensees engaged in inter-state transmission of electricity as may be specified by the Central Commission."*(www.cercind.gov.in)

The functions of POSOCO have been evolving with the expansion of footprint of Indian grid, increase in electrical energy demand; growth in the economy and paradigm shift in technology, regulations, market design, administration, and management of the power system. POSOCO is a knowledge based control center oriented organization and is fulfilling various other functions assigned by the Government of India, from time to time. POSOCO is facilitating and enabling Power Sector Reforms by Ministry of Power, regular feedback is given to the Central Regulator, Authority, Central Transmission Utility and other stakeholders on design and operational aspects pertaining to Power System Operation and Power Market Operation.

3.4 RESPONSIBILITIES OF POSOCO

- Open Access in Inter-state transmission: Open Access in Inter-state Transmission has been introduced by CERC in the year 2004 after enactment of the Indian Electricity Act in 2003. The present Regulation in vogue was notified in 2008, which was subsequently amended w.e.f. 15.06.2009.
- Nodal agency for collective transactions: NLDC has been designated as nodal agency for collective transactions through Power Exchanges as per Open Access in Inter-state Transmission Regulations and Power Market Regulations. RLDCs have been designated as nodal agency for bilateral transactions.

- Congestion management: CERC has notified Regulations on Measures to relieve congestion in real time operation on 22.12.2009. NLDC and RLDCs are required to asses Total Transfer Capability (TTC), Available Transfer Capability (ATC) and Transmission Reliability Margin (TRM) of inter-regional links / corridors and put the same on their websites. In case of congestion in real time, congestion charge is imposed by NLDC and RLDCs. RLDCs maintain separate accounts for congestion charges collected from and disbursed to different entities.
- Nodal agency for Ancillary Services: In India explicit ancillary services market is not there at present. In the Unscheduled Interchange (UI) Charges Regulations, CERC has specified that surplus funds left in UI pool account can be utilized for providing Ancillary Services, as identified by Regional Load Dispatch Centers. A proposal has been submitted to CERC in this regard. POSOCO would have to gradually develop Ancillary Services with approval of CERC commensurate with maturing of Indian Power Market.
- Implementing agency for Sharing of Inter-State Transmission Charges and Losses: As per CERC Regulations dated 15.06.2010 on Sharing of Inter-State Transmission Charges and Losses, NLDC has been designated as Implementing Agency (IA). Data required for carrying out studies and computation is collected from different transmission licensees and Designated ISTS customers (DICs). The data is validated by a Validation Committee constituted by the CERC and thereafter results are submitted to CERC. After approval by CERC, the results and rate of charges and losses are published on the website of NLDC.
- Central agency for Renewable Energy Certificates (REC): In accordance with the CERC Regulations, NLDC has been designated as the Central Agency for implementation of the REC Mechanism in the country. The responsibilities entrusted to NLDC are Registration of eligible Renewable Energy Generation Facilities, issuance of REC, maintenance and settlement of REC Account, repository of transactions, and such other activities incidental to implementation of REC Mechanism as may be assigned by CERC from time to time. For further information for the public the following site: https://www.recregistryindia.nic.in/has been made.
- Energy Savings Certificates (ESCerts): Ministry of Power vide order dated 05.01.2016 assigned the responsibility of Registry of ESCerts trading to the POSOCO and authorized POSOCO to discharge all activities of Registry under Perform Achieve and Trade (PAT) scheme. The important activities

of the Registry are Registration of Designated Consumers, issue of ESCerts, etc.

- Power System Development Fund: CERC has notified the Power System Development Fund Regulations on 04.06.2010. The Power System Development Fund Regulations also provide for a managing committee headed by Head of NLDC. (CERC Power System Development Fund Notification 04.06.2010)
- Disaster Management: As per Ministry of Power letter dated 27th May 2009, NLDC is required to act as Central Control Room in case of natural and man-made emergencies / disasters.
- Forum of Load Dispatchers (FOLD): FOLD has been constituted by the Forum of Regulators (FOR) in November 2008. NLDC is providing secretarial services to the FOLD. Regular meetings and Workshops are being conducted under the aegis of FOLD.
- Maintenance of Pool Accounts: Operation of Regional UI Pool accounts, regional reactive energy account and congestion charge account are maintained by RLDCs as per IEGC, 2010. Operation of Congestion account by NLDC as per CERC Power Market Regulations effective from 20.01.2010.
- Regulation of power supply: In case of default in payment or non-maintenance of payment security mechanism as per agreement, RLDCs prepares an implementation plan for regulation of power supply based on request of generating company or transmission company, as per CERC (Regulation of Power Supply) Regulations, 2010.

3.5 DEPARTMENTS

The different Departments in POSOCO are:

- System Operation
- Market Operation
- Decision support systems
- Human resource management
- Finance and accounts
- Infrastructure Services, Contracts & Materials
- Legal & regulatory affairs
- Information technology
- Renewable Energy Management Centers

POSOCO is managing the Grid and conducts various activities in accordance with 18 Regulations of CERC, which encompass the multi-dimensional facets of load dispatching such as system operation, market operation, etc. and Technical Standards notified by CEA.

A list of CERC Regulations is as follows: (Refer CERC Website- www.cercind.gov.in)

1. *CERC (Open Access in inter-State Transmission) Regulations, 2008*
2. *CERC (Grant of Connectivity, Long-term Access and Medium-term Open Access in interState Transmission and related matters) Regulations, 2009*
3. *CERC (Measures to relieve congestion in real time operation) Regulations, 2009*
4. *CERC (Procedure, Terms and Conditions for grant of trading license and other related matters) Regulations, 2009*
5. *CERC (Power Market) Regulations, 2010*
6. *CERC (Terms and Conditions for recognition and issuance of Renewable Energy Certificate for Renewable Energy Generation) Regulations, 2010*
7. *CERC (Indian Electricity Grid Code) Regulations, 2010*
8. *CERC (Sharing of Inter State Transmission Charges and Losses) Regulations, 2010*
9. *CERC (Regulation of Power Supply) Regulations, 2010*
10. *CERC (Fixation of Trading Margin Regulations), 2010*
11. *CERC (Rates, Charges and Terms and Conditions for use of Intervening Transmission Facilities) Regulations, 2010*
12. *CERC (Standards of Performance of inter-State transmission licensees) Regulations, 2012*
13. *CERC (Terms and Conditions of Tariff) Regulations, 2014*
14. *CERC (Power System Development Fund) Regulations, 2014*
15. *CERC (Deviation Settlement Mechanism and related matters) Regulations, 2014*
16. *CERC (Fees and Charges of Regional Load Dispatch Centre and other related matters) Regulations, 2015*
17. *CERC (Ancillary Services Operations) Regulations, 2015*
18. *CERC (Terms and Conditions for Dealing in Energy Savings Certificates) Regulations, 2016*

The Central Electricity Authority (CEA) Regulations on Grid Standards are as follows:

1. *CEA (Technical Standards for Connectivity of the Distributed Generation Resources) Regulations, 2012*

2. *CEA (Grid Standards) Regulations, 2010*
3. *CEA (Technical Standards for Connectivity to the Grid), Regulations, 2007*
4. *CEA (Installation and Operation of meters) Regulations, 2006*
5. *Central Electricity Authority (Measures relating to Safety and Electricity Supply) Regulations, 2010*
6. *Central Electricity Authority (Technical Standards for Construction of Electrical Plants and Electric Lines) Regulations, 2010*

3.6 OPERATIONAL EXCELLENCE

The average All India energy met during 2019-20 was 3547 Million units per day (MU/day), as compared to 3527 MU/day during 2018-19, marking an increase of 0.6%. The highest All India Demand recorded during 2019-20 was 182610 MW (on 30th May 2019), as compared to 175590 MW in 2018-19 (on 18th Sep 2018), marking an increase of 4.0%.

Hydro generation increased by 16.3% from 385 MU/day during 2018-19 to 447 MU/day during 2019-20. Wind generation increased by 3.7% from 170 MU/day during 2018-19 to 176 MU/day during 2019-20. Solar generation increased by 25.6% from 108 MU/day during 2019 to 127 MU/day during Jan-Jun 2019.

Inter-regional exchanges during 2019-20 were 195 Billion units (BU), marking an increase of 7.2% as compared to 182 BU during 2018-19.

A consultation paper on Security Constrained Economic Dispatch(SCED) of Inter State Generating Stations (ISGS) pan India was prepared by POSOCO which primarily focuses on enhancing the scope of optimization of ISGS schedules in India. The objective of the optimization exercise is to minimize the total generation cost while honoring the technical constraints of the power plants and the grid. CERC vide its order on 31st Jan 2019, directed POSOCO to implement SCED for all thermal ISGS on pilot basis for 6 months w.e.f. 1st Apr 2019. POSOCO formulated the detailed procedure for implementation of SCED as directed by CERC. Requisite framework and infrastructure for implementation of SCED and its integration with scheduling has been put in place across all RLDCs and NLDC. A detailed feedback report was prepared by POSOCO based on the experience of the pilot from April-December 2019 and it was submitted to CERC on 31st January 2020.

POSOCO helped in maintaining the grid resilience during the Extremely Severe Cyclonic Storm 'Fani' which struck Odisha on 3rd May 2019 resulting in extensive damage to transmission and distribution infrastructure in the state and Severe Cyclonic Storm 'Bulbul' which hit West Bengal and Odisha coast on 9th Nov 2019.

With the operationalization of AGC (Automatic Generation Control) pilot project at Bongaigaon (NER) on 19th November 2019, AGC pilots are operational in all 5 regions. The total generation capacity under AGC pilot is 4800 MW. Projects in all 5 regions are under continuous operation and signals are being sent from NLDC every 4 seconds to control the generation at these plants. Continuous meetings and interaction are being held with power plants and CTU for operationalization of AGC pan-India.

India experienced Annular Solar Eclipse on 26th December 2019 between 0805 to 1130 hrs. Annularity was visible mainly in Southern India in the states of Kerala, Tamil Nadu and Karnataka, while the rest of the country witness partial eclipse. It was envisaged that the reduction in solar generation due to the eclipse would approximately 7.8 GW, considering clear sky conditions. Advisories were prepared and issued by NLDC and RLDCs listing various measures to be taken to ensure power system security and reliability during the eclipse. The maximum reduction in solar generation observed on 26th December 2019 was 6.5 GW less than 25th December 2019, which was a cloudy day. Sharp reduction or increase in solar output was handled by regulating gas and hydro generation. Additional thermal capacity was also brought on-bar to manage net-demand.

To maintain operations reliably in the wake of outbreak of COVID-19 pandemic, periodic advisories have been issued to ensure adequate hygiene measures and effective social distancing across POSOCO and to mitigate any possible impact on the power system. Numerous steps have been taken to facilitate control room operations in a safe and secure environment.

An artificial neural network (ANN) based algorithm has been developed at NLDC for forecasting All India Demand. Day-ahead forecasting with real-time correction on hourly basis has been implemented. Weather parameters for multiple locations across all regions have been incorporated in the model. The tool has been operationalized and it is generating forecasts on daily basis.

A vibrant electricity market is operating in the country. About 10% of the total energy generated in the country is traded in the Short Term Electricity Market which comprises of Bilateral Transactions (direct or through traders) and Collective Transactions through Power Exchanges. Two Power Exchanges (IEX and PXIL) are operational in the country. During FY 2019-20, over 50,000 transactions and around 117 Billion Units (BU) of energy was approved under Short Term Open Access (STOA) which has been facilitated by the RLDCs/NLDC.

The regulatory framework for ancillary services was introduced for the first time in India in 2015 and implemented in April 2016. With the help of in-house development of customized software solution, Reserve Regulation Ancillary Services (RRAS) has addressed the congestion management issues and optimization at regional & pan-India level, thereby, facilitates integration of renewables.

NLDC has been designated as the Implementing Agency for Sharing of Inter State Transmission Charges and Losses (POC Charges and Losses Regulation of CERC dated 15th June 2010) w.e.f. 1st July 2011. The computations of Point of Connection (PoC) Charges and Losses are carried out on a quarterly basis.

The RLDCs and NLDC have been giving feedback and inputs at various stages of formulation of the policies and regulations pertaining to the power system design and operational aspects. The RLDCs and NLDC make best efforts towards implementing these policies & regulations in letter and spirit through feedback and participation in the process.

POSOCO is one of the members of the group of GO15 comprising of 18 large international power grid operators. POSOCO actively participates in the CIGRE (International Council on Large Electric Systems) which is one of the premier organizations on Electric Power Systems, covering their technical, economic, environmental, organizational and regulatory aspects. POSOCO is an active participant in the North American SynchroPhasor Initiative (NASPI) which has the mission to foster the use and capabilities of synchrophasor technology.

As part of capacity building, basic and specialist level training is being imparted to all the SLDCs, RLDCs and NLDC through the National Power Training Institute (NPTI), an autonomous body under the MoP. An international level capacity building program for power system operators from Bhutan and Saudi Arabia was also organized. For furthering capability enhancement for System Operators and developing research capacity by promoting Industry-academia partnership, POSOCO signed an MoU with Indian Institute of Technology, Kanpur, Indian Institute of Technology, Kharagpur and Jamia Milia Islamia (JMI).

3.7 DETAILS OF INVESTMENT

National Open Access Registry (NOAR) would be an integrated IT based system accessible to all stakeholders including open access participants, traders, National/ Regional/ State Load Dispatch Centers (LDCs) with system for automated Short Term Open Access (STOA) approvals. It would help in maintaining a repository of information such as open access granted to all customers, balance margin available per corridor, availed STOA as per corridor limit in an electronic form. It will facilitate fast exchange of information which in turn would make the approval process efficient and would help in reducing the gate closure time for executing a short-term open access transaction. The NOAR project is going to be a mission critical application which will administer the Electricity Market in India. Therefore, it requires a high end technical compliance so that the reliability and integrity of the system is maintained. It will facilitate implementation of Real Time Electricity

Market in India. Looking into system criticality and dependency of stake holders like NLDC, RLDC, SLDC, CERC and all market players in the NOAR system, a robust solution through NOAR is envisaged. POSOCO Board has already accorded investment approval for implementation of NOAR.

3.8 SKILL INVENTORY

Human resource is the key asset in a knowledge oriented organization like POSOCO. At present, there are 592 employees in POSOCO comprising of Corporate Centre, NLDC and RLDCs. Capacity building of the human resource is paramount for building POSOCO as a sustainable institution that would keep track with the ever changing regulatory regime & technological up gradation in the Indian Power Sector. Performance & efficiency of the power system operation requires continuous training & capacity building for skill up gradation of the all the personnel on the Load Dispatch Centers. CERC (Fees and Charges) Regulations, 2019 allocates sufficient funding for Human Resource Development (HRD) personnel of LDCs.

In addition to the engineering knowledge, new skill-sets are required in terms of hard skills and soft skills. Hard skills include MS Office applications, Forecasting, Network Simulation, Market Simulation, Software Development, Optimization, Economics, Law, Meteorology, Communication, Research Methodology, Statistics, Data Science, Analytics etc.

On the other hand, soft skills include Cognitive, verbal and written communication, interpersonal communication, public speaking, emotional intelligence, report writing, analytical, aesthetics, public relations etc.

POSOCO is committed to creating value proposition for its employees by developing a culture that incubates innovation and excellence through capacity building and catalyzing its Human Capital. Manpower/Human Resource is an integral part. POSOCO, as an organization, focuses on developing a well devised talent pool for a better and smarter future.

As on date, following is the diversity of the employees of POSOCO w.r.t. their qualifications:

Table 3.1: Diversity of the employees of POSOCO w.r.t. their qualifications

SN	Degree	Nos.
1	Degree in Electrical Engg.	326
2	Diploma in Electrical Engg.	42
3	Degree in CS/IT Engg.	32
4	Diploma in CS/IT Engg.	4

Table 3.1: Continue

SN	Degree	Nos.
5	Degree/Graduates in HR	35
6	Diploma in HR	1
7	Degree/Graduates in Finance	41
8	12th pass or below/other qualifications	111
	TOTAL	592

POSOCO focuses on contributing to an individual's functional proficiency and encouraging Continued Professional Development.

3.9 UNIQUENESS OF POSOCO

Indian grid is one of the largest synchronous grids and emerging electricity markets in the world. It is also unique due to diversity, federal and decentralized approach of governance in grid management. The mandate regarding load dispatch centers in the Indian Electricity Act 2003, introduction of open access, the recommendations post grid disturbance of 2012 and the national commitment towards renewable and clean energy have been the key Drivers for capacity development of load dispatching in India.

Today, the electricity landscape is changing faster than ever before. The achievement of a reliable and secure grid requires new rules, new technologies, and new ways of operating the power system. Closer co-operation among all players, be it generators, consumers, power exchanges, power suppliers or technology providers is key to the optimization of the overall system. Power System Operators manage the backbone of the electricity supply for the benefit of the society.

Socio-technical systems are complex systems. They comprise of several sub-systems with interrelationships that mutually influence each other's performance. The coordination services offered by the power system operators are unique and mission critical. While the performance of the subsystems can be improved by requisite investments in technology and other infrastructure, the performance of the power system operators would be a function of their domain knowledge, problem solving skills and motivation to deliver. Unlike the commercial organization, competition in power system operation is not against any other organization but against the randomly occurring combination of expected and unexpected events.

The role of Load Dispatch Centers falls under the realm of essential public service and is presently being carried out within the government set up and under regulatory oversight. The activities have to be limited within a code of discipline and commercial rules specified by the regulators. A diverse constituency has a stake in power system operation. This includes generating utilities, transmission utilities, distribution companies, consumers, manufacturers, market intermediaries, academic institutions, technologists and economists, lending agencies, planners, administrators, government authorities, regulatory bodies, legislature, judiciary and many others. Decisions are arrived at after a considerable formal and informal interaction among stakeholders and System Operators are subject to heightened value-laden expectations for neutrality, fairness, transparency and accountability. This makes power system operation a multidisciplinary in nature and calls for an understanding of all related areas apart from the technical aspects.

The country has set an ambitious target of adding 175 GW of renewable generation capacity by 2022. It includes Solar (utility-scale, distributed, off-grid / mini-grid - 100 GW), Wind (utility-scale - 60 GW), Small hydro (5 GW) and Bioenergy (10 GW). In this direction, a high level Technical committee, constituted by Ministry of Power, for Large Scale Integration of Renewable energy submitted its recommendations in April-2016. Several actions are being taken covering regulatory, transmission, system operation and capacity building. In order to facilitate grid integration of renewables at inter-state level, the CERC regulatory framework for forecasting, scheduling and deviation settlement for renewables at inter-state level has been implemented in November - 2015. At present, a total of about 5 GW of renewable generation is being scheduled by RLDCs at inter-state level.

Maintaining frequency within the stipulated Indian Electricity Grid Code (IEGC) band without adequate primary response, secondary control and ancillary services has been challenging for POSOCO.

Managing power system in natural disasters such as earthquakes and cyclones has been quite challenging. The cyclones and floods in India are an alarm for the safety and reliability of Indian Grid. The immediate effects of such natural disasters on the power system are system faults and loads throw off. This leads to high voltages and frequency in the system which if uncontrolled may lead to cascade failure. The proactive and fast response from POSOCO has averted cascading failures in both the cases. Such low probability high impact events bring out the need for a resilient grid and design of such a resilient grid at the planning horizon itself.

POSOCO also signed MoU with Earth System Science Organization - India Meteorological Department (ESSO-IMD), Ministry of Earth Sciences on 18th May 2015 for synergy in the management of Indian Power System and weather related impact.

3.10 BUSNIESS MODEL

POSOCO uses the Business Services Model by adding value which entails that the company uses all the three components of Intellectual Capital viz. Human Capital, Structural or Organizational Capital and Social Capital. Accordingly, POSOCO adds value to the service it provides to its clients by using first and foremost, its human capital. KM is the most crucial and critically important factor in the revenue generation. Human Resource vertical of POSOCO also takes of organizational capital and social capital for stakeholders 'WOW SATISFACTION'.

3.11 REVENUE FROM OPERATIONS

POSOCO derives revenue primarily by providing services of system operation and market operation, short term open access, Energy saving certificates, Renewable energy certificates and registrations.

In order to ensure an independent revenue stream and financial autonomy for POSOCO, the CERC notifies Fees and Charges Regulations from time to time on five-year control period basis. For the present control period 2019-24, the CERC has notified the Regulations on Fees and Charges on 5th April, 2019. In the previous control period, i.e. 2014-19, Regulations notified on 18th May, 2015 were applicable. The revenue is being realized by levying the Fees and Charges on the Users like Generating stations, Discoms, Sellers, Buyers, and the Transmission Licensees towards the services provided to them.

Revenue from system operation and market operations comprising of RLDC fees and charges is recognized as a performance obligation satisfied over time as the customer simultaneously receives and consumes the benefit provided by the Company. It is based on tariff approved by Central Electricity Regulatory Commission (CERC) and is recognized on monthly basis.

Income from short term open access is recognized as a performance obligation satisfied over time as the customer simultaneously receives and consumes the benefit provided by the Company for as and when the bilateral / collective transactions take place. Non-Refundable Application money is accounted as income on receipt of application along with the fee, It is based on regulations notified by CERC and is recognized on monthly basis.

Revenue from application fee, registration fee and issuance of certificates is recognized at the point in time on satisfaction of performance obligation.

3.12 REVENUE REALIZATION PROCESS

The process of Revenue i.e. Fees & Charges, Billing & realization of Power System Operation Corporation Limited is detailed below:

Central Electricity Regulatory Commission notifies Regulations governing the Revenue stream of RLDCs/NLDC under POSOCO on five year control period basis. For the control period 2019-24, CERC vide notification dated 5th April 2019 issued the Central Electricity Regulatory Commission (Fees and Charges of Regional Load Dispatch Centre and other related matters) Regulations, 2019.These fees and charges include Return on equity, Interest on loan capital, Depreciation, Operation and Maintenance expenses excluding human resources expenses, Operational Expenditure (OPEX), Human Resource expenses, NLDC charges and Corporate Office expenses and Interest on working capital. These fees and charges are collected from the beneficiaries/ Users of the services of the RLDCs and NLDC on monthly basis. The Users of RLDCs are the generating companies, distribution licensees, buyers, Bulk consumers (SEZ), sellers and inter-State transmission licensees, Demand Response Consumers, Qualified Coordinating Agency (QCA), or any other such existing (or envisaged in future)entity who use the inter-State transmission network or the associated facilities and services of National Load Dispatch Centre and Regional Load Dispatch Centers.

All generating stations, distribution licensees and inter-State transmission licensees or any other user intending to avail the Grid Access need to be registered themselves with concerned Regional Load Dispatch Centre responsible for scheduling, metering, energy accounting and switching operations, not less than 30 days prior to intended date of commencement of Grid access. The Registration fees of distribution licensees and interState transmission licensees are 10 lakh and for generating station it is based on the installed capacity of the plant.

The monthly LDC charges to be calculated for the inter-State transmission licensees, generating stations and sellers, distribution licensees and buyers as under:

(a) The LDC Charges for inter-State transmission licensees to be determined on the basis of(1/3) of approved annual charges and to be worked out on the basis of the circuit kilometers (ckt-km) of the lines owned by inter-State transmission licensees;

(b) The LDC Charges for the inter-State Generating station and sellers to be determined on the basis of (1/3) of annual LDC charges and to be worked out on the basis of installed capacity in case of the generating station and long term and / or medium term contracted capacity in case of sellers;

(c) The LDC Charges for the distribution licensees and buyers to be determined on the basis of (1/3) of annual charges and shall be worked out on the basis of sum of aggregate allocated capacity and / or contracted capacities in case of distribution licensee including deemed distribution licensees.

Based on the above, RLDCs raise the bill to the Users on monthly basis and realization generally takes up to 45 days from the date issuance of the bill. A rebate of 1.5% mayis allowed to the Users on the gross bill amount settled through RTGS, NEFT, Letter of Credit or cheque up to fifth day (i.e. T+5 day) from the date of issuance of the bills, where T is the date of issuance of the bill. The rebate of 1% may be allowed when payment is made from T+6 to T+30 days from issuance of the bill.

No rebate shall be allowed for payment made from T+31 days till T+45 days from the date of issuance of the bill.

In case the payment is delayed by a user beyond a period of 45 days from the date of billing, a late payment surcharge at the rate of 1.5%per month to be levied from the users.

Realization is generally more than 95% on annual basis.

3.13 CASH COW

According to the Webster Dictionary "Cash Cow is a business, investment, or product that provides a steady income or profit."

POSOCO is a statutory organization that provides essential services to the country. POSOCO is a utility and its functions are indispensable to the sector and to the country. Its revenue model ensures steady Income. It is not dependent on market forces, nor is highly fluctuating. Hence, POSOCO can be classified as a Cash Cow.

However, POSOCO is a profit neutral organization and its revenue entail recouping of its expenses and are budgeted as recovery/ reimbursement of expenditure required for its uninterrupted activities. Its functions are as defined by various regulatory/ statutory bodies are not dependent on innovations and are not market sensitive.

3.14 MEMORANDUM OF UNDERSTANDING (MOU)

POSOCO signs a MoU with Ministry of Power, Govt. of India on annual basis for various qualitative and quantitative parameters with stipulated performance levels.

POSOCO signed a MoU with Earth System Science Organization - India Meteorological Department (ESSOIMD), Ministry of Earth Sciences for synergy in the management of Indian Power System and weather related impact. (Source: POSOCO Annual Report 201819)

In order to increase collaborative research work in the Area of Power System an MOU between ERLDC and IIT Patna was also signed. (Source: POSOCO Annual Report 201819)

MoU between Power System Operation Corporation Limited (POSOCO) and Ministry of Power (MoP)

MoU is a negotiated agreement and contract between the Administrative Ministry/ Department/ Holding Company i.e. the majority shareholder and the management of the CPSE on selected parameters having targets decided normally before the beginning of the financial year and results evaluated at the end of the financial year. All CPSEs (Holding as well as Subsidiaries) are required to sign MoUs. The Apex/Holding companies sign MoUs with their administrative Ministries/ Departments, while the subsidiary companies sign MoUs with their respective Apex/ Holding companies.

The purpose of the MoU is to measure the performance of the management of the CPSEs on key selected parameters against the targets set so as to increase the improvements of the critical financial indicators of the organization.

POSOCO has been signing MoU with Administrative Ministry/ Holding Company from FY 2011-12 onwards. Till 2017-18, POSOCO was a subsidiary company of its erstwhile holding company POWERGRID, therefore, MoUs prior to FY 2017-18 were signed with it. POSOCO became an independent company in FY 2017-18, therefore, subsequent MoUs have been signed with Ministry of Power.

This whole mechanism of MoU is governed through Guidelines issued by Department of Public Enterprises (DPE), in this regard. CPSEs work in various sectors under different conditions and therefore uniform parameters cannot be prescribed. In view of this, in the MoU of any CPSE, there are uniform parameters for measuring financial performances such as revenue from operations, operating profit and return on investment (e.g. ratio of PAT/Net-worth). 50% weightage in the MoU is assigned to these financial parameters.

For the remaining 50% weightage, a list of parameters has been suggested in the DPE guidelines for selection depending on the sector in which the CPSE is operating. The parameters most appropriate and relevant for measuring performance are negotiated and finalized after consultations at two levels i.e. the Pre-Negotiation Committee (PNC) and the Inter-Ministerial Committee (IMC). The role of the Pre-negotiation Committee (earlier known as Standing Committee on MoU) is to assist IMC in determining the most appropriate and relevant parameters for measuring improvement in performance and for fixing targets. Meetings of the Pre-negotiation Committee are held before the meetings of IMC to look at the trends, discuss, negotiate and recommend MoU parameters and targets. With a view to distinguish "Excellent Performance" from the "Poor Performance", DPE has prescribed five different categories:

Table 3.2: Performance Scores given by DPE (Source: dpemou.nic.in)

Aggregated Score	Rating
90< Score< 100	Excellent
70< Score< 90	Very Good
50< Score< 70	Good
33< Score< 50	Fair
0< Score< 33	Poor

POSOCO has been consistently rated 'Excellent' since beginning except in FY 2016-17 and FY 2018-19 in which it was rated as 'Very Good' for reasons not in operational control of the company. (Source: dpe.gov.in)

3.15 TECHNOLOGY INITIATIVES

Real-time data acquisition from various stations across the country is a challenging task and it involves implementation of state-of-the art technology in SCADA / EMS system and WAM systems, strong communication network along-with rigorous planning to achieve it. System Operators relies on the real-time data made available to them through SCADA / EMS & WAM systems for grid monitoring and decision making in day to day Grid Operation. It is desired that the system operators are equipped with latest tools to facilitate real time decision making process. Accordingly, SCADA / EMS systems at all the control centers on all India basis including at RLDCs, SLDCs have been replaced / upgraded in order to equip the system operators with latest available visualization and power system application tools. Availability of SCADA / EMS systems are being maintained above 99.9% to provide the interruption free data to the operators. Backup of each control centers have also been established as a disaster recovery system to take over system operation function by back-up control center in case of any contingency in main control center. As a part of emergency preparedness for disaster management, the operation of all the regional back-up Control Centre are being tested through various mock drills by respective control centers.

To provide dynamic visibility of the grid, Wide Area Management Systems (WAMS) are being installed nationwide under the Unified Real Time Dynamic State Measurement (URTDSM) project. Presently, under the URTDSM project about 1460 PMUs are commissioned and reporting to the regional control centers.

Establishment of Renewable Energy Management Centers (REMCs) is under implementation with the guidance of Ministry of Power and Ministry of New and Renewable Energy, GoI. 3 nos. have been established at Regional Level and one at National Level.

POSOCO facilitated the development of two applications, named as "Vidyut PRAVAH"- Electricity, Price Availability and Highlights and "MERIT" - Merit Order Dispatch of Electricity for Rejuvenation of Income and Transparency, for the Ministry of Power.

ERLDC has developed Power Information Portal and EASTGRID Mobile App for providing information to its stakeholders & interested parties. Built on latest Angular & CMS platforms, the ERLDC information portal is an interactive Data visualization and an analytical platform in graphical forms(https: / / erldc.in /).

In order to facilitate better management of weather data, a dedicated Web-portal has been developed by POSOCO in collaboration with IMD for all regions/ states. Subsequently, workshop-cum-knowledge sharing program has been conducted at various levels for better understanding. The information available in the Portal regarding weather forecast shall help State Discoms to take pro-active steps regarding short term and medium term management processes and supply planning requirements and also for better planning for infrastructure availability to ensure cost effective and reliable supply.

3.16 REAL TIME OPERATIONS

The Load Dispatch Centers (LDC) make mission critical decisions in real time for reliable operation of the electricity grid. The IEEE (Institute of Electrical and Electronics Engineers) proceedings Volume 93 titled "'Power System Control Centers Past Present and Future' by Felix F Wu et.al. (2005) have noted that "The control center is the nerve system of the power system. It senses the pulse of the power system, adjusts its conditions, coordinates its movements and provides defense against exogenous events." The importance of real time operation is recognized with nearly 25-30% of the LDC strength involved in this critical activity.

The real time operation includes close monitoring of the system parameters, such as frequency, voltages, line loadings, while facilitating inter-state / inter-regional power exchanges in accordance with Indian Electricity Grid Code (IEGC). Energy Management system modules implemented in the different control centers (NLDC/RLDCs/SLDCs) consists of various applications covering wide spectrum of functions like Pre-dispatch, Real time dispatch and Post-dispatch functions. The Energy Management System (EMS) tools such as state estimation, contingent analysis, optimum power flow, load forecasting, resources scheduling has provided system operators greater flexibility in taking appropriate and judicious decisions during the course of operation. The control room operator has been equipped with latest technological tools to manage the grid for Frequency Control, Voltage control, Tie line loading or congestion management, Ensuring N-1 security at all times, Ancillary Services, Balancing Services, Automatic Generation Control, Real Time Contingency Analysis, Dynamic Security Assessment, Monitoring weather updates, handling emergency outage requests, Restoration of network after tripping, Rescheduling of generation, Information dissemination to authorities in case of a grid disturbance/grid event, Periodic communication with relevant stakeholders and sensitizing in case of emergencies and de-briefing after an extreme event.

The Supervisory Data Acquisition (SCADA) system which was implemented pan India during the 2002 - 2005 has been renovated during 2014-16 by all the LDCs pan-India to deal with obsolescence of the equipment and to implement the latest technology. Wide Area Measurement (WAM) Systems which includes around 1400 Phasor Measurement Units have been implemented at different LDCs which let the LDC operator visualize dynamic behaviour of the power systems. Visualization tools are available for the real time data as implemented in SCADA/WAM system.

The real time grid operator is regularly updated on weather data such as temperature, pressure, humidity, rain fall etc. at key load centers to assess the expected demand trend. Demand forecasting is a key input for preparation of day-ahead schedules which in turn requires accurate weather information from large geographical areas. With increase in renewable energy penetration in the grid, there is added emphasis on providing accurate weather data such as wind speed, solar insolation etc. to the LDC control rooms. Further, for managing the grid during inclement weather conditions such as storms, cyclones (Hud-hud, Phailin, Titli etc.) & earthquakes that adversely impact the power system, the LDCs need to prepare in advance. Hence to improve crisis-preparedness they require advance information from weather service providers.

3.17 CORPORATE SOCIAL RESPONSIBILITY (CSR)

At POSOCO, all efforts towards the true measure of growth and progress are best echoed in the impact that the company makes to the lives of people and society as a whole. POSOCO has always endeavored to ensure that the CSR activities are effective and positively contribute in bettering the lives of people through environmental sustainability, educational and health related initiatives. There is a POSOCO CSR and Sustainability policy for smooth execution of the activities taken up by the company. The CSR initiatives taken up by the company are in line with the schedule-VII of the Companies Act 2013. The POSOCOCSR and Sustainability Policy of the company is available on POSOCO website.

POSOCO commits towards creating a community of responsible and educated citizens who are environmentally conscious, practice social responsibility in their daily lives and inspire others to do the same. POSOCO will endeavor for uplifting of the underprivileged and marginalized sections of the society through promoting preventive health care, education including special education, employment enhancing vocational skills, promoting gender equality and empowering women. POSOCO will also promote innovation, research and excellence in the area of Powers Systems through collaborations with technology incubators located within academic institutions.

The key projects undertaken under CSR activities during FY 2018-19 are:

(a) Promoting research and studies related to Power Systems in the engineering institutions to encourage excellence in the area

(b) Capacity Building in the field of Computer education

(c) Construction of a waiting hall for patients and their attendants at Safdarjung Hospital

(d) Organizing camps for providing Aids and Assistive devices to Persons with Disabilities and (e) Participation in Swachh Bharat Abhiyan.

3.18 AWARDS & RECOGNITION

In the last 2-3 years, the performance of POSOCO has been recognized at various levels in the form of awards and accolades in various categories.

POSOCO has consistently got "Excellent Rating" on the basis of self - evaluation on the parameters of Corporate Governance in terms of the DPE Guidelines on Corporate Governance for CPSEs. POSOCO has been recognized and awarded, nationally and internationally, for its performance amongst the PSUs. The Company has also been rated 'Excellent' for its performance for most of the years.

POSOCO got the ISGF Innovation Award for Best Smart Grid Pilot Project in India in March, 2020.

POSOCO was awarded with "Best in class for Training & Development (PSUs)" Award on September, 2019 by Asia Pacific HRM Congress.

POSOCO was presented India's Most Trusted Company in Electricity Transmission Services for year 2019 by International Brand Consulting Corporation USA on August, 2019.

POSOCO was bestowed with "Best Power System Operator Award" in January, 2019 by Central Board of Irrigation and Power (CBIP).

Women's Team from POSOCO bagged the Gold Medal among Women Employee's, AIMA Corporate Olympiad quiz competition which was organized by AIMA in January, 2019.

"North India Best Employer Brand Award" 2018 by World HRD Congress was awarded to POSOCO.

POSOCO was awarded for "Innovation in HR" in September, 2018 at 17th Asia Pacific HRM Congress.

3.19 JOURNEY OF KNOWLEDGE MANAGEMENT IN POSOCO

This part of the thesis will give the journey of Knowledge Management in POSOCO right from envisioning to evaluation.

POSOCO which was earlier a part of POWERGRID was made a subsidiary of POWERGRID in 2008 and so we followed the policy of Knowledge Management which was there in POWERGRID. However, the implementation, the Yellow pages, the Knowledge matrices and maps were differently done suited to the need of POSOCO. POSOCO started by establishing a Knowledge Management cell, subsequently the Knowledge Management policy was implemented followed by Knowledge Bank, Knowledge Maps and Matrices, Knowledge Portal, etc.

3.19.1 Knowledge Management Cell

A Knowledge Management Cell was created in 2009 to manage the Knowledge assets of POSOCO. POSOCO had enormous amounts of data both tacit & explicit further managing the grid was and still is full of complexities. Transfers and superannuation of experienced employees was the main reason and another was attrition of youngsters. Any of these three factors would have led to loss of knowledge which was so critical to manage the grid. To mitigate the loss of knowledge caused by these factors Knowledge Management became an essential critical activity. The Knowledge Management cell was headed by the Head of Human Resources and had two members each form IT Department, Market Operation Department & System Operation Department. Along with the personnel deployed in the Knowledge Management cell of POWERGRID the personnel in the Knowledge Management cell of POSOCO visited many organizations both in the Public Sector & Private Sector, understood their Knowledge Management policies and implementation. Finally after much discussion and deliberation the Knowledge Management policy was formulated for POSOCO.

3.19.2 Knowledge Management Policy

The Knowledge Management Policy included the policy statement, definition of Knowledge Management, Objectives, and Rationale for Knowledge Management, Strategy, Virtual Knowledge Management organization, Knowledge Management procedure; Knowledge

Management Bank, Knowledge Management practices; Incentives and Recognition. The Policy also listed the role of the Knowledge Management Cell, and the role of the individual staff, role of Nodal Officers, and the role of HODs.

3.19.2.1 Mission of Knowledge Management Policy

Knowledge Management promotes an integrated approach to identifying, capturing, retrieving, sharing & evaluating an enterprises knowledge wealth. These assets may include databases, documents, policies, procedures as well as the tacit expertise and experience available with the individuals.

3.19.2.2 Objectives of Knowledge Management Policy

a) *Harnessing potential of Information and Communication Technology.*
b) *Increasing the organizational process efficiency and accuracy for maximizing the returns.*

c) *Enriching knowledge content for establishing and creating new ways and means in business process of organization.*
d) *Facilitating and managing organizational innovation and learning.*
e) *Leveraging the expertise of people across the organization.*
f) *Increasing the knowledge exchange among employees.*
g) *Managing intellectual capital and intellectual assets in the work force.*
h) *Adopting new Knowledge Management tools, techniques and technologies to keep the KM system in POSOCO intact, robust and going.*
i) *Increasing employee satisfaction by facilitating employee learning.*

3.19.3 Nodal Officers for Knowledge Management

The Head of HR was the Nodal Officer of the concerned RLDC. He also identified a nodal officer from every department- viz. Information Technology, System Operation, Market Operation and Finance. These nodal officers were well versed with knowledge of computers as well as knowledge about their own department. They would also help in identifying the people who would capture the knowledge. This formed the task force for implementation of Knowledge Management.

3.19.4 Knowledge Management Awareness programs

Knowledge Management Awareness programs were conducted throughout the RLDCs, to educate employees about the Knowledge Management policy and its purpose. By 31st March, 2011 all RLDCs had completed the one day Knowledge Management awareness programs.

3.19.5 Pilot Implementation of Knowledge Management Policy

The Pilot Implementation of Knowledge Management was done in the southern region in September, 2011. It was successful except in the areas of finance and accounts. These issues were then addressed and the policy was revised by December, 2011.

3.19.6 Knowledge Management Technology

The existing technology needed to be upgraded. The technology for Knowledge Management was subsequently upgraded in 2010 and a homepage, page for online discussions repository for documents and reports and a directory of domain experts was provided.

Enterprise Resource Planning Technology form SAP was also implemented.

3.19.7 Knowledge Bank

Knowledge Bank was created in 2012 to enable implementation of the Knowledge Management processes including creation, acquisition, collations, storage, use and reuse and dissemination employees were encouraged to post tacit knowledge which they had because of their experience on the Knowledge Management portal which was called the Knowledge Bank. All employees of POSOCO were given access to the Knowledge Portal.

The Knowledge Bank also had information about subject matter experts, training material, technical reports, books, manuals, research articles, discussion and external resources like links to other websites.

3.19.8 Knowledge Maps and Matrices

Knowledge Maps and Matrices were organized as under the heads of Knowledge requirements, Knowledge gaps, Knowledge assets, Knowledge domains. These alsoindicate what Knowledge is needed, who needs it, who has it, whether it is explicit or tacit; routine or non-routine. The vertical wise formats were used for mapping the 'organizational knowledge'. (Appendix 'E' as adopted from POWERGRID website)

3.19.9 Corporate Yellow Pages

POSOCO is a Knowledge driven organization. To leverage the Knowledge assets Corporate Yellow Pages were prepared that had the details of all the domain experts and their area of expertise.

This activity also had to ensure that the domain experts were available and ready to help inspite of their busy schedule. The yellow pages were then uploaded on the Knowledge Bank. This facilitated the availability of knowledge to the personnel at right time and at the right place. (Appendix 'F')

3.19.10 Communities of Practice

Communities of Practice were then created for all Departments. These communities were to prepare an annual plan of implementation of Knowledge Management processes and suggest any change in policy if required.

3.19.11 Training on Knowledge Management

Training Programs on Knowledge Management were incorporated in the HRD Action Plan w.e.f. 2012. These programs were for the Nodal Officers, the members of the Knowledge Management Task Force as well as employees in the Middle

Management. As the time has progressed training on Knowledge Management became an integral part of the HRD action plan and is being conducted every year. Even the Engineer Trainees are trained on the aspects of Knowledge Management during their one year long training programs.

3.19.12 Structure

It was decided to have Knowledge Management implemented as a virtual department where everyone while doing his routine jobs would contribute towards the Knowledge Management portal. Every RLDC had the Head of HR as the nodal officer and a task force of experts from various Departments. The nodal officers of the RLDC coordinated the functions of Knowledge Management. Every Head of Department has been delegated the power to decide about the content and of information and about to whom and how much the information is to be shared, both within the organization and with external stakeholders.

3.19.13 Top Management support

The Top Management of POSOCO is extremely concerned about the organizations knowledge needs. Therefore, there is a lot of support from the Top Management. The Top Management has not only encouraged the employees but has also made it a imperative for all HODs to ensure that the Knowledge Management Policy is implemented. The top management has also encouraged all trainings on Knowledge Management.

3.19.14 Recognition, Rewards & Incentives

The following rewards & incentives are proposed to be introduced in POSOCOto encourage contribution to Knowledge Management.

1. Contribution to the Knowledge Management portal is proposed to be considered as a Key Performance Indicator in the Appraisal System.
2. It is proposed to highlight the names of the Top Contributors to the Knowledge Management Portal.
3. It is also proposed to give titles every month to the Top Contributors to the Knowledge Management portal.

Information used in this chapter is from Secondary Sources. Any primary data has been used with the permission of POSOCO.

CHAPTER 4

RESEARCH METHODOLOGY

4.1 INTRODUCTION

This chapter elaborates the Research Methodology adopted in this study in order to assess the Drivers shaping the Knowledge Management implementation with special reference to POSOCO. Primarily, the chapter entails the research design, sampling methodology, instrument design and development and the techniques used for data analysis required to meet the objectives of the study in a systematic and coherent manner.

Research is "creative and systematic work undertaken to increase the stock of knowledge, including knowledge of humans, culture and society, and the use of this stock of knowledge to devise new applications. "According to Clifford Woody (1961), "research comprises defining and redefining problems, formulating hypotheses or suggested solutions; collecting, organizing and evaluating data; making deductions and reaching conclusions; and at last carefully testing the conclusions to determine whether they fit the formulating hypothesis". As per Kothari, C.R. (2004) "Research methodology is a method to systematically solve the research problem. It may be understood as a science of studying how research is done scientifically". Thus, it is a systematic and structured process to arrive at the conclusion of a defined problem.

In furtherance of realizing the basic aim and purpose of this study- i.e. to identify Knowledge Management Drivers from the point of view of HR towards an implementation perspective in POSOCO, both qualitative and quantitative research approaches have been adopted in this study besides reasoning as a part of triangulation method. Triangulation, in the context of research in social sciences; "refers to the application and combination of several research methods", especially; when a study is undertaken of a particular phenomenon from various angles. So, both inductive and deductive approaches in varied methods were adopted to arrive at the desired result outcomes using statistical analysis through NVivo v.12 for qualitative data and SPSS 26 and AMOS 26 softwares for quantitative data. In this study, a descriptive research design contrived from a deductive approach was used which initiated from deducing logical relationships between concepts through exploration of the extant theoretical studies posited in the review of literature, and then finally; the research moved towards establishing concrete empirical evidence based on the premises drawn for the study. It was complied with exploratory investigation. To recapitulate, the basic aim and purpose of this study is to identify Knowledge Management Drivers from the perspective of implementation in various departments of POSOCO.

In order to achieve the expected outcome of the study, hypotheses were developed and tested using statistical analysis for quantitative instrument through SPSS AMOS 26 software. The data was thoughtfully generated using the questionnaire method in the area of survey research and some interviews were also conducted to yield rich insight into the study at the initial stages of instrument designing and development. In this study, structured interviews were also conducted to ascertain the validity of the questionnaire scale items in the context of the KM. This was aimed to elicit actual KM implementation aspects from senior level executives like Executive Directors (EDs), HODs of Operations, HR Executive (HOPs) who are either championing KM initiatives or supervising software development projects in POSOCO. This led to deciphering the intricate relationship between the Drivers effectuating the KM implementation in POSOCO, especially; the onerous responsibility on HR. The detailed research methodology is presented in the following sections.

4.2 RESEARCH OBJECTIVES

The main objectives of this study are as:-

1. To examine the various 'Drivers of Knowledge Management' by focusing the role of HR impacting organizational processes and structural make-up for Knowledge Management orientation in POSOCO.
2. To validate the 'Drivers of Knowledge Management' in order to help in the theory- building effort of Knowledge Management Implementation.
3. To identify the relationship between the 'Drivers of Knowledge Management' and the overall 'effectiveness of KM implementation' in POSOCO.

4. To ascertain the relationship of the Drivers of KM and the overall effectiveness of KM implementation across the demographic variables.
5. To provide a Technology Acceptance Model for man-machine amelioration in the domain of Knowledge Management.

4.2.1 Case Study

In order to undertake an empirical enquiry, the case study research method has been adopted by academicians of various business schools. It becomes more important to use this method when an organization has uniqueness. POSOCO is such an organization. An exhaustive case study research method and its requirement had been undertaken by Viale (2010) and he established that ' generalization' of the outcome of a single case study research is not only relevant but also can to be emulated in management parlance.

Though Yin had propounded this concept in 2004 itself; the invigorated study was undertaken by Yin (2014) again and he established the 'universality of an outcome' of a single case study. Accordingly, this case study has been proposed on the premise of uniqueness of POSOCO.

4.2.2 Hypothesis

A hypothesis is a proposed explanation for executing this research towards the fulfillment of the objectives in part. For a hypothesis to be scientific in nature, the scientific method is to be adopted and same requires that one tests it thoroughly. Even though the words like "hypothesis" and "theory" are often used synonymously, a scientific hypothesis is not the same as a scientific theory. A working hypothesis is a provisionally accepted hypothesis proposed for future research.

A good hypothesis should have three crucial aspects. The three aspects are as follows:

- Assumption: It is a possible explanation for the problem.
- Condition: It tells how the researcher will conduct the experiment.
- Prediction: It tells what the researcher thinks will happen in due course of time.

In this study, various KM Drivers were postulated to be related to the overall effective implementation of KM in POSOCO. So each of the Drivers, (as extracted from the factor analysis results), were taken up to constitute the corresponding hypothesis.

First was its relationship with the effective implementation of KM in POSOCO. Second was its relationship with the effectiveness of KM implementation across the demographic variables.

Accordingly, several hypotheses and their sub-hypotheses were articulated to present the results in a systematic manner. All the hypotheses testing in this study was conducted at 95% confidence level. This is presented in the following tables as:-

H1: There is a relationship between all the KM Drivers and overall effectiveness of KM implementation.

Table 4.1: Relationship between KM Drivers and overall effectiveness of KM implementation (Hypotheses)

S. No.	Hypothesis
1	H1a: There is a relationship between Structures and overall effectiveness of KM implementation
2	H1b: There is a relationship between Assets and overall effectiveness of KM implementation
3	H1c: There is a relationship between Processes and overall effectiveness of KM implementation
4	H1d: There is a relationship between Culture and overall effectiveness of KM implementation
5	H1e: There is a relationship between Technology and overall effectiveness of KM implementation
6	H1f: There is a relationship between Strategy and overall effectiveness of KM implementation
7	H1g: There is a relationship between Deterrents and overall effectiveness of KM implementation
8	H1h: There is a relationship between Incentives and overall effectiveness of KM implementation
9	H1i: There is a relationship between Enablers and overall effectiveness of KM implementation
10	H1j: There is a relationship between Training and overall effectiveness of KM implementation

Table 4.2: Relationship between KM Drivers and overall effectiveness of KM implementation across Genders (Hypotheses)

S. No.	Hypothesis
1	H2a: There is a relationship between Structures and overall effectiveness of KM implementation across Genders

Table 4.2: Continue

S. No.	Hypothesis
2	H2b: There is a relationship between Assets and overall effectiveness of KM implementation across Genders
3	H2c: There is a relationship between Processes and overall effectiveness of KM implementation across Genders
4	H2d: There is a relationship between Culture and overall effectiveness of KM implementation across Genders
5	H2e: There is a relationship between Technology and overall effectiveness of KM implementation across Genders
6	H2f: There is a relationship between Strategy and overall effectiveness of KM implementation across Genders
7	H2g: There is a relationship between Deterrents and overall effectiveness of KM implementation across Genders
8	H2h: There is a relationship between Incentives and overall effectiveness of KM implementation across Genders
9	H2i: There is a relationship between Enablers and overall effectiveness of KM implementation across Genders
10	H2j: There is a relationship between Training and overall effectiveness of KM implementation across Genders

Table 4.3: Relationship between KM Drivers and overall effectiveness of KM implementation across Age Groups (Hypotheses)

S. No.	Hypothesis
1	H3a: There is a relationship between Structures and overall effectiveness of KM implementation across Age Groups
2	H3b: There is a relationship between Assets and overall effectiveness of KM implementation across Age Groups
3	H3c: There is a relationship between Processes and overall effectiveness of KM implementation across Age Groups
4	H3d: There is a relationship between Culture and overall effectiveness of KM implementation across Age Groups
5	H3e: There is a relationship between Technology and overall effectiveness of KM implementation across Age Groups

Table 4.3: Continue

S. No.	Hypothesis
6	H3f: There is a relationship between Strategy and overall effectiveness of KM implementation across Age Groups
7	H3g: There is a relationship between Deterrents and overall effectiveness of KM implementation across Age Groups
8	H3h: There is a relationship between Incentives and overall effectiveness of KM implementation across Age Groups
9	H3i: There is a relationship between Enablers and overall effectiveness of KM implementation across Age Groups
10	H3j: There is a relationship between Training and overall effectiveness of KM implementation across Age Groups

Table 4.4: Relationship between KM Drivers and overall effectiveness of KM implementation across varied Levels of Education (Hypotheses)

S. No.	Hypothesis
1	H4a: There is a relationship between Structures and overall effectiveness of KM implementation across varied Levels of Education
2	H4b: There is a relationship between Assets and overall effectiveness of KM implementation across varied Levels of Education
3	H4c: There is a relationship between Processes and overall effectiveness of KM implementation across varied Levels of Education
4	H4d: There is a relationship between Culture and overall effectiveness of KM implementation across varied Levels of Education
5	H4e: There is a relationship between Technology and overall effectiveness of KM implementation across varied Levels of Education
6	H4f: There is a relationship between Strategy and overall effectiveness of KM implementation across varied Levels of Education
7	H4g: There is a relationship between Deterrents and overall effectiveness of KM implementation across varied Levels of Education
8	H4h: There is a relationship between Incentives and overall effectiveness of KM implementation across varied Levels of Education
9	H4i: There is a relationship between Enablers and overall effectiveness of KM implementation across varied Levels of Education
10	H4j: There is a relationship between Training and overall effectiveness of KM implementation across varied Levels of Education

H5: There is a relationship between KM Drivers and overall effectiveness of KM implementation across Levels of Hierarchy in the organization. Levels of Hierarchy are in terms of pay scales, with E-1 being the lowest Executive level of employee designated as Assistant Officer and E-9 being the level just below the Board of Directors. E-9 level of Executives are designated as Executive Directors.

Table 4.5: Relationship between KM Drivers and overall effectiveness of KM implementation across Levels of Hierarchy (Hypotheses)

S. No.	Hypothesis
1	H5a: There is a relationship between Structures and overall effectiveness of KM implementation across Levels of Hierarchy
2	H5b: There is a relationship between Assets and overall effectiveness of KM implementation across Levels of Hierarchy
3	H5c: There is a relationship between Processes and overall effectiveness of KM implementation across Levels of Hierarchy
4	H5d: There is a relationship between Culture and overall effectiveness of KM implementation across Levels of Hierarchy
5	H5e: There is a relationship between Technology and overall effectiveness of KM implementation across Levels of Hierarchy
6	H5f: There is a relationship between Strategy and overall effectiveness of KM implementation across Levels of Hierarchy
7	H5g: There is a relationship between Deterrents and overall effectiveness of KM implementation across Levels of Hierarchy
8	H5h: There is a relationship between Incentives and overall effectiveness of KM implementation across Levels of Hierarchy
9	H5i: There is a relationship between Enablers and overall effectiveness of KM implementation across Levels of Hierarchy
10	H5j: There is a relationship between Training and overall effectiveness of KM implementation across Levels of Hierarchy

Table 4.6: Relationship between KM Drivers and overall effectiveness of KM implementation across number of years of Experience (Hypotheses)

S. No.	Hypothesis
1	H6a: There is a relationship between Structures and overall effectiveness of KM implementation across number of years of Experience
2	H6b: There is a relationship between Assets and overall effectiveness of KM implementation across number of years of Experience

Table 4.6: Continue

S. No.	Hypothesis
3	H6c: There is a relationship between Processes and overall effectiveness of KM implementation across number of years of Experience
4	H6d: There is a relationship between Culture and overall effectiveness of KM implementation across number of years of Experience
5	H6e: There is a relationship between Technology and overall effectiveness of KM implementation across number of years of Experience
6	H6f: There is a relationship between Strategy and overall effectiveness of KM implementation across number of years of Experience
7	H6g: There is a relationship between Deterrents and overall effectiveness of KM implementation across number of years of Experience
8	H6h: There is a relationship between Incentives and overall effectiveness of KM implementation across number of years of Experience
9	H6i: There is a relationship between Enablers and overall effectiveness of KM implementation across number of years of Experience
10	H6j: There is a relationship between Training and overall effectiveness of KM implementation across number of years of Experience

Likewise other hypotheses, H1 to H6, were postulated. More importantly, the constructs ought to be validated which was achieved through Confirmatory Factor Analysis, using the AMOS software. This would yield rich insight for further analysis and implications for the study. Not only this, the study aims at a thorough integration of the KM Drivers that are widely accepted in the literature. Since this is an empirical study, the researcher went through the vast literature abounding Knowledge Management and also probed the intellectual capital of POSOCO with respect to various Drivers actually enforcing Knowledge Management implementation therein.

4.2.3 Research approach of Study

This research study was conducted in two ways involving:

- ❖ Qualitative approach, and
- ❖ Quantitative approach

In the first phase, the Qualitative tools like Focus Group Discussion, In-depth interviews, Elite Interviews and Participant's Observation (since the researcher is a part of the organization) were used in this study for collating extensive information and insight into the KM Drivers and implementation related aspects at POSOCO. Qualitative themes/ antecedents of Knowledge Management were also extracted using the qualitative tools.

Next, a quantitative approach was adopted and statistical analysis was adminstratered on the data obtained using a structured questionnaire from the executives of POSOCO.

4.2.3.1 Focus Group

The Focus Group is a rich source of primary data and also the most lucid style of extracting information (Sekaran & Bougie, 2010). According to Sekaran & Bougie, "focus groups consist typically of eight to ten members with a moderator leading the discussions for about two hours on a particular topic, concept, or product. Members are generally chosen on the basis of their expertise in the topic on which information is sought."

The focus group sessions are aimed at obtaining respondents' impressions, interpretations, and opinions; as the members talk about the event, concept and service. It is pertinent to note that the moderator's role is pivotal in steering the discussions in the right direction to elicit the required information and to keep the members on track so that they don't digress from the topic of discussion. The unstructured and spontaneous responses are expected to reflect the genuine opinions, ideas and feelings of the members participating in focus group about the topic under discussion. The focus group discussions involve minimal cost, and provides a fairly dependable data within a short span of time. In this study, the focus group was conducted by the researcher herself by involving the Nodal Officers of every department at Corporate Center and all the Regional Load Dispatch Centers of POSOCO.

The transcripts for the same have been placed at Appendix- A.

4.2.3.2 Interview

An interview is a method of data collection that may be described as an interaction involving the interviewer and the interviewee, the purpose of which is to obtain valid and reliable information. Interviews may range from casual conversation of brief questioning to more formal, lengthy interactions, formal interviews are sometimes necessary in research, in order to, standardize interview topics and general questions. "The most important aspect of an interviewer's approach concerns conveying the idea that the participant's information is acceptable and valuable" (Marshall & Rossman, 2006). Interview entails a session of formal questioning of a group of people.

In this study, the researcher has conducted two types of interviews; (i) In-depth Interview of the committee members who have been entrusted with the work of implementation of Knowledge Management policies of POSOCO and (ii) the Elite Interview of Chief Executive Officer known as Chairman and Managing Director in POSOCO.

4.2.3.3 In-Depth Interview

In-depth interviewing is another effective means of data collection techniques used extensively in qualitative research. It is described as "a conversation with a purpose" (Kahn and Cannell, 1957). Typically, qualitative in-depth interviews are more like conversations rather than formal structured interview through which the researcher explores a few general topics to help uncover the participant's perspective of meaning. The researcher respects as to how the participant frames and structures his responses". An interview is a useful way to get large amounts of data quickly. When more than one person is used as an informant, the interview process allows for a wide variety of information through a large number of subjects. It also allows for immediate follow-up questions and, if necessary for clarifications; follow-up interviews can also be scheduled at a later date. In-depth interview of Knowledge Management Implementation Committee members of POSOCO was conducted.

The same has been appended as Appendix B.

4.2.3.4 Elite Interview

Marshall & Rossman (2006) have advocated another variant of interview, known as the 'Elite Interview' which is an interview with an 'elite' person and is a specialized case of interviewing that focuses on a particular type of interviewee. Elite individuals are considered to be influential, prominent, and/or well-informed in an organization or community; they are selected for interviews on the basis of their expertise in areas relevant to the research. In this study, Elite interview was specifically conducted by asking specific questions on KM from Mr. KVS Baba, CMD, POSOCO.

The elite interview has been transcribed and the transcription is available in Appendix C.

4.2.3.5 Internal Observation

Luders (2004) highlighted the importance of observation in qualitative research where one can make an empirical investigation of other persons, their everyday practices by holding conversations with the participants about their actions or through his/her own observations. Being on the rolls of POSOCO and being in the organization under this study; the 'subject' becomes a direct participant. Since this researcher herself is a member of the Knowledge Management Implementation Committee of POSOCO, it is pertinent to take into account her own (participant) observations. So, "Participant's observations" method is also used in this dissertation for qualitative inputs. The role of this method is that "researcher began to see participant observation in a broader sense as a flexible, methodologically plural and context related strategy that could incorporate widely different procedures".

Besides, the qualitative tools as discussed above, the quantitative research approach has also been adopted in this study to make it more comprehensive. For this, the structured questionnaire as a survey tool was tool designed as delineated in Section 4.6 and administered to the Executives in POSOCO as per the given sample size.

4.3 RESEARCH DESIGN

At present, the evidence-based research is in vogue as explained by Burkholder & Burbank, (2019). They advocated that both qualitative and quantitative approaches are to be used in the research to be "doubly sure" about the findings and hence triangular methodology has been used in this study. Research design is a kind of blueprint to conduct the research and the various methods and methodologies that have to be followed to complete the research. The purpose of research design is to provide for the collection of relevant evidence with minimal expenditure of effort, time and money. Research design elaborates the steps followed to study the problem and reasoning behind it. There are two techniques in which research can be designed. The first is exploratory research and the other is conclusive research (Cooper & Schindler, 2006).

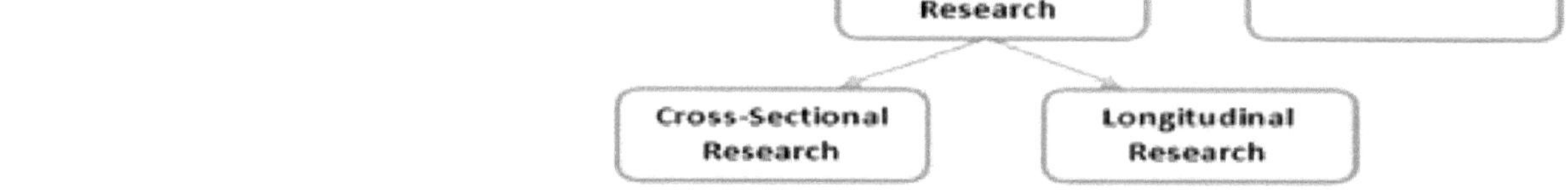

Figure 4.1: Types of Research Design

Figure 4.1 has been Adapted from the googling source as described in the following parenthetical portion.

Source: https://assets.pubpub.org/tv5qu5gn/01521405490221.pdf

Exploratory Research is used to define the problem clearly, to identify possible alternatives and to make deeper hypotheses.

Conclusive Research design is formal and structured and the information needed is explained in a proper manner to test the hypotheses and intends to examine the relationship between variables. Conclusive research design is further categorized into - Causal Research and Descriptive Research.

Causal Research is used to predict relationships between the observed variables and primarily to explain the nature of cause and effect relationship.

Descriptive Research, on the other hand, intends to describe phenomena and thus, define and explain explicitly the nature of relationship between the hypothesized variables. This is classified as: Cross-sectional Research and Longitudinal Research.

Cross-Sectional Research is where the data is collected from subjects only once at a particular time.

Longitudinal Research where data is captured from the group of respondents during a specific time interval to collate whether there is a change in the behavior of the same group over a period of time or not.

Normally, most research studies proceed first with an exploratory research design to fine tune and understand the problem at hand and to identify the different variables (dependent and independent variables) which help in formulating hypotheses for the study. So, this leads to descriptive research or causal research to prove and validate the hypothesized relationships among the stated variables.

In this study, an Exploratory-cum-Descriptive research design is used to understand the research problem, leading to identification of variables and formulation of hypotheses. It uses the technique of exploratory research to gain familiarity with the research problem. Descriptive analysis is used to further validate and establish the role and impact of the KM Drivers- Culture, Strategy, Enablers, Structure, Processes, Technology, Assets, Deterrents, Training, Technology on the effective KM implementation in POSOCO. So, the data is collected mainly through quantitative survey instrument comprising of questionnaires; and to some extent, through focus group discussions and interviews of senior executives who head the KM implementation process therein to elicit the actual KM Drivers in POSOCO. The data was analyzed statistically using the SPSS AMOS 26 software for testing the hypotheses for drawing the final conclusions.

Explanatory Research entails deductive reasoning for which measuring and evaluating qualities of the data is required especially from qualitative data obtained by using the qualitative tools e.g. Focus Group Discussion, In-depth interview, Elite interview, observation by practitioner who happens to be the researcher (Participative Observation). Accordingly, Explanatory research methodology has been used in research design in this study.

4.4 SAMPLING METHODOLOGY

4.4.1 Sampling Design

An explicit plan for obtaining samples from a given population is known as sampling design. It is an overall plan for selecting objects from the universe before the survey is undertaken. Sample designing process requires the items to be defined clearly because they are closely interrelated and relevant to all aspects of research, from problem definition to the presentation of the results.

A Sampling element comprises a single member of the population. For present study, all executives of POSOCO who were aware of and following the KM practices formed the sampling element to reduce the response errors.

Further, the sampling technique was chosen carefully. The Sampling technique is of two types:-

Probability Sampling

Non-Probability Sampling

Probability sampling uses random sampling techniques to create a sample. In probability sampling every member of the population gets a fair chance of selection which is not in the case with non-probability sampling.

Non-Probability sampling refers to the sampling technique where not all members of the population have an equal chance of participating in the study, unlike Probability Sampling where each and every member of a population has a known and equal chance of being selected. Non- Probability Sampling techniques use non-random processes like researcher's judgment or convenience. Non-Probability sampling provides the best chance to create a sample that is truly representative of the population but it is constrained due to enormous cost and time involved in gathering responses from all.

In this study, Convenience sampling was resorted to as it was the apt alternative to get adequate responses from the Executives in POSOCO who were willing to participate in the process of survey. They were requested to fill the structured questionnaire as per their availability and willingness and the purpose of the study was also communicated to them.

4.4.2 Sample Size

Sample is a subset of the population. It comprises only some elements of the population which is a true representation of the entire population. On the basis of research development, population size of the executive class of employees was adhered to. Leaving 92 nonexecutives out of population. In total, out of 592 population of POSOCO, 489 were executive category of employees- "knowledge workers". Out of 500 knowledge worker, 12 were seniors and directors who did not fill up the survey and 56 were executive trainees who were not asked to fill up the questionnaire. Hence, structured close-ended questionnaire involving five-point Likert scale had been developed and distributed among 432 executives covering all the Department in POSOCO. Out of these 432 executives, 403 responses were found valid which were taken up for this study. The formula for Sample Size is-

$$n = \frac{z^2_{\alpha/2} x p(1-p)}{e^2}$$

4.5 DATA COLLECTION

For this research study, both Primary and Secondary Data have been used for analysis. Secondary data was necessary to understand the theoretical foundation and derive the variables from the extant literature related to Knowledge Management. Secondary data was collected from documented literary sources mainly management journals, online repositories, and company annual reports.

Primary data is original data collected for the specific Research Objectives as spelt out in 4.2 earlier by the researcher. In this study, the approach has been adopted for quantitative data collection through collecting the self-administered structured questionnaire from the executives including senior executives in POSOCO. The personally-administered questionnaire establishes rapport and motivates the respondents when respondents are sitting in a group. It also ensures both the anonymity of the respondents and responses. It is also inexpensive.

The data was collected into two phases.

The data in *phase I* was collected using the qualitative approach. The qualitative data collection included the tools of Focus Group Discussion, In-depth Interview, Elite Interview, and Participant Observation. In *phase II,* a quantitative approach is followed through administering the structured questionnaire which was the tool to obtain quantifiable data. This was completed by the Executives of POSOCO under active interaction with the researcher.

"Participant Observation" has been taken recourse to while Analyzing Data for peppering the inferences while the causal component was inexplicable. This 'tool' has also been used to help provide the cues for buttressing the interpretation of the collected data studiously as required by triangulation method; well beyond quantitative and qualitative needs for comprehension.

4.5.1 Qualitative Tools

4.5.1.1 Focus Group Discussion

It is a good source of obtaining the Primary Data. Sekaran & Bougie (2010) in their studies have opined the same so far as the qualitative aspect of research is concerned. The unstructured and spontaneous responses are expected to reflect the genuine opinions, ideas and feelings of the members about the topic under discussion. Focus Groups are also used to 'feel the pulse and friction where the rubber meets the road.'

The researcher conducted the Focus Group Discussion with the Nodal officers earmarked for Knowledge Management. These were the Heads of HR in all the RLDCs and the Head of HRM and Head of HRD at Corporate Office. So, in total there were HOPs of five RLDCs, one HOP from NLDC, one Head of HR and one Head of HRD i.e. a total of eight officers. During the Focus Group Discussion, the Researcher was the Moderator. The Researcher appraised the Nodal officers about the topic. Discussions were done through Video Conferencing (VC) and the discussions we recorded. The researcher encouraged the members to participate equally. Care was taken that no member dominated the group. The researcher ensured that she was not a part of the discussion nor did she influence any of the participants. This data has provided qualitative input to the study.

The transcription of the Focus Group Discussion is available at Appendix A.

4.5.1.2 In-Depth Interview

In-depth interview has been described by Kahn and Cannel (1957) as "a general conversation with a purpose". The in-depth interviews are more like a conversational discussion. In the instant case, HR aspects of Knowledge Management were discussed to get the perspective of the participants. In this case, the participants were the Executive Directors of the RLDCs and the NLDC.

The questions asked were semi structured to get a qualitative perspective about the Knowledge Management in POSOCO.

The same has been transcribed and the details are delineated as in Appendix B.

4.5.1.3 Elite Interview

An interview with an 'Elite' person is called an 'Elite Interview'. A person who is prominent and well-informed in the organization and society is identified for this. In this study, Mr. KVS Baba, CMD, POSOCO is the head of the company. Because of his valuable experience in POSOCO, awareness about the future trends in the Power

Sector and his frequent interactions with the Ministry of Power as well as the Power Secretaries of all the States; he was considered as an Elite person for this research. Mr. Baba could give the overall picture of Knowledge Management and its importance as well as enablers of Knowledge Management at the organizational level.

The interview is transcribed and the same is appended as Appendix C.

4.5.2 Quantitative Tools-Survey Instrument [Questionnaire]: Design and Development

While designing the survey tool, it was kept in mind that the questionnaire must be simple, understandable and valid to meet the purpose of the study. The questionnaire consisted of structured, close-ended questions to enable the accuracy of the responses. All the scale items were extracted from the prominent studies related to KM and were further subjected to reliability tests also, which is discussed in the rubric ahead.

4.5.2.1 Pilot Study- Piloting of Survey Instrument (Cronbach's Alpha Value).

The survey instrument has two sections: (i) Personal Information (ii) KM Drivers. The first section contained 10 questions, and the second section contained 77 questions. Table 4.7 depicts the description of the Constructs with its variables and sources from where it has been extracted. To improve the validity, multiple sources were taken into account in the study. However, since it is a study for a company in power industry, the survey instrument has been adapted from the research published by Pandey (2016). Nevertheless, during the process of adaption, the reliability and validity have been verified for all the seventy seven questions. In order to avoid redundancy, the table 4.7 has not been elaborated apropos the original source as quoted by Pandey (2016) in his seminal work. Further, the instrument reliability was ascertained using the widely accepted Cronbach Alpha (which is presented in detail in the following section 4.7) from Table Number 4.8 to Table Number 4.18.

Table 4.7: Constructs description with its variables and Source(s) [Adapted from Pandey (2016)]

Constructs	Statements	Reference Source(s)
Asset	Knowledge is treated as a resource/asset in POSOCO Knowledge is treated as an object in my department	KM as an asset --Teece (2001), Grant (2001) Chen et.al (2012)
	Knowledge is used as an important and critical resource in my department	

Table 4.7: Continue

Constructs	Statements	Reference Source(s)
	Transfer of Knowledge and Best Practices are taking place in day-to-day working of employees	
	Innovation and Knowledge Creation are a way of life in my Company	
Culture	Knowledge Management has taken place in POSOCO In my department, Knowledge Management activities are taking place satisfactorily My organization periodically gives special awards to employees who make significant contributions to the organization The mission and objectives of Knowledge Management are clearly understood by employees propagated throughout POSOCO There are appropriate values and mindset towards Knowledge Management amongst employees of my Company	KM as Culture — Swanson (20050, Wood (20050, Anderson (2009), Fullan (2011), Tryon Jr. (2012)
	The personnel in POSOCO are oriented towards Knowledge Management very positively	
	Aesthetically oriented culture for Knowledge Management is a way of life in POSOCO	
	Employees in POSOCO are having informal, open-minded and collaborative working	
	The organization continuously strives for Knowledge acquisition, dissemination and capture for its employees	
	I visit Power Portal for my knowledge needs	
	I have free access to any information I want irrespective of where it resides in my organization	
	I feel that I have got support from Management for Knowledge Management	

Table 4.7: Continue

Constructs	Statements	Reference Source(s)
Deterrents	In my opinion, there are very few Subject Matter Experts available in my department	KM Enablers (or facilitating factors)—Klein (1998), Almeida (2008), Pasher & Ronen (2011), Upadhyay (2011), Tryon Jr. (2012)
	I have come across situations in work where the same mistake done by someone in the past is being repeated	
	There are lots of documents/reports lying unutilized in my department	
	Most of the time I find that it is pretty time consuming to access any document in my department	
	Information about the outcome of implementing Best Practices is translated in practice in my department / company	
	I contact subject matter experts by using my Corporate Yellow Pages	
	All programs have periodic team meetings to review the progress and discuss issues pertaining to the work	
	My organization's newsletter/bulletin will inform me about the latest happenings in your organization and outside	
	My organization has a directory of personnel containing information of names of people, their designation, division, program, phone number, email, etc.	
	Use of knowledge is a way of work life in every employees' job	
	Company has got proper facility for Research & Development	
	My superiors fully endorse my way of handling Knowledge Management related issues	
	Dedicated staff for Knowledge capture and acquisition are earmarked in my department	

Table 4.7: Continue

Constructs	Statements	Reference Source(s)
	Information regarding relevant topics are readily available to the employees in my Company	
	Information regarding process description can be uploaded in the Organization's Knowledge Bank at Power Portal, the intranet of Company	
	'Personal best practices can be shared with other employees easily' can be said as a part of job in POSOCO	
	Employees can upload their documents or reports to Power Portal	
	Employees can download any document they want from the Intranet site/portal	
	My organization has a 'Chief Knowledge Officer' (or equivalent) who is responsible for managing the knowledge-related activities	
	I use Knowledge maps and matrices of my Company for knowledge requirements	
Incentives	Reward and recognition for suggestion of Best Practices, have been incorporated in POSOCO's annual plan	KM Incentives—Peachey (23006), Armstrong (2012)
	The organization provides incentives to motivate users to learn from experiences and use the Knowledge Management System of POSOCO	
	In my organization, it is mandatory for every employee to document insights (in the form of best practices, lessons learnt etc.) from the work/project	
	Recognition in form of titles, certificates & commendation letters are periodically awarded to the contributors of knowledge	
	My organization actively promotes a 'culture of experimentation' that encourages employees to try new ideas and take risks	

Table 4.7: Continue

Constructs	Statements	Reference Source(s)
Processes	In my department/organization, every program has a closure meeting to critically review the performance	KM Processes—Anderson (2009), Asian productivity Organization (2010)
	Within the team/department, employees share their knowledge in an informal manner	
	There is very good interaction between departments/ groups in my organization	
	All important communications in my organization are sent to me through circulars or memos in electronic environment	
	A Communities of Practice exists in POSOCO.	
	Acquisition of knowledge is a regular practice in our Company	
Strategy	POSOCO has got a vision in Knowledge Management which properly articulates its knowledge needs	KM strategy—Shih & Chiang (2005), Chen et.al (2012)
	Knowledge Management is being used constantly as a business strategy	
	A cohesive and powerful vision of the organization is shared across the workforce to promote the need for strategic thinking at all levels	
	Our Company has got collegial, flat, team based, open door policy	
Structure	The organization has enabling structures in terms of hierarchy and communication flows that facilitates knowledge sharing	KM Structure—Conway & Sligar (2002), Brauner & Becker (2006), Jones & George (2011)
	POSOCO publishes regular intellectual achievements and reports it to its external stakeholders	
	The evaluation of work/projects that are completed successfully has been done in my organization from KM point of view.	

Table 4.7: Continue

Constructs	Statements	Reference Source(s)
	We strive to have matrix form of structure of Company	
	Brick-and-mortar model (dealing with the customer face-to-face) structure is followed in our Company	
	My organization has a central repository / library where all the necessary documents/ reports are stored	
	Documents pertaining to past research programs are arranged in such a manner that they can be easily accessed and used as and when necessary	
	There are enough Meeting/Conference rooms available for Team meetings and discussions	
	Notice boards kept at various vantage points in my organization plays an important role in informing me of various news and events	
	Information about locations of project reports, research facilities and equipment available are displayed prominently in my organization	
	In my organization, every employee is encouraged to periodically produce documents in the form of technical reports, journal papers, presentations, articles, etc.	
Technology	Employees are provided 'instant messenger' or 'chat' – video conferencing facilities through which they can have conversations with their colleagues	KM Technology—Hasnali (2005), Burg, et.al (2008), Man et.al. (2008)
	The Intranet site provides an Online Discussion Forum in which employees can share information and post their doubts	
	My organization has an Experts Database that can be used by Employees to locate experts within the organization	

Table 4.7: Continue

Constructs	Statements	Reference Source(s)
	Employees are provided the 'blogging' platform wherein they can share their experiences through blogs	
	All important documents in my organization are available in the electronic format	
	Employees/Teams can discuss work through Tele-Conferencing (i.e. through telephones, VOIP, Mobile, etc.)	
	My organization's intranet/website plays a vital role in disseminating information to the employees	
	My organization measures and manages its intellectual capital (IC) in a systematic way	
	There is Knowledge Management Cell in POSOCO which collects knowledge nuggets and disseminates it through Power Portal	
Training	Every employee is imparted training required by him for his job	KM Training—Bates (1998), Jones & George (2011)
	Knowledge Management related training is identified as part of organizational training need assessment	
	My organization arranges seminars/ lectures by external experts on a periodic basis	
	All employees in my department are willing to share their knowledge with others	
	My organization sponsors trips for employees to international/national conferences and seminars	

Thus, extensive and broad array of constructs used in the KM literature have been used to assess the KM implementation in POSOCO.

4.6 REALIABILITY AND VALIDITY

Reliability is one of the essential characteristics of sound research tools. A scale must yield a reliable estimate of the activity. If a tool gives the same result on different occasions, according to the ability of those to whom it is applied to, it is said to be reliable. Reliability hence means consistency of the result. Reliability refers to the consistency of scores obtained from the same persons "when they are reexamined with the same test on different occasions or with different sets of equivalent items, or under other variable examining conditions."

In this study, the Reliability of the responses were generated for the Five Point Likert-scaled responses using the Cronbach Alpha test, which is the most widely used test for measuring Reliability. The Cronbach scores above.75 were accepted as Reliable measures for further treatment and analysis.

In conjunction with this, to explore the dimensionality of the scale items (to see whether more than one construct is needed to account for the pattern of item scores), the use of factor analysis has been done, the results of which are presented below:-

Table 4.8: Reliability of Constructs

Reliability of Constructs			
Constructs	**Cronbach's Alpha**	**Cronbach's Alpha Based on Standardized Items**	**No. of Items**
Asset	0.877	0.879	5
Culture	0.932	0.934	12
Deterrents	0.786	0.791	4
Enablers	0.957	0.958	16
Incentives	0.887	0.887	5
Processes	0.866	0.867	6
Strategy	0.859	0.86	4
Structures	0.929	0.929	11
Technology	0.897	0.893	9
Training	0.867	0.871	5
Overall Reliability	0.945	0.95	77

The threshold value for reliability and co-efficient in Cronbach's Alpha has been used as 0.7 in the early stages. When the applied form is brought into play, it increases to 0.8 and while 'final decision' entails 0.9 and above. With this in view, it is found to always be above 0.7 (in case of deterrents only it is 0.7 being a negative enumeration by the respondents but it has been used for authenticity). All other constructs are at 0.8 or above.

Table 4.9: Item-Total Statistics of Asset Construct

Item-Total Statistics					
	Scale Mean if Item Deleted	Scale Variance if Item Deleted	Corrected Item- Total Correlation	Squared Multiple Correlation	Cronbach's Alpha if Item Deleted
ASSET1	14.95	11.851	0.603	0.375	0.878
ASSET2	14.52	11.643	0.757	0.575	0.84
ASSET3	14.54	11.811	0.692	0.491	0.854
ASSET4	14.44	11.426	0.764	0.606	0.837
ASSET5	14.49	11.529	0.735	0.578	0.844

Table 4.10: Item-Total Statistics of Culture Construct

Item-Total Statistics					
	Scale Mean if Item Deleted	Scale Variance if Item Deleted	Corrected Item-Total Correlation	Squared Multiple Correlation	Cronbach's Alpha if Item Deleted
CULT1	42.37	48.059	0.777	0.636	0.924
CULT2	42.61	48.478	0.574	0.358	0.932
CULT3	42.27	50.085	0.568	0.362	0.931
CULT4	42.16	47.889	0.765	0.622	0.924
CULT5	42.29	47.844	0.754	0.579	0.924
CULT6	42.26	48.222	0.751	0.595	0.924
CULT7	41.98	47.912	0.709	0.582	0.926
CULT8	42.59	49.063	0.54	0.298	0.933
CULT9	42.08	47.382	0.78	0.675	0.923
CULT10	42.28	47.935	0.76	0.611	0.924
CULT11	42.34	47.652	0.747	0.574	0.924
CULT12	42.33	47.663	0.774	0.616	0.923

Table 4.11: Item-Total Statistics of Deterrents Construct

Item-Total Statistics					
	Scale Mean if Item Deleted	Scale Variance if Item Deleted	Corrected Item- Total Correlation	Squared Multiple Correlation	Cronbach's Alpha if Item Deleted
DETE1	8.25	7.841	.455	.211	.808
DETE2	8.76	7.122	.723	.607	.669
DETE3	8.68	7.636	.614	.475	.724
DETE4	8.41	7.356	.605	.440	.727

Table 4.12: Item-Total Statistics of Enablers Construct

Item-Total Statistics					
	Scale Mean if Item Deleted	Scale Variance if Item Deleted	Corrected Item- Total Correlation	Squared Multiple Correlation	Cronbach's Alpha if Item Deleted
ENAB1	52.85	111.827	.751	.704	.954
ENAB2	53.61	110.856	.649	.506	.956
ENAB3	53.19	109.767	.766	.607	.954
ENAB4	53.16	110.281	.782	.644	.954
ENAB5	53.61	109.816	.691	.540	.955
ENAB6	53.41	110.188	.748	.594	.954
ENAB7	53.21	110.366	.763	.627	.954
ENAB8	53.01	111.069	.745	.688	.954
ENAB9	53.06	109.292	.802	.708	.953
ENAB10	53.46	109.965	.775	.644	.954
ENAB11	52.98	109.994	.816	.713	.953
ENAB12	53.21	109.256	.810	.707	.953
ENAB13	53.34	110.523	.751	.618	.954
ENAB14	53.31	110.519	.757	.644	.954
ENAB15	53.46	111.836	.733	.586	.954
ENAB16	53.65	112.697	.619	.426	.957

Table 4.13: Item-Total Statistics of Incentives Construct

Item-Total Statistics					
	Scale Mean If Item Deleted	Scale Variance if Item Deleted	Corrected Item Total Correlation	Squared Multiple Correlation	Cronbach's Alpha if Item Deleted
INCE1	13.90	10.312	.673	.455	.874
INCE2	14.14	9.384	.759	.629	.855
INCE3	14.09	9.522	.781	.653	.850
INCE4	13.74	10.380	.705	.509	.868
INCE5	14.00	9.776	.718	.530	.865

Table 4.14: Item-Total Statistics of Processes Construct

Item-Total Statistics					
	Scale Mean if Item Deleted	Scale Variance if Item Deleted	Corrected Item Total Correlation	Squared Multiple Correlation	Cronbach's Alpha if Item Deleted
PROC1	17.44	18.685	.660	.467	.844
PROC2	17.39	17.727	.696	.511	.837
PROC3	17.40	18.191	.698	.496	.837
PROC4	17.31	18.509	.639	.423	.848
PROC5	17.64	18.306	.617	.402	.852
PROC6	17.68	18.341	.667	.465	.843

Table 4.15: Item-Total Statistics of Strategy Construct

Item-Total Statistics					
	Scale Mean if Item Deleted	Scale Variance if Item Deleted	Corrected Item Total Correlatioi	Squared Multiple Correlation	Cronbach's Alpha if Item Deleted
STRA1	8.93	6.196	.632	.416	.851
STRA2	8.86	5.760	.778	.606	.789
STRA3	9.03	6.103	.714	.528	.817
STRA4	8.67	6.071	.697	.502	.823

Table 4.16: Item-Total Statistics of Structures Construct

Item-Total Statistics					
	Scale Mean if Item Deleted	Scale Variance if Item Deleted	Corrected Item-Total Correlation	Squared Multiple Correlation	Cronbach's Alpha if Item Deleted
STRU1	30.98	54.288	.702	.583	.923
STRU2	30.88	53.809	.718	.554	.922
STRU3	31.00	53.527	.742	.591	.921
STRU4	30.87	54.325	.698	.611	.923
STRU5	31.03	54.474	.651	.438	.925
STRU6	31.55	54.000	.717	.586	.922
STRU7	31.19	53.850	.715	.563	.922
STRU8	31.42	54.826	.677	.513	.924
STRU9	31.07	53.309	.710	.552	.923
STRU10	30.80	55.275	.714	.533	.923
STRU11	31.27	53.780	.759	.621	.920

Table 4.17: Item-Total Statistics of Technology Construct

Item-Total Statistics					
	Scale Mean If Item Deleted	Scale Variance if Item Deleted	Corrected Item Total Correlation	Squared Multiple Correlation	Cronbach's Alpha if Item Deleted
TECH1	27.07	55.221	.198	.068	.915
TECH2	27.32	45.831	.763	.608	.877
TECH3	27.35	45.185	.802	.804	.874
TECH4	27.33	46.298	.709	.558	.881
TECH5	27.26	47.425	.650	.491	.886
TECH6	27.55	46.507	.671	.496	.885
TECH7	27.34	44.567	.834	.822	.871
TECH8	27.30	45.704	.776	.651	.876
TECH9	27.53	49.344	.528	.331	.895

Table 4.18: Item-Total Statistics of Training Construct

Item-Total Statistics					
	Scale Mean if Item Deleted	**Scale Variance if Item Deleted**	**Corrected Item Total Correlation**	**Squared Multiple Correlation**	**Cronbach's Alpha if Item Deleted**
TRAI1	15.63	7.084	.627	.429	.861
TRAI2	15.34	7.678	.704	.510	.836
TRAI3	15.11	7.645	.728	.580	.831
TRAI4	15.29	7.075	.758	.582	.821
TRAI5	15.09	7.818	.660	.460	.846

Thus, the constructs were taken as such based on their reliability values for further analysis in this study.

4.7 TECHNIQUES FOR ANALYSIS

4.7.1 Quantitative Techniques

The tools for analyzing the data are comprised of MS Excel for data entry and quality checks in the data; SPSS 26 for data analysis and AMOS software for Confirmatory Factor Analysis (CFA). The technique of data analysis included: Editing (field editing and office editing), Coding, and Tabulation, along with cleaning of data and checking the normality and assumptions for tests. The tests mainly comprised of:-

- Multivariate Techniques of Exploratory Factor Analysis & the Confirmatory Factor Analysis.
- Univariate Techniques: for descriptive statistics using frequency, mean and standard deviation computations.
- Multiple Regression for deriving the regression equation.

4.7.2 Qualitative Techniques

- NVivo Result for Thematic Value
- Word Frequency
- Word Frequency Layout

4.8 CONCLUSION

This chapter enumerated the research methodology adopted for this study in detail. It examined the various steps taken to conduct the research in a systematic manner providing a clear understanding on theoretical concepts of research. Various tools and formulae used in this study have the metamorphosed form in accordance with the triangulation methodology.

The next chapter presents the Analysis and Findings of the study.

CHAPTER 5

ANALYSIS AND FINDINGS

5.1 INTRODUCTION

This chapter presents the analysis for understanding the Drivers of Knowledge Management and its perceived effectiveness in POSOCO.

The chapter is divided into various sections to present the analysis in a systematic manner. In this chapter the analysis of both the Qualitative and Quantitative data and the related aspects have been presented. The qualitative analysis has been carried out through the N Vivo Result for the Thematic value, Word Frequency, Word Frequency Layout of the transcribed interview and responses of the participants. The quantitative analysis is explained through the various statistical treatments of data for explaining the relationship with demographic profile, Drivers of KM and thereafter the hypotheses testing to ascertain the relational impact of these Drivers of KM on the implementation related effectiveness of Knowledge Management in POSOCO.

Both descriptive and inferential statistics have been employed to arrive towards achieving the objectives of the study in a comprehensive manner. All the statistical analyses were conducted at 95% confidence level and the assumption of normality and multicollinearity were tested while administering the tests. The data was also checked for 'skewness and kurtosis' for meeting the criterion of the normal distribution of the data so that the results generated thereby are accurate and reliable. It was found that the data was normally distributed as the values of skewness fell within the acceptable range -2 to +2 and for kurtosis in the range of -1.96 to +1.96.

5.1 A-Qualitative Analysis

The focus group discussion, in-depth interview and elite interview were conducted and thereby the texts of these interviews and discussions were subjected to qualitative analysis with NVivov. 12 software. In the qualitative study infographics plays an important role and thus has been taken into account.

The results were analyzed with word frequency, weighted percentage, and similar words. Tree map and frequency layout were analyzed and the results are presented below.

Table A-5.1 NVivo Result for Thematic Value

Word	Length	Count	Weighted Percentage (%)	Similar Words
Knowledge	9	146	6.16	initially, knowledge, learn, learning, letter, letters
Management	10	81	3.33	achieved, achievements, caring, dealing, deals, director, directors, handle, handling, manage, managed, management, manages, managing
Organization	12	51	2.07	arranged, arranges, coordinator, coordinators, establishment, format, organization, system, systems
Employees	9	39	1.71	employee, employees, employees'
POSOCO	6	39	1.71	POSOCO
Sharing	7	38	1.47	contributed, contributing, contributions, dealing, deals, share, shared, sharing

Table A-5.1 Continue

Word	Length	Count	Weighted Percentage (%)	Similar Words
Information	11	28	1.23	conversations, inform, informal, information, informing
Researcher	10	28	1.23	research, researcher
Experts	7	34	1.05	expert, expertise, experts, practice, practices, skills, technical
Department	10	23	0.98	department, departments, quite, started
Policy	6	20	0.88	policies, policy
Power	5	26	0.86	electricity, officer, officer', officers, power, powerful, right, strongly
Company	7	17	0.75	company
Training	8	20	0.72	development, educational, groom, taking, trained, training
Documents	9	22	0.69	certificates, document, documented, documents, paper, papers, support
Discussion	10	15	0.66	discuss, discussion, discussions
Issues	6	30	0.66	emerged, events, issue, issues, matter, outcome, public, publish, published, publishes, subject, taking, topic, topics
Available	9	18	0.64	access, accessed, availability, available, helped, helps

Table A-5.1 Continue

Word	Length	Count	Weighted Percentage (%)	Similar Words
Important	9	15	0.64	crucial, importance, important, significant
implementation	14	15	0.63	executives, implement, implementation, implemented, implementing
Practices	9	29	0.63	executives, exercise, operation, operator, practice, practices, useful, using
Resources	9	13	0.57	resource, resources
Response	8	13	0.57	response, responses, responsibility, responsible
Ensure	6	15	0.56	assure, control, ensure, ensured, ensures, secure
Meetings	8	16	0.55	contact, meeting, meetings, played, plays
Encourage	9	15	0.52	encourage, encouraged, encouragement, encourages, promote, promotes, support
Number	6	16	0.52	issue, issues, number, routine, total
External	8	14	0.48	external, international, outside, project, projects
Portal	6	11	0.48	portal, portals
Years	5	11	0.48	annual, years
Question	8	12	0.46	doubts, heads, interview, question, questions

Table A-5.1 Continue

Word	Length	Count	Weighted Percentage (%)	Similar Words
Operation	9	25	0.44	control, functioning, operation, operator, performance, procedure, procedures, process, running, worked, working
Tacit	5	10	0.44	tacit, understood
Technology	10	11	0.44	technical, technology
Circulars	9	10	0.42	circulars, circulate, circulated, disseminate, disseminates, disseminating, dissemination, propagated
Learning	8	23	0.41	acquire, acquisition, learn, learning, study, taking, teach
Concerned	9	15	0.38	caring, concerned, interest, interested, pertain, pertaining, refers, related
Business	8	11	0.37	business, concerned
Identified	10	13	0.37	describe, identified, identify, names, place
Culture	7	8	0.35	culture
Needs	5	17	0.35	asked, involved, involvement, motivate, motivation, needs, require, required, requirement, requirements, taking
Officers	8	18	0.35	agencies, functioning, officer, officer', officers, place, positively, situations

Table A-5.1 Continue

Word	Length	Count	Weighted Percentage (%)	Similar Words
Areas	5	10	0.34	areas, countries, domains, field, regional, regions
Corporate	9	9	0.34	collected, collects, corporate, corporation, incorporated, material
Activities	10	9	0.33	actively, activities, activity, participants, participate, participation, trips
Communication	13	9	0.33	communication, communications, communities, national
Process	7	18	0.33	procedure, procedures, process, progress, treated, treating, worked, working
Program	7	8	0.32	planning, platform, program, programs
Asset	5	7	0.31	asset, assets
Followed	8	10	0.31	followed, following, follows, observations, pursuing, survey
Provided	8	7	0.31	caters, provide, provided, provider, provides
Strategy	8	7	0.31	strategy
Nodal	5	7	0.31	nodal
Papers	6	13	0.29	paper, papers, reports
Periodically	12	9	0.29	flows, period, periodic, periodically, point, points

Table A-5.1 Continue

Word	Length	Count	Weighted Percentage (%)	Similar Words
Place	5	14	0.29	investing, locate, locations, place, point, points, positively, range, sites, situations
Subject	7	16	0.29	dependent, field, national, study, subject, topic, topics
Advantage	9	7	0.27	advantage, positively, reward, rewarded, vantage
Human	5	7	0.27	human, world
Various	7	7	0.27	diverse, respect, various
Enabling	8	6	0.26	enabled, enabler, enablers, enables, enabling
Explicit	8	6	0.26	explicit
Group	5	6	0.26	group, groups
Improving	9	6	0.26	better, betterment, improve, improving
Intranet	8	6	0.26	intranet
Matrices	8	6	0.26	matrices
Objectives	10	6	0.26	object, objectively, objectives
Pages	5	6	0.26	pages
People	6	6	0.26	people
Seminars	8	6	0.26	seminars
Yellow	6	6	0.26	yellow
Experiences	11	7	0.25	experience, experiences, experimentation', getting
Facilitating	12	9	0.25	facilitates, facilitating, helped, helps

Table A-5.1 Continue

Word	Length	Count	Weighted Percentage (%)	Similar Words
Opinions	8	8	0.25	opinion, opinions, rules, views
Based	5	7	0.24	based, basis, establishment, found
Conducting	10	11	0.23	conduct, conducting, dealing, deals, imparted, leading, taking
Evaluation	10	8	0.23	assess, assessment, evaluation, measure, measured, measures, values
Innovation	10	10	0.23	creation, design, designated, designation, found, initially, innovation
Presentations	13	8	0.23	awarded, awards, displayed, presentations, representative, sponsors
Related	7	10	0.23	associate, associated, dealing, deals, links, related
Reports	7	13	0.23	accounts, covered, describe, reports, study
Right	5	11	0.23	appropriate, completed, correctly, entire, entired, proper, properly, right, total, whole
Disagree	8	5	0.22	different, disagree
Interactions	12	5	0.22	interacted, interacting, interaction, interactions

Table A-5.1 Continue

Word	Length	Count	Weighted Percentage (%)	Similar Words
Project	7	10	0.22	design, designated, designation, envisioning, planning, project, projects, visualize
RLDCs	5	5	0.22	RLDCs
SRLDC	5	5	0.22	SRLDC
WRLDC	5	5	0.22	WRLDC
Close	5	6	0.21	close, closure, completed, finalization, finalized, nearing
Conferences	11	5	0.20	conference, conferences, consultancy
Create	6	6	0.20	create, created, making, produce
First	5	6	0.20	first, initially, started
Level	5	7	0.20	equal, level, levels, point, points
Thank	5	5	0.20	appreciation, thank
Adequate	8	5	0.19	adequate, enough, equal
Aspects	7	6	0.19	aspects, views
Capture	7	6	0.19	appropriate, capture, captured, getting
Regarding	9	9	0.19	considered, involved, involvement, regarding, respect, views
Structure	9	5	0.19	integration, structure, structures
Treated	7	11	0.19	covered, dealing, deals, handle, handling, treated, treating
Across	6	4	0.18	across

Table A-5.1 Continue

Word	Length	Count	Weighted Percentage (%)	Similar Words
Agree	5	4	0.18	accordingly, agree
Aware	5	4	0.18	aware, awareness
Board	5	4	0.18	board, boards, rooms
Capital	7	4	0.18	capital, capitalize
Critical	8	5	0.18	critical, critically, crucial, vital
Forum	5	4	0.18	forum, forums
Matter	6	7	0.18	affairs, matter, thing
Personal	8	4	0.18	person, personal, someone
Purpose	7	9	0.18	deliberate, design, designated, designation, functioning, purpose, useful, using
Recognition	11	4	0.18	recognition
Uploaded	8	4	0.18	upload, uploaded
Vision	6	4	0.18	vision
Within	6	4	0.18	within
Towards	7	4	0.18	towards
Assigned	8	7	0.17	assigned, assignments, design, designated, designation, names, transfer
Gives	5	11	0.17	contributed, contributing, contributions, establishment, gives, giving, imparted, making, presentations
Working	7	13	0.17	exercise, influence, making, played, plays, worked, working

Table A-5.1 Continue

Word	Length	Count	Weighted Percentage (%)	Similar Words
Acquisition	11	8	0.16	acquire, acquisition, skills
Support	7	7	0.16	endorse, friendly, sponsors, support, sustained
Dedicated	9	5	0.15	dedicated, gives, giving
Dispatch	8	4	0.15	dispatch, dispatcher, despatchers, dispatch
Efforts	7	4	0.15	drive, effort, efforts
Focus	5	4	0.15	centers, focus
Regular	7	4	0.15	regular, regulations
State	5	6	0.15	countries, declare, formalized, positively, state
Study	5	13	0.15	considered, study, survey, worked, working
System	6	6	0.15	system, systematic, systems
Necessary	9	7	0.14	necessary, require, required, requirement, requirements
Approved	8	3	0.13	approved, commendable, commendation
Articles	8	3	0.13	articles
Choice	6	3	0.13	choice, optional
Competitive	11	3	0.13	challenge, competitive
Current	7	5	0.13	current, flows, presentations
Exchange	8	3	0.13	central, exchange
Facilities	10	3	0.13	facilities, facility
Finance	7	3	0.13	finance
Intellectual	12	3	0.13	intellectual

Table A-5.1 Continue

Word	Length	Count	Weighted Percentage (%)	Similar Words
Library	7	3	0.13	library
Market	6	3	0.13	market
organizational	14	3	0.13	organizational
Personnel	9	3	0.13	personnel
Secure	6	6	0.13	certificates, dependent, secure, strongly
Suggestions	11	3	0.13	suggestion, suggestions
Survey	6	8	0.13	review, reviews, survey, views
Terms	5	3	0.13	terms
Verticals	9	3	0.13	verticals
Visit	5	3	0.13	chat', visit
Workforce	9	3	0.13	manpower, workforce
ERLDC	5	3	0.13	ERLDC
Especially	10	4	0.12	especially, particular, special, specialization
Limited	7	4	0.12	limited, modified, special, specialization
Considered	10	4	0.11	considered, deliberate, think, thinking
Emerged	7	5	0.11	emerged, growth
Energy	6	3	0.11	energy, vital
Heads	5	6	0.11	chief, heads, leading, point, points
Helped	6	8	0.11	helped, helps, support
Multiple	8	3	0.11	multiple, propagated, times
Spirit	6	3	0.11	hearted, spirit
Translate	9	3	0.11	translate, translated, understand
Acquire	7	8	0.10	acquire, development, getting, produce, taking

Table A-5.1 Continue

Word	Length	Count	Weighted Percentage (%)	Similar Words
Appropriate	11	4	0.10	appropriate, proper, properly, suitable
Attitude	8	3	0.10	attitude, positively
Creation	8	4	0.10	creation, exists, world
Earmarked	9	3	0.10	appropriate, earmarked
Findings	8	6	0.10	findings, getting, happenings, notice, observations, rules
Harness	7	3	0.10	harness, harnessing, rules
Oriented	8	4	0.10	oriented, point, points
Performance	11	7	0.10	executives, performance, played, plays
Played	6	7	0.10	played, plays, representative, running
Requirements	12	6	0.10	mandatory, require, required, requirement, requirements
Taking	6	7	0.10	consuming, containing, drive, getting, making, taking
Achieved	8	3	0.09	achieved, achievements, successfully
Affairs	7	5	0.09	affairs, functioning, involved, involvement, occasions
Agents	6	2	0.09	agents, factor
Along	5	2	0.09	along
Attend	6	2	0.09	attend
Blogging'	9	2	0.09	blogging', blogs
Books	5	2	0.09	books, records
Certain	7	2	0.09	certain

Table A-5.1 Continue

Word	Length	Count	Weighted Percentage (%)	Similar Words
Classify	8	2	0.09	classify, classifying
Conjunction	11	3	0.09	conjunction, continuously, cooperation
Consideration	13	2	0.09	consideration
Division	8	2	0.09	division, segment
Easily	6	2	0.09	easily, easily'
Electronic	10	2	0.09	electronic
Extremely	9	2	0.09	extremely, members
Financial	9	2	0.09	financial
Frequency	9	2	0.09	frequency
Fruitful	8	2	0.09	fruitful, fruits
Future	6	2	0.09	future
Graduation	10	2	0.09	graduation
Incentives	10	3	0.09	incentives, motivate, motivation
Included	8	2	0.09	included
Insight	7	2	0.09	insight, insights
Inter	5	2	0.09	inter
Loaded	6	2	0.09	loaded, loading
Manner	6	2	0.09	manner
Measure	7	4	0.09	measure, measured, measures, steps
Memos	5	2	0.09	memos
Mention	7	5	0.09	mention, names, notes, observations, refers
Model	5	2	0.09	model
Monitoring	10	2	0.09	monitoring
Online	6	2	0.09	online
Parameter	9	2	0.09	parameter, parameters
Phone	5	2	0.09	phone, telephones
Potential	9	2	0.09	potential, voltages
Primarily	9	2	0.09	primarily

Table A-5.1 Continue

Word	Length	Count	Weighted Percentage (%)	Similar Words
Problem	7	2	0.09	problem, problems
Public	6	5	0.09	public, publish, published, publishes, world
Relevant	8	2	0.09	relevant
Review	6	4	0.09	comments, review, reviews
Rotation	8	2	0.09	rotation
Sector	6	2	0.09	sector
Senior	6	2	0.09	senior
Sessions	8	2	0.09	sessions
Single	6	2	0.09	single
Sought	6	2	0.09	sought
Strive	6	2	0.09	strive, strives
Superannuated	13	2	0.09	superannuated, superannuation
Teams	5	2	0.09	teams
Together	8	2	0.09	together
Users	5	2	0.09	users
Write	5	2	0.09	write, writing
Amongst	7	2	0.09	amongst
Brought	7	2	0.09	brought
Davar	5	2	0.09	davar
Highest	7	2	0.09	highest
NRLDC	5	2	0.09	NRLDC
Build	5	4	0.08	build, establishment, framing, making
Continuously	12	3	0.08	continuously, covered, remain
Control	7	5	0.08	accounts, containing, control, moderator
International	13	5	0.08	incorporated, international, national

Table A-5.1 Continue

Word	Length	Count	Weighted Percentage (%)	Similar Words
Involved	8	5	0.08	involved, involvement, participants, participate, participation
National	8	5	0.08	countries, national, state
Sites	5	3	0.08	sites, situations, website
Views	5	5	0.08	considered, perspective, positively, views
Almost	6	2	0.07	almost, nearing
Articulates	11	2	0.07	articulates, joining
Caring	6	5	0.07	caring, deliberate, measure, measured, measures
Clearly	7	3	0.07	clearly, making, understand
Collaborative	13	2	0.07	collaborative, cooperation
Contributed	11	5	0.07	contributed, contributing, contributions, imparted, leading
Courses	7	3	0.07	courses, flows, running
Entire	6	4	0.07	entire, entired, integration, total
Establishment	13	4	0.07	establishment, found, making, proved
Progress	8	3	0.07	build, progress
Special	7	3	0.07	special, specialists, specialization
Celebrate	9	3	0.06	celebrate, notes, observations

Table A-5.1 Continue

Word	Length	Count	Weighted Percentage (%)	Similar Words
Consultancy	11	3	0.06	consultancy, interview, refers
Design	6	6	0.06	design, designated, designation, planning, point, points
Functioning	11	4	0.06	functioning, procedure, procedures, routine
Interest	8	4	0.06	interest, interested, involved, involvement
Making	6	3	0.06	making, names, qualification
Promote	7	3	0.06	promote, promotes, public
Unanimous	9	2	0.06	unanimous, whole
Ahead	5	2	0.05	ahead, leading
Balanced	8	2	0.05	balanced, equal
Become	6	2	0.05	become, getting
Development	11	3	0.05	development, growth
Equal	5	2	0.05	equal, equivalent
Leadership	10	2	0.05	leadership, leading
Normal	6	2	0.05	normal, rules
Aesthetically	13	1	0.04	aesthetically
Another	7	1	0.04	another
Appreciation	12		0.04	appreciation, values
Barriers	8	1	0.04	barriers
Basically	9	1	0.04	basically
Benefits	8	1	0.04	benefits
Birthdays	9	1	0.04	birthdays
Borne	5	1	0.04	borne
Bottom	6	1	0.04	bottom
Brick	5	1	0.04	brick

Table A-5.1 Continue

Word	Length	Count	Weighted Percentage (%)	Similar Words
Briefings	9	1	0.04	briefings
Bulletin	8	1	0.04	bulletin
Categorization	14	1	0.04	categorization
Centers	7	2	0.04	centers, hearted
Chairman	8	1	0.04	chairman
Classroom	9	1	0.04	classroom
Codifying	9	1	0.04	codifying
Cohesive	8	1	0.04	cohesive
Colleagues	10	1	0.04	colleagues
Collegial	9	1	0.04	collegial
Comfortable	11	1	0.04	comfortable
Comments	8		0.04	comments, notice, observations
Committees	10	1	0.04	committees
Completed	9		0.04	completed, dispatch
Concrete	8	1	0.04	concrete
Confidential	12	1	0.04	confidential
Constantly	10	1	0.04	constantly
Contact	7		0.04	contact, links
Context	7	1	0.04	context
Contributors	12	1	0.04	contributors
Customer	8	1	0.04	customer
Database	8	1	0.04	database
Dealing	7		0.04	considered, dealing, deals, taking
Description	11	1	0.04	description
Difficulties	12	1	0.04	difficulties
Directory	9	1	0.04	directory
Disturbances	12	1	0.04	disturbances
Doctorate	9	1	0.04	doctorate

Table A-5.1 Continue

Word	Length	Count	Weighted Percentage (%)	Similar Words
Download	8	1	0.04	download
Eclipses	8	1	0.04	eclipses
Economic	8	1	0.04	economic
Educational	11	2	0.04	educational, teach
Efficiency	10	1	0.04	efficiency
Elite	5	1	0.04	elite
Email	5	1	0.04	email
Enclosed	8	1	0.04	enclosed
Enhancing	9	1	0.04	enhancing
Entrants	8	1	0.04	entrants
Environment	11	1	0.04	environment
Envisaged	9	1	0.04	envisaged
Equipment	10	1	0.04	equipment
Guidelines	10	1	0.04	guidelines
Happenings	10		0.04	happenings, material
Happy	5	1	0.04	happy
Hierarchical	12	1	0.04	hierarchical
Hierarchy	9	1	0.04	hierarchy
Ideally	7	1	0.04	ideally
Ideas	5	1	0.04	ideas
Impartial	9	1	0.04	impartial
Implicit	8	1	0.04	implicit
Industry	8	1	0.04	industry
Inertia	7	1	0.04	inertia
Influence	9		0.04	influence, regulations
Instant	7	1	0.04	instant
Interventions	13	1	0.04	interventions
Inviting	8	1	0.04	inviting
Irrespective	12	1	0.04	irrespective
Joining	7		0.04	joining, links

Table A-5.1 Continue

Word	Length	Count	Weighted Percentage (%)	Similar Words
Journal	7	1	0.04	journal
Latest	6	1	0.04	latest
Lectures	8	1	0.04	lectures
Lessons	7	1	0.04	lessons
Leverage	8	1	0.04	leverage
Lifelong	8	1	0.04	lifelong
Liftman	7	1	0.04	liftman
Lying	5	1	0.04	lying
Mails	5	1	0.04	mails
Major	5	1	0.04	major
Matrix	6	1	0.04	matrix
Messenger	10	1	0.04	messenger
Methods	7	1	0.04	methods
Ministry	8	1	0.04	ministry
Mission	7	1	0.04	mission
Mistake	7	1	0.04	mistake
Mobile	6	1	0.04	mobile
Mortar	6	1	0.04	mortar
Neighboring	11	1	0.04	neighboring
Neither	7	1	0.04	neither
Network	7	1	0.04	network
Newsletter	10	1	0.04	newsletter
Nuggets	7	1	0.04	nuggets
Owner	5	1	0.04	owner
Pilot	5	1	0.04	pilot
Pivot	5	1	0.04	pivot
Previously	10	1	0.04	previously
Professional	12	1	0.04	professional
Prominently	11	1	0.04	prominently
Quarter	7	1	0.04	quarter

Table A-5.1 Continue

Word	Length	Count	Weighted Percentage (%)	Similar Words
Readily	7	1	0.04	readily
Really	6	1	0.04	really
Reaps	5	1	0.04	reaps
Renewable	9	1	0.04	renewable
Repeated	8	1	0.04	repeated
Repository	10	1	0.04	repository
Residential	11	1	0.04	residential
Resides	7	1	0.04	resides
Resistance	10	1	0.04	resistance
Respond	7	1	0.04	respond
Reuse	5	1	0.04	reuse
Risks	5	1	0.04	risks
Satisfactorily	14	1	0.04	satisfactorily
Scale	5	1	0.04	scale
Sensitive	9	1	0.04	sensitive
Smooth	6	1	0.04	smooth
Software	8	1	0.04	software
Solar	5	1	0.04	solar
Sometimes	9	1	0.04	sometimes
Staff	5	1	0.04	staff
Stakeholders	12	1	0.04	stakeholders
Stored	6	1	0.04	stored
Strategic	9	1	0.04	strategic
Subsequently	12	1	0.04	subsequently
Suffice	7	1	0.04	suffice
Superiors	9	1	0.04	superiors
Supervisory	11	1	0.04	supervisory
Taken	5	1	0.04	taken
Teleconferencing	16	1	0.04	teleconferencing
Throughout	10	1	0.04	throughout
Titles	6	1	0.04	titles

Table A-5.1 Continue

Word	Length	Count	Weighted Percentage (%)	Similar Words
Tools	5	1	0.04	tools
Transmission	12	1	0.04	transmission
Types	5	1	0.04	types
Umbrella	8	1	0.04	umbrella
Verbal	6	1	0.04	verbal
Video	5	1	0.04	video
Whatever	8	1	0.04	whatever
Willing	7	1	0.04	willing
Written	7	1	0.04	written
Biggest	7	1	0.04	biggest
Comradeire	10	1	0.04	comradeire
Conferencing	12	1	0.04	conferencing
Everyone	8	1	0.04	everyone
Largest	7	1	0.04	largest
Learnt	6	1	0.04	learnt
NERLDC	6	1	0.04	NERLDC
POWERGRID	9	1	0.04	POWERGRID
SCADA	5	1	0.04	SCADA
SLDCs	5	1	0.04	SLDCs
Unutilized	10	1	0.04	unutilized
Containing	10	2	0.03	containing, incorporated
Domains	7	2	0.03	domains, world
Experimentation	16	2	0.03	experimentation, observations
Format	6	2	0.03	format, initially
Integration	11	2	0.03	integration, whole
Leading	7	3	0.03	leading, moderator, running

Table A-5.1 Continue

Word	Length	Count	Weighted Percentage (%)	Similar Words
Notes	5	3	0.03	notes, notice, observations
Range	5	2	0.03	range, running
Respect	7	2	0.03	respect, values
Executives	10	2	0.02	executives, running
Incorporated	12	2	0.02	incorporated, integration
Observations	12	2	0.02	observations, respect
Regulations	11	2	0.02	regulations, rules

Word Frequency Layout of the major words was performed to get a clear idea of the themes of discussions and interviews. Larger count and the percentage are indicative of the relative importance of the concept. It can be inferred from the above table that the term 'Knowledge' and 'Management' have received the highest percentage of 6.16% and 3.33% respectively. Repetition of words in terms of count and percentages as captured in the focus group discussions and interviews have been represented in the Word Frequency Layout A-5.1given below. This corroborates the prevalence of Knowledge Management in POSOCO along with sharing, and organization/systems and employees which is seen in the core. The terms that have registered higher frequency counts are—training, practices, policy, implementation, documents, experts, available, information, issues, discussions, resources, meetings, and portals.

Besides this, the Word Frequency Layout also indicates these terms in the outer rung- strategy, technology, resources, portal, tacit, communication, meetings, encourage, periodically, program, learning, circulars, culture, operations, and assets.

This means that in POSOCO, information sharing systems, training, practices and culture are in place for facilitating 'Knowledge Management'. It is also elicited that there are ample KM enablers in POSOCO for managing the knowledge-related activities, through meetings, circulars, documents, experts, discussions, available information, and power portals for facilitating effective KM implementation.

Figure A-5.1: Word Frequency Layout

To further supplement the above findings, the tree map is also presented in the Figure A-5.2 given below. The figure explicitly highlights the importance of knowledge at the core of POSOCO management and that is set in its systems and practices besides it's culture. It is pertinent to note herein that these findings and insights of the qualitative research analysis have been used for exploratory purposes in this study.

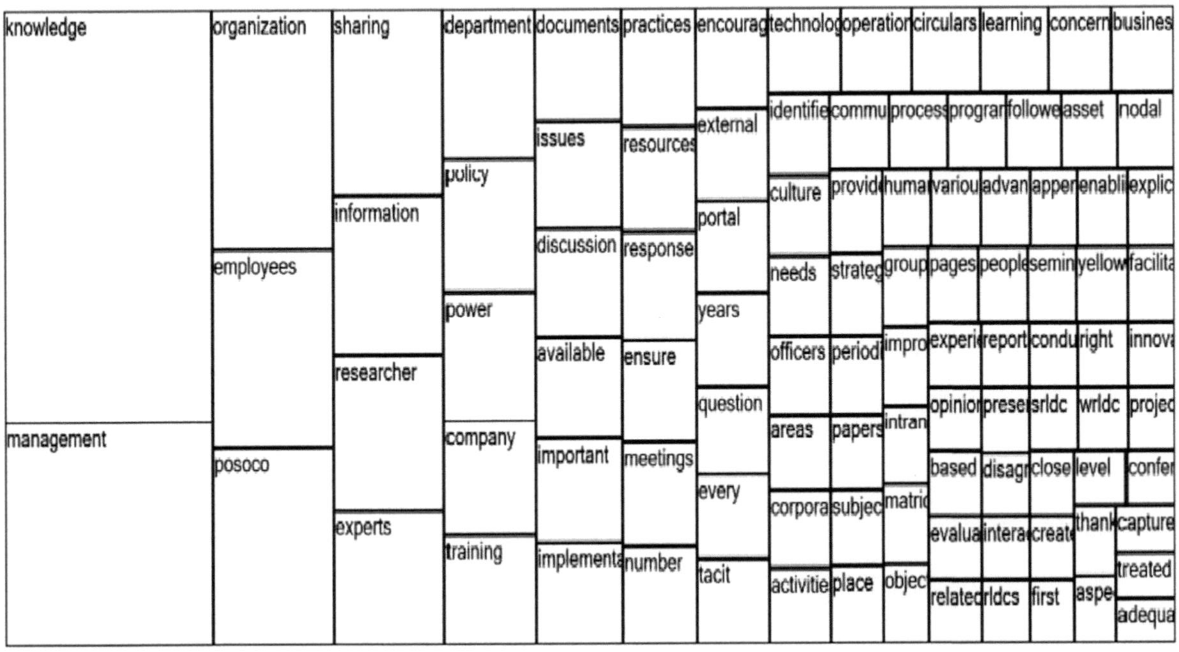

Figure A-5.2: Word Frequency Query

5.1 B- Quantitative Analysis

In addition, to qualitative analysis as discussed above, the next phase of data analysis is the quantitative research analysis, which is discussed in the subsequent paragraphs.

5.2 DEMOGRAPHIC PROFILE

A total of 403 valid responses were obtained from the respondents who participated in the survey meant to accomplish the objectives of this study. The descriptive analysis depicting the demographic constitution of the respondents is presented in the tables as follows:-

5.2.1 Gender Distribution

Table 5.1: Gender

Gender		
	Frequency	**Percent**
Male	343	85.1
Female	60	14.9
Total	403	100

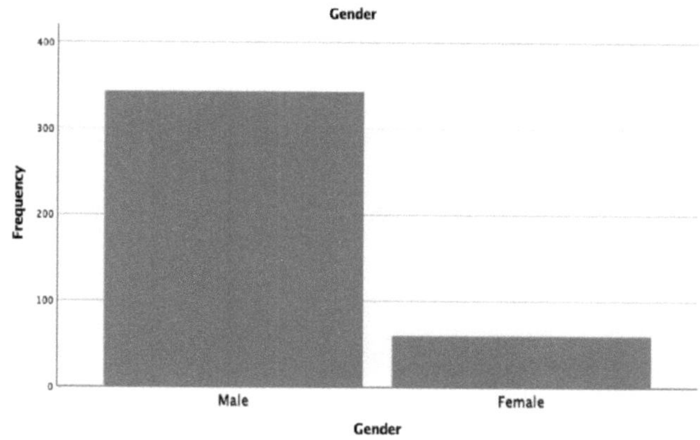

Figure 5.1: Gender

Interpretation

Out of the 403 respondents who participated in this survey, it was found that there were 343 male and 60 females.

5.2.2 Age Distribution

Table 5.2: Age

Age		
	Frequency	**Percent**
23-30 years	174	43.2
31-38 years	97	24.1
39-46 years	53	13.2
47-54 years	39	9.7
55 years or above	40	9.9
Total	403	100

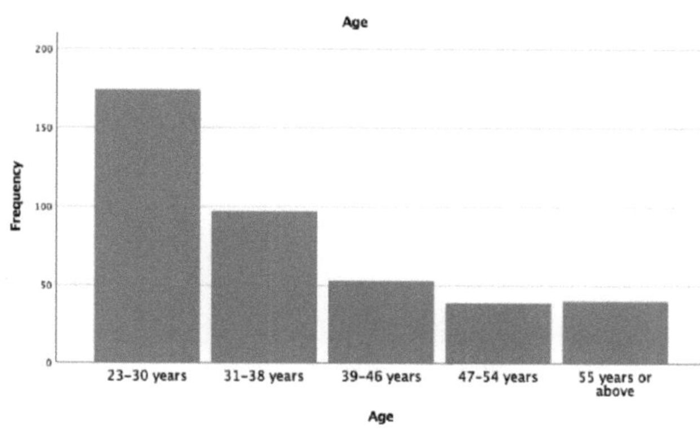

Figure: 5.2 Age

Interpretation

It can be inferred from above that the majority of the respondents belonged to 23-30 years (43.2%) followed by those in the age group of 31-38 years (24.1%), 39-46 years (13.2%).. There are relatively few senior age group respondents who were above 55 years (9.9%) or in the 47-54 years (9.7%) age bracket.

5.2.3 Education Distribution

Table 5.3: Education

Education		
	Frequency	**Percent**
Graduation	261	64.8
Post-Graduation	141	35
Doctorate	1	0.2
Total	403	100

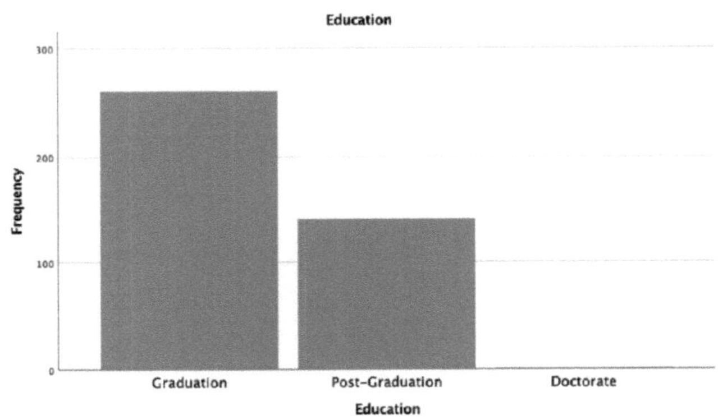

Figure: 5.3 Education

Interpretation

From the above, it can be inferred that the majority of the respondents were well-educated, either graduates (64.8%) and/or post-graduates (35%).

5.2.4 Levels of Hierarchy Distribution:

Levels of Hierarchy in the organization are in terms of pay scales, with E-1 being the lowest Executive level of employee designated as Assistant Officer and E-9 being the level just below the Board of Directors. E-9 level of Executives are designated as Executive Directors.

Table 5.4: Level

Level		
	Frequency	**Percent**
E1-E3	135	33.5
E4-E5	139	34.5
E6-E7A	80	19.9
E8 & above	49	12.2
Total	403	100

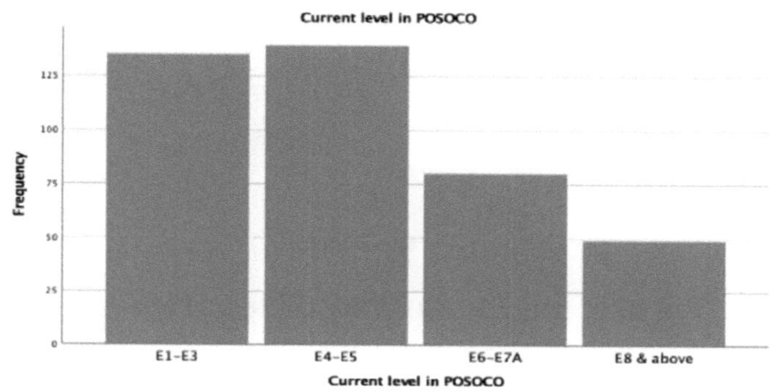

Figure: 5.4 Level

Interpretation

From the above, it can be inferred that as per the Level in the POSOCO, the respondents pertained to levels E1-E3 level (33.5%), E4-E5 (34.5%), E6-E7 A (19.9%) and E8 and above (12.2%).

5.2.5 Department Distribution

Table 5.5: Department

Department		
	Frequency	**Percent**
Market Operation	47	11.7
System Operation	184	45.7
SCADA/IT	60	14.9
Finance	33	8.2
Human Resource	26	6.5
Contracts and Materials	14	3.5
Law	2	0.5

Table 5.5: Continue

Department		
	Frequency	Percent
Any Other	37	9.2
Total	403	100

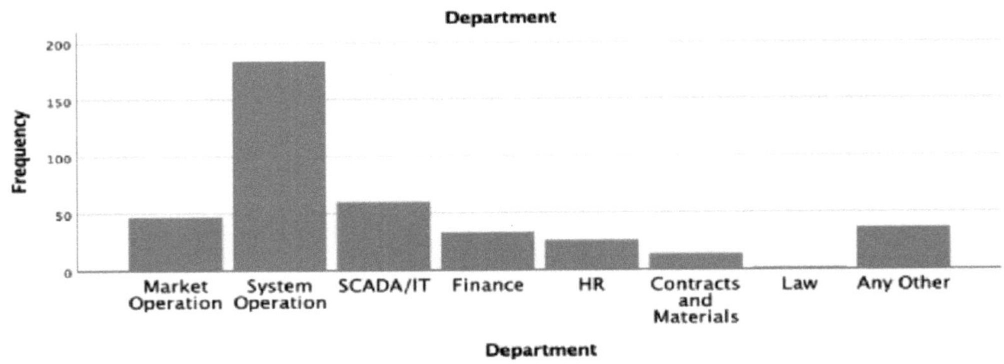

Figure: 5.5 DepartmentDepartment

Interpretation

As per the departments, it can be inferred from above that the respondents were spread over varied departments in POSOCO, i.e. System Operation (45.7%), SCADA/IT (14.9%), Market Operation (11.7%), Finance (8.2%), HR(6.5%), Contracts and Materials (3.5%), Law (o.5%) and other departments (9.2%).

5.2.6 Experience Distribution

Table 5.6: Experience

Experience		
	Frequency	Percent
0-7 years	189	46.9
8-14 years	102	25.3
15-21 years	32	7.9
22-28 years	28	6.9
29 years & above	52	12.9
Total	403	100

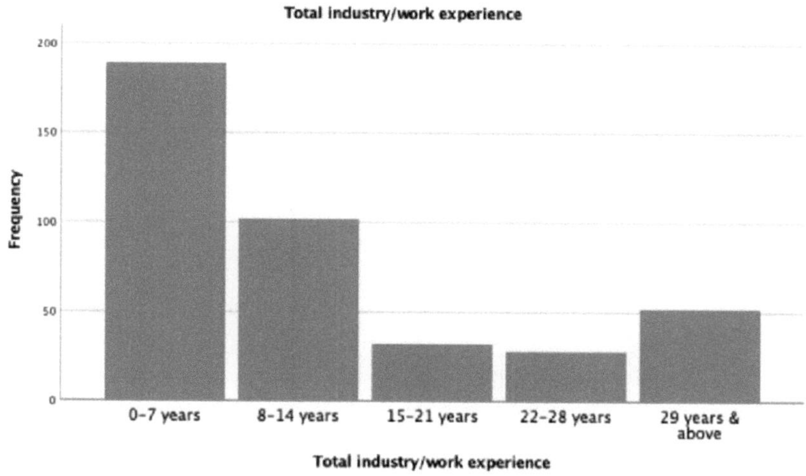

Figure: 5.6 ExperienceTotal industry/work experience

Interpretation

As per the Total industry / work experience, it can be inferred from above that majorly the respondents had a work experience of less than 7 years (46.9%), followed by 8-14 years of work experience (25.3%). Overall it can be observed that the senior experienced employees with more than 15 years of total work experience were collectively 27.7% only.

5.2.7 Worked in PSU Distribution

Table 5.7: Worked in PSU

Work PSU		
	Frequency	**Percent**
Yes	186	46.2
No	217	53.8
Total	403	100

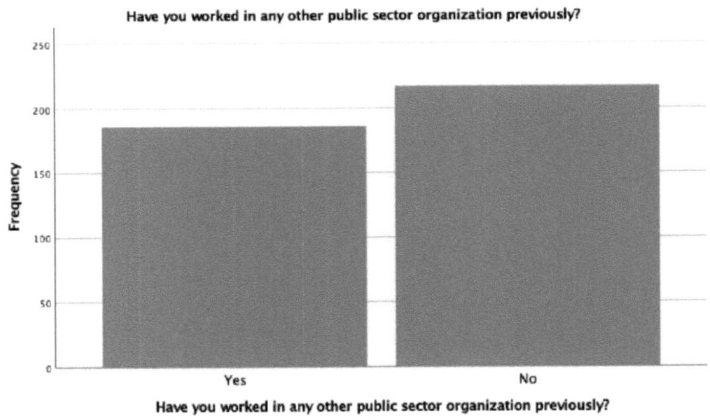

Figure: 5.7 Worked in PSU

Interpretation

Further, it can be that (53.8%) respondents did not have any prior work experience in a public sector organization while only 46.2% stated that they had worked in the public sector organization.

5.2.8 Association with Knowledge Management Distribution

Table 5.8: Association with Knowledge Management

Association KM		
	Frequency	**Percent**
Yes	403	100
No	0	0
Total	403	100

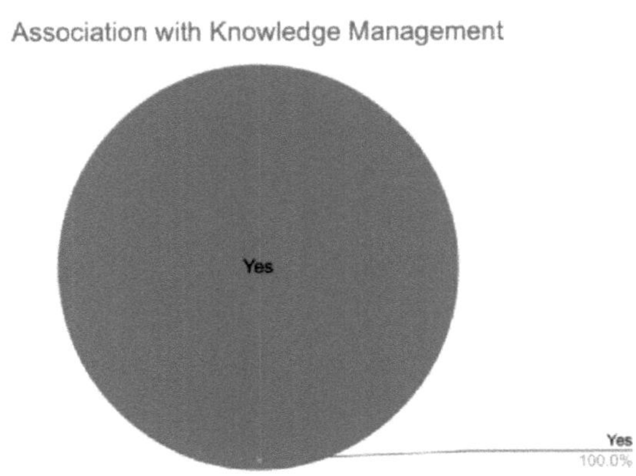

Figure: 5.8 Association with Knowledge Management

Interpretation

This is due to the fact that only executives who were associated with KM implementation in POSOCO were administered in this study.

5.2.9 Place of Posting Distribution

Table 5.9: Place of Posting

Place of Posting		
	Frequency	**Percent**
CC/NLDC	77	19.1
ERLDC	60	14.9
NERLDC	65	16.1
NRLDC	62	15.4
SRLDC	72	17.9
WRLDC	67	16.6
Total	403	100

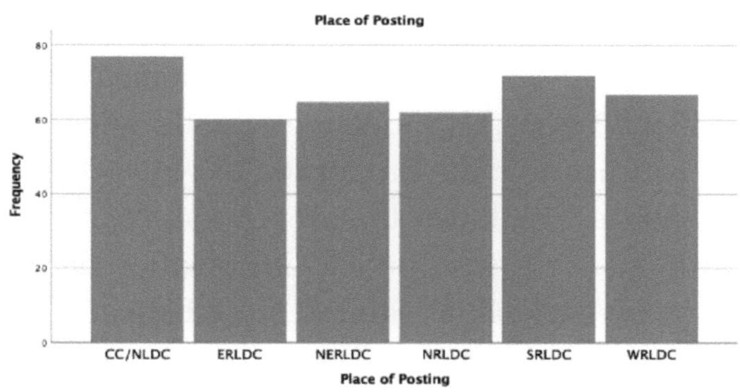

Figure: 5.9 Place of PostingPlace of Posting

Interpretation

It may be seen from the figure number 5.9 that the highest concentration of the personnel is in Delhi because the headquarters of the company is located in Delhi and in the RLDCs the population is more or less similar.

5.3 CONSTRUCTS: MEASURES OF CHARACTERISTICS

Constructs can be conceptually defined as composite of several indicators apropos variables that measure characteristics, or traits. Constructs thus explain how well the observed variable items predict the outcome expected. In this case, it was also imperative to gain insight into the Drivers shaping the Knowledge Management implementation in POSOCO. This involved a two-step treatment by administering one, Exploratory Factor Analysis with the idea of reducing the number of items and group similar items into distinct factors for further analysis, and two, Confirmatory Factor Analysis, i.e. a statistical technique used to verify the factor structure of a set of observed variables. This was used primarily to test the hypothesized relationship between the observed variables with their underlying latent constructs i.e. the 'Driver factors' in explaining the KM in POSOCO. This is presented in the following paragraphs.

5.4. DETERMINANTS OF KNOWLEDGE MANAGEMENT IN POSOCO

5.4.1 Exploratory Factor Analysis

As discussed above, the technique of Exploratory Factor Analysis (EFA) was performed using the Principal Component Analysis method. This technique is primarily used to reduce the statement items and to group similar items under distinct factor sets for better analysis. But prior to administering EFA, the data is checked to see whether it is suitable for factor analysis using the Kaiser-Meyer-Olkin (KMO) Test for sampling adequacy vis-a-vis population besides finding out the suitability of data for Factor Analysis and to measure the adequacy of the sampling. The KMO statistic is a measure of the proportion of variance among variables that might be common variance. The lower the proportion, the more suited the data is to use the Factor Analysis. This would yield information about the suitability of the data in conducting EFA which is required to be between 0.8 and 1 as used in research according to the rule of thumb. The value found after administering the test as recorded in Table 5.10. Bartlett's test of Sphericity is conducted to find out the redundancy between variables by summarizing the factors. In order to test the hypotheses, the Bartlett's test was also run to test the hypothesis as whether the correlation matrix is an identity matrix; which

indicates that the variables are unrelated. In this case, small values (<0.05) of the significance level indicate that a factor analysis is useful for identifying the emanated specified data set. So, here also in this study, the results of KMO and Bartlett's test of Sphericity, were run which indicates the outcome as presented in the table given below:-

Table 5.10: KMO

KMO and Bartlett's Test		
Kaiser-Meyer-Olkin Measure of Sampling Adequacy.		0.929
Bartlett's Test of Sphericity	Approx. Chi- Square	21931.636
	df	2926
	Sig.	0

From the above table 5.10, it can be inferred that Bartlett's test of Sphericity, establishes that 'the variances of the differences between all combinations of related groups (levels), are equal.' These tests have given the overall significance of all the correlations within the correlation matrix; that was significant (x 2 (2926) = 21931.636, p<.05) as is evident in figure 5.10 as given above. The Kaiser-Meyer-Olkin measure of sampling adequacy indicated that the strength of the relationships among variables was also reported to be high (KMO =.929), thus it was acceptable to proceed with the analysis.Pattern Matrix has been presented in Table 5.11.

Table 5.11: Pattern Matrix

Pattern Matrix					
Factor	**Statement**	**Item Code**	**Factor Loading**	**Variance (%)**	**Reliability**
Structures	The organization has enabling structures in terms of hierarchy and communication flows that facilitates knowledge sharing	STRU1	0.65	7.958	0.886
	We strive to have matrix form of structure of Company	STRU2	0.693		
	Brick-and-mortar model (dealing with the customer face-to-face) structure is followed in our Company	STRU3	0.745		

Table 5.11: Continue

Pattern Matrix					
Factor	**Statement**	**Item Code**	**Factor Loading**	**Variance (%)**	**Reliability**
	My organization has a central repository / library where all the necessary documents/ reports are stored	STRU4	0.693		
	Documents pertaining to past research programs are arranged in such a manner that they can be easily accessed and used as and when necessary	STRU5	0.702		
	There are enough Meeting/Conference rooms available for Team meetings and discussions	STRU6	0.816		
	Notice boards kept at various vantage points in my organization plays an important role in informing me of various news and events	STRU7	0.82		
	Information about locations of project reports, research facilities and equipment available are displayed prominently in my organization	STRU8	0.757		

Table 5.11: Continue

Pattern Matrix					
Factor	**Statement**	**Item Code**	**Factor Loading**	**Variance (%)**	**Reliability**
	In my organization, every employee is encouraged to periodically produce documents in the form of technical reports, journal papers, presentations, articles, etc.	STRU9	0.766		
	POSOCO publishes regular intellectual achievements and reports it to its external stakeholders	STRU10	0.588		
	The evaluation of work/projects that are completed successfully has been done in my organization from KM poin of view.	STRU11	0.811		
Assets	Knowledge is treated as a resource/asset in POSOCO	ASST1	0.684	3.858	0.773
	Knowledge is treated as an object in my department	ASST2	0.858		
	Knowledge is used as an important and critical resource in my department	ASST3	0.794		

Table 5.11: Continue

Pattern Matrix					
Factor	**Statement**	**Item Code**	**Factor Loading**	**Variance (%)**	**Reliability**
	Transfer of Knowledge and Best Practices are taking place in day-to-day working of employees	ASST4	0.885		
	Innovation and Knowledge Creation are a way of life in my Company	ASST5	0.831		
Processes	In my department/ organization, every program has a closure meeting to critically review the performance	PROC1	0.744	4.02	0.807
	Within the team/ department, employees share their knowledge in an informal manner	PROC2	0.805		
	There is very good interaction between departments/ groups in my organization	PROC3	0.805		
	All important communications in my organization are sent to me through circulars or memos in electronic environment	PROC4	0.721		
	A Community of Practice exists in POSOCO.	PROC5	0.714		
	Acquisition of knowledge is a regular practice in our Company	PROC6	0.743		

Table 5.11: Continue

Pattern Matrix					
Factor	**Statement**	**Item Code**	**Factor Loading**	**Variance (%)**	**Reliability**
Culture	Knowledge Management has taken place in POSOCC	CULT1	0.688	5.697	0.894
	Aesthetically oriented culture for Knowledge Management is a way of life in POSOCO	CULT4	0.817		
	Employees in POSOCO are having informal, open-minded and collaborative working	CULT5	0.65		
	The organization continuously strives for Knowledge acquisition, dissemination and capture for its employees	CULT6	0.763		
	I visit Power Portal for my knowledge needs	CULT7	0.884		
	I have free access to any information I want irrespective of where it resides in my organization	CULT8	0.629		
	I feel that I have got suppon from Management for Knowledge Management	CULT9	0.895		
	In my department, Knowledge Management activities are taking place satisfactorily	CULT10	0.722		

Table 5.11: Continue

Pattern Matrix					
Factor	**Statement**	**Item Code**	**Factor Loading**	**Variance (%)**	**Reliability**
	My organization periodically gives special awards to employees who make significant contributions to the organization	CULT11	0.658		
	The mission and objectives of Knowledge Management are clearly understood by employees propagated throughout POSOCO	CULT12	0.769		
Technology	The Intranet site provides an Online Discussion Forum in which employees can share information and post their doubts	TECH2	0.793	4.944	0.876
	My organization has an Experts Database that can be used by Employees to locate experts within the organization	TECH3	0.865		
	Employees are provided the 'blogging' platform wherein they can share their experiences through blogs	TECH4	0.805		
	All important documents in my organization are available in the electronic format	TECH5	0.746		

Table 5.11: Continue

Pattern Matrix					
Factor	**Statement**	**Item Code**	**Factor Loading**	**Variance (%)**	**Reliability**
	Employees/Teams can discuss work through TeleConferencing (i.e. through telephones, VOIP, Mobile, etc.)	TECH6	0.777		
	My organization's intranet/website plays a vital role in disseminating information to the employees	TECH7	0.88		
	My organization measures and manages its intellectual capital (IC) in a systematic way	TECH8	0.853		
	There is Knowledge Management Cell in POSOCO which collects knowledge nuggets and disseminates it through Power Portal	TECH9	0.632		
Strategy	POSOCO has got a vision in Knowledge Management which properly articulates its knowledge needs	STRA1	0.783	3.175	0.778
	Knowledge Management is being used constantly as a business strategy	STRA2	0.881		

Table 5.11: Continue

Pattern Matrix					
Factor	**Statement**	**Item Code**	**Factor Loading**	**Variance (%)**	**Reliability**
	A cohesive and powerful vision of the organization is shared across the workforce to promote the need for strategic thinking at all levels	STRA3	0.852		
	Our Company has got collegial, flat, team based, open door policy	STRA4	0.82		
Deterrents	In my opinion, there are very few Subject Matter Experts available in my department	DETE1	0.649	2.858	0.762
	I have come across situations in work where the same mistake done by someone in the past is being repeated	DETE2	0.863		
	There are lots of documents/reports lying unutilized in my department	DETE3	0.805		
	Most of the time I find that it is pretty time consuming to access any document in my department	DETE4	0.791		
Incentives	Reward and recognition for suggestion of Best Practices, have been incorporated in POSOCO's annual plan	INCE1	0.804	3.325	0.821

Table 5.11: Continue

Pattern Matrix					
Factor	**Statement**	**Item Code**	**Factor Loading**	**Variance (%)**	**Reliability**
	The organization provides incentives to motivate users to learn from experiences and use the Knowledge Management System of POSOCO	INCE2	0.838		
	In my organization, it is mandatory for every employee to document insights (in the form of best practices, lessons learnt etc.) from the work/project	INCE3	0.843		
	Recognition in form of titles, certificates & commendation letters are periodically awarded to the contributors of knowledge	INCE4	0.793		
	My organization actively promotes a 'culture of experimentation' that encourages employees to try new ideas and take risks	INCE5	0.802		
Enablers	Information about the outcome of implementing Best Practices is translated in practice in my department / company	ENAB1	0.96	26.221	0.913

Table 5.11: Continue

Pattern Matrix					
Factor	**Statement**	**Item Code**	**Factor Loading**	**Variance (%)**	**Reliability**
	Dedicated staff for Knowledge capture and acquisition are earmarked ir my department	ENAB2	0.524		
	Information regarding relevant topics are readily available to the employees in my Company	ENAB3	0.738		
	Information regarding process description can be uploaded in the Organization's Knowledge Bank at Power Portal, the intranet of Company	ENAB4	0.798		
	'Personal best practices can be shared with other employees easily' can be said as a part of job in POSOCO	ENAB5	0.616		
	Employees can upload their documents or reports to Power Portal	ENAB6	0.696		
	Employees can download any document they want from the Intranet site/portal	ENAB7	0.823		

Table 5.11: Continue

Pattern Matrix					
Factor	**Statement**	**Item Code**	**Factor Loading**	**Variance (%)**	**Reliability**
	My organization has a 'Chief Knowledge Officer' (or equivalent) who is responsible for managing the knowledge-related activities	ENAB8	0.872		
	I use Knowledge maps and matrices of my Company for knowledge requirements	ENAB9	0.837		
	I contact subject matter experts by using my Corporate Yellow Pages	ENAB10	0.666		
	All programs have periodic team meetings to review the progress and discuss issues pertaining to the work	ENAB11	0.842		
	My organization's newsletter/bulletin will inform me about the latest happenings in your organization and outside	ENAB12	0.779		
	My organization has a directory of personnel containing information of names of people, their designation, division, program, phone number, email, etc.	ENAB13	0.744		

Table 5.11: Continue

Pattern Matrix					
Factor	**Statement**	**Item Code**	**Factor Loading**	**Variance (%)**	**Reliability**
	Use of knowledge is a way of work life in every employees' job	ENAB14	0.755		
	Company has got proper facility for Research & Development	ENAB15	0.737		
	My superiors fully endorse my way of handling Knowledge Management related issues	ENAB16	0.638		
Training	Knowledge Management related training is identified as part of organizational training need assessment	TRAI2	0.717	2.078	0.803
	My organization arranges seminars/ lectures by external experts on a periodic basis	TRAI3	0.832		
	All employees in my department are willing to share their knowledge with others	TRAI4	0.721		
	My organization sponsors trips for employees to international/national conferences and seminars	TRAI5	0.707		

Interpretation

On running the Exploratory Factor Analysis tests, it was found from the Pattern Matrix, as per table; that 10 main factors with Eigenvalues >1 can be extracted as the principal Drivers of KM practices. From the above factor analysis tables, it can be interpreted that there are ten major Drivers of KM practices that can be extracted that explains a total of 64.13% of the variance for the entire set of variables. The ten Drivers were labeled as Structures, Assets, Processes, Culture, Technology, Strategy, Deterrents, Incentives, Enablers, Training and their reliability was also determined by using the Cronbach's alpha score which is 0.886, 0.773, 0.807, 0.894, 0.876, 0.778, 0.762, 0.821, 0.913 and 0.803 respectively. The description of these is as follows:-

Factor 1: 'Enablers' are the most important Drivers of KM practices in POSOCO that explained 26.22% of the variance.

Factor 2: 'Structures' are the second Drivers of KM practices in POSOCO and it explained 7.95% of the variance.

Factor 3: 'Culture' is the third Driver of KM practices in POSOCO and it explained 5.69% of the variance.

Factor 4: 'Technology' is the fourth Driver of KM practices in POSOCO and it explained 4.94% of the variance

Factor 5: 'Processes' together are the fifth Driver of KM practices in POSOCO and it explained 4.02% of the variance

Factor 6: 'Assets' are the sixth Driver of KM practices in POSOCO which explained 3.85% of the variance.

Factor 7: 'Incentives' are the seventh Driver of KM practices in POSOCO which explained 3.32% of the variance.

Factor 8: 'Strategy' is the eighth Driver of KM practices in POSOCO which explained 3.17% of the variance.

Factor 9: 'Deterrents' are the ninth Drivers of KM practices in POSOCO which explained 2.85% of the variance.

Factor 10: 'Training' is the last Driver of KM practices in POSOCO which explained 2.07% of the variance.

5.5 CONFIRMATORY FACTOR ANALYSIS (CFA)

As the next step, CFA is used to examine the hypothesized relationship between Drivers shaping the KM in POSOCO. Constructs should only be used if they have good measurement characteristics and this aspect was examined before estimating the various models of interest. On the basis of theory and literature review and exploratory factor analysis, CFA is used to examine the hypothesized relationship amongst constructs. As per the nature of the latent variables or constructs, key model constructs are shown in figure 5.10.

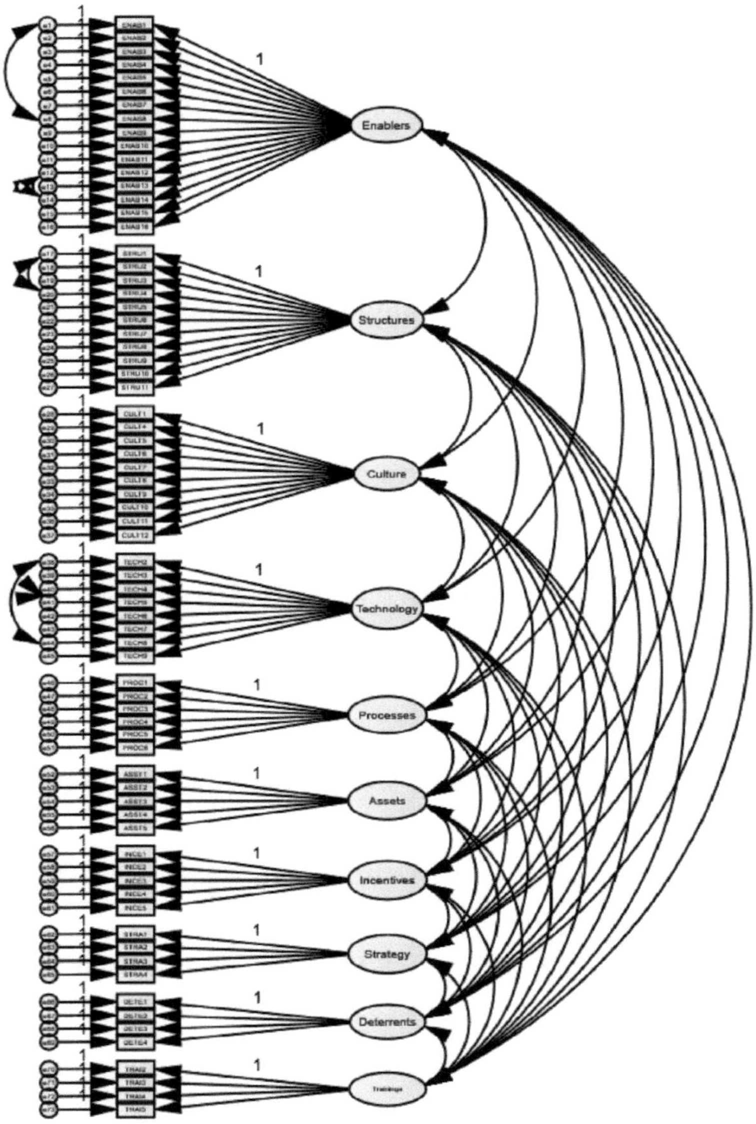

Figure 5.10: Confirmatory Model of Constructs (Determinants)

The present study used AMOS statistical software v26 to conduct the confirmatory factor analysis to test the efficiency of the ten constructs. According to Holtzman and Leich (2014), when running CFA; there are various fit statistics which help to examine the model fitness for the data as shown in Table 5.12.

The ratio of Goodness of Fit to Degrees of Freedom should not be more than 3 (Maclver & Carmines, 1981), and the value of Root Mean Square Error of Approximation (RMSEA) should be less than 0.08, with the *Goodness of Fit Index*

(GFI), Indicators of Financial Integration (IFI), Incremental measure of Goodness of Fit Index (NFI), Comparative Fit Index(CFI) exceeding 0.9 (Bagozzi and Yi, 1988). Furthermore, Root Mean Square Residual (RMR) is associated with the residual in the attitude model. The range of RMR value is zero to one where a smaller RMR shows better model fit.

Table 5.12: Model Fit Measures

Model Fit Measures			
	Estimate	**Threshold**	**Interpretation**
CMIN	4677.129	--	--
DF	2505	--	--
CMIN/DF	1.867	Between 1 and 3	Excellent
CFI	0.9	>0.95	Acceptable
SRMR	0.054	<0.08	Excellent
RMSEA	0.046	<0.06	Excellent
PClose	0.998	>0.05	Excellent

In the table 5.12 above the CMIN/DF is 1.867 which is well below 3 and this is considered to be excellent for the overall performance of the model. CFI is 0.91 which is though below 0.95 but more than 0.90 and acceptable value for the fit of the model. Furthermore SRMR (0.054), RMSEA (0.046) and P Close i.e. P of close fit (0.998) are excellent values contributing to the overall fit of the model. Those values indicate a good fit between the model and the observed data.

Table 5.13 shows that there is convergent and discriminant validity in the factors of the measurement model as the value of all ten constructs on Credibility Ratio (CR), Average Variance Extracted (AVE) and Maximum Shared Variance (MSV) are acceptable and are CR>AVE>MSV.

Table 5.13: Validity Measures

Validity Measures			
	CR	**AVE**	**MSV**
Enablers	0.958	0.586	0.372
Structures	0.929	0.543	0.418
Culture	0.934	0.59	0.421
Technology	0.909	0.563	0.022
Processes	0.867	0.522	0.123
Assets	0.881	0.599	0.058

Table 5.13: Continue

Validity Measures			
	CR	AVE	MSV
Incentives	0.887	0.612	0.197
Strategy	0.862	0.611	0.026
Deterrents	0.799	0.514	0.022
Trainings	0.863	0.612	0.421

Standardized parameter estimates are provided in the table 5.14 along with unstandardized estimates. The results show that all items have P more than 0.6 and most of the items have P more than 0.7. The unstandardized parameters of the items of all constructs are significant at $p<0.05$.

Table 5.14: Regression Weights

Regression Weights: (Group number 1 - Default model)							Standardized Regression Weights
			Estimate	S.E.	C.R.	P	
ENAB1	<—	Enablers	1				0.762
ENAB2	<—	Enablers	1.069	0.077	13.962	***	0.667
ENAB3	<—	Enablers	1.164	0.069	16.792	***	0.782
ENAB4	<—	Enablers	1.137	0.065	17.394	***	0.806
ENAB5	<—	Enablers	1.155	0.077	15	***	0.711
ENAB6	<—	Enablers	1.133	0.069	16.378	***	0.766
ENAB7	<—	Enablers	1.117	0.067	16.692	***	0.778
ENAB8	<—	Enablers	1.063	0.052	20.491	***	0.761
ENAB9	<—	Enablers	1.21	0.068	17.819	***	0.822
ENAB10	<—	Enablers	1.15	0.068	17.026	***	0.791
ENAB11	<—	Enablers	1.164	0.064	18.318	***	0.841
ENAB12	<—	Enablers	1.204	0.067	17.857	***	0.823
ENAB13	<—	Enablers	1.114	0.067	16.575	***	0.774
ENAB14	<—	Enablers	1.091	0.067	16.285	***	0.763
ENAB15	<—	Enablers	0.998	0.063	15.815	***	0.744
ENAB16	<—	Enablers	0.915	0.07	13.003	***	0.627
STRU1	<—	Structures	1				0.714
STRU2	<—	Structures	1.064	0.074	14.382	***	0.741

Table 5.14: Continue

Regression Weights: (Group number 1 - Default model)							Standardized Regression Weights
			Estimate	S.E.	C.R.	P	
STRU3	<—	Structures	1.096	0.074	14.856	***	0.765
STRU4	<—	Structures	0.988	0.056	17.588	***	0.704
STRU5	<—	Structures	0.998	0.076	13.217	***	0.681
STRU6	<—	Structures	1.063	0.073	14.6	***	0.752
STRU7	<—	Structures	1.072	0.074	14.489	***	0.746
STRU8	<—	Structures	0.975	0.071	13.797	***	0.711
STRU9	<—	Structures	1.126	0.078	14.443	***	0.744
STRU10	<—	Structures	0.944	0.065	14.632	***	0.753
STRU11	<—	Structures	1.086	0.071	15.357	***	0.791
CULT1	<—	Culture	1				0.804
CULT4	<—	Culture	1.027	0.056	18.326	***	0.8
CULT5	<—	Culture	1.02	0.058	17.723	***	0.78
CULT6	<—	Culture	0.998	0.055	18.155	***	0.794
CULT7	<—	Culture	1.022	0.061	16.707	***	0.747
CULT8	<—	Culture	0.821	0.072	11.429	***	0.547
CULT9	<—	Culture	1.086	0.058	18.75	***	0.813
CULT10	<—	Culture	1.012	0.056	17.938	***	0.787
CULT11	<—	Culture	1.031	0.06	17.294	***	0.766
CULT12	<—	Culture	1.05	0.057	18.504	***	0.805
TECH2	<—	Technology	1				0.755
TECH3	<—	Technology	1.222	0.062	19.787	***	0.916
TECH4	<—	Technology	0.934	0.066	14.233	***	0.689
TECH5	<—	Technology	0.839	0.065	12.953	***	0.633
TECH6	<—	Technology	0.903	0.068	13.3	***	0.648
TECH7	<—	Technology	1.272	0.063	20.322	***	0.94
TECH8	<—	Technology	1.051	0.053	19.812	***	0.797
TECH9	<—	Technology	0.693	0.065	10.684	***	0.53
PROC1	<—	Processes	1				0.727
PROC2	<—	Processes	1.146	0.081	14.225	***	0.761
PROC3	<—	Processes	1.069	0.076	14.144	***	0.756

Table 5.14: Continue

Regression Weights: (Group number 1 - Default model)							**Standardized Regression Weights**
			Estimate	**S.E.**	**C.R.**	**P**	
PROC4	<—	Processes	1.008	0.077	13.083	***	0.698
PROC5	<—	Processes	1.016	0.081	12.532	***	0.668
PROC6	<—	Processes	1.034	0.077	13.513	***	0.721
ASST1	<—	Assets	1				0.651
ASST2	<—	Assets	1.103	0.082	13.524	***	0.811
ASST3	<—	Assets	1.052	0.083	12.709	***	0.747
ASST4	<—	Assets	1.169	0.085	13.794	***	0.834
ASST5	<—	Assets	1.151	0.085	13.543	***	0.812
INCE1	<—	Incentives	1				0.705
INCE2	<—	Incentives	1.322	0.085	15.575	***	0.841
INCE3	<—	Incentives	1.293	0.081	15.907	***	0.863
INCE4	<—	Incentives	0.992	0.072	13.737	***	0.734
INCE5	<—	Incentives	1.144	0.081	14.117	***	0.756
STRA1	<—	Strategy	1				0.693
STRA2	<—	Strategy	1.221	0.082	14.893	***	0.868
STRA3	<—	Strategy	1.076	0.077	13.971	***	0.787
STRA4	<—	Strategy	1.076	0.079	13.695	***	0.769
DETE1	<—	Deterrents	1				0.448
DETE2	<—	Deterrents	1.828	0.208	8.796	***	0.928
DETE3	<—	Deterrents	1.421	0.167	8.508	***	0.722
DETE4	<—	Deterrents	1.442	0.173	8.343	***	0.687
TRAI2	<—	Trainings	1				0.753
TRAI3	<—	Trainings	1.07	0.066	16.131	***	0.817
TRAI4	<—	Trainings	1.197	0.075	15.955	***	0.808
TRAI5	<—	Trainings	1	0.068	14.739	***	0.749
*Item Code elaboration in the Table No. 5.14 has been given in the Pattern Matrix Table 5.11.							

It has been found that in order to depict the results drawn for KM Drivers the Technology Acceptance Model as represented in the figure 5.11; delineates the coherence of all the factors which are ameliorated and have consonance with each other.

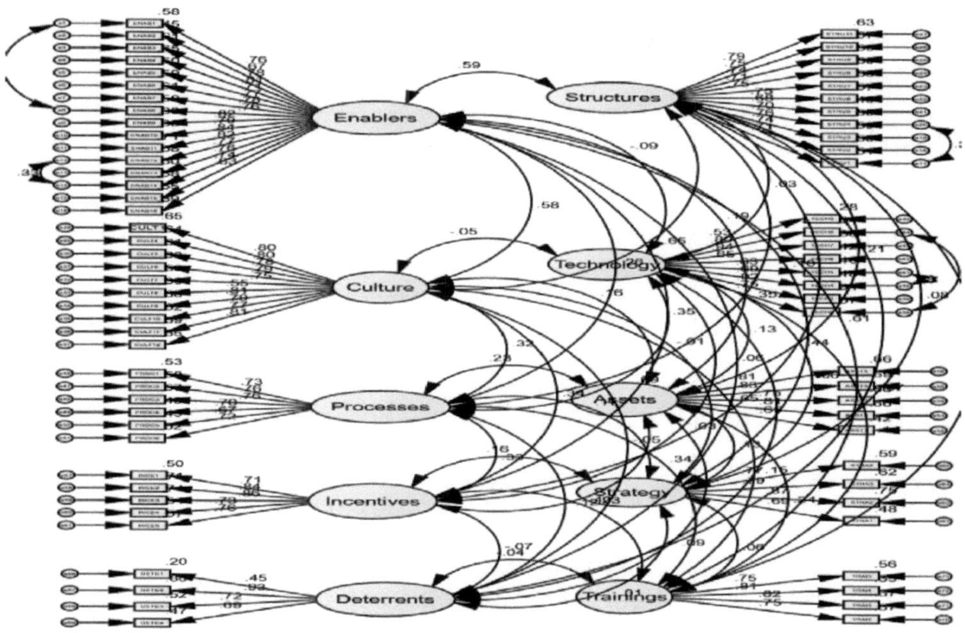

Figure 5.11: TAM Model

Technology Acceptance Model proves that the Chi-Square goodness of fit along with associated degrees are having the normal distribution apropos the actual population. This point is brought to the fore by Model Fit measures as described in Table 5.12 of this dissertation. It also demonstrates the "perceived usefulness and its usage" and "its intentions for its social influence". The AMOS value based Technology Acceptance Model also depicts as how the "characteristic of abstractness is independent from a specific time and place" (Walliman 2005). In this research endeavour, the achievement iteration is minimum which clearly indicates that the estimation process has fructified into an acceptable solution. The interrelatedness of the constructs and their variables having the correlation with the items grouped under each construct have also been taken into consideration through pattern matrix as depicted in Table 5.11 earlier.

5.6 RELATIONSHIP OF THE DRIVERS OF KM AND THE OVERALL EFFECTIVENESS OF KM IMPLEMENTATON PRACTICES IN POSOCO

In order to achieve the objective of this study apropos effectiveness of KM, Regression analysis was conducted on all ten Drivers aka factors (as extracted from Factor Analysis) to understand their relative impact shaping the KM implementation in POSOCO. This led to the formulation of the regression equation showing the predictive strength of the relationships between these Drivers and the KM implementation in POSOCO. Accordingly, the following hypotheses were proposed as:-

Table 5.15: Relationship between KM Drivers and overall effectiveness of KM implementation

H1a: There is a relationship between Structures and overall effectiveness of KM implementation.
H1b: There is a relationship between Assets and overall effectiveness of KM implementation.
H1c: There is a relationship between Processes and overall effectiveness of KM implementation.
H1d: There is a relationship between Culture and overall effectiveness of KM implementation.
H1e: There is a relationship between Technology and overall effectiveness of KM implementation.
H1f: There is a relationship between Strategy and overall effectiveness of KM implementation.
H1g: There is a relationship between Deterrents and overall effectiveness of KM implementation.
H1h: There is a relationship between Incentives and overall effectiveness of KM implementation.
H1i: There is a relationship between Enablers and overall effectiveness of KM implementation.
H1j: There is a relationship between Training and overall effectiveness of KM implementation.

The results of the Multiple Regression are presented in the tables (5.16 - 5.17) below:-

Table 5.16 ANOVA

ANOVA					
	Sum of Squares	**df**	**Mean Square**	**F**	**Sig.**
Regression	91.526	10	9.153	82.906	0
Residual	43.276	392	0.11		
Total	134.802	402			
Dependent Variable: KME calculation of measures of Fuzzy Module Membership (KME)					
Predictors: (Constant), Trainings, Deterrents, Strategy, Technology, Assets, Processes, Incentives, Enablers, Culture, Structures					

Table 5.17: Model Summary

Model Summary			
R	**R Square**	**Adjusted R Square**	**Std. Error of the Estimate**
0.824	0.679	0.671	0.33226

Table 5.18: Coefficients and Significance of Determinants

Model	Unstandardized Coefficients		Standardized Coefficients		
Male	**B**	**Std.Error**	**Beta**	**t**	**Sig.**
(Constant)	-0.507	0.157		-3.223	0.001
Structures	0.116	0.034	0.147	3.432	0.001
Assets	0.124	0.021	0.18	5.86	0
Processes	0.119	0.022	0.174	5.483	0
Culture	0.169	0.037	0.184	4.555	0
Technology	0.093	0.021	0.138	4.548	0
Strategy	0.144	0.021	0.199	6.784	0
Deterrents	0.122	0.019	0.186	6.264	0
Incentives	0.112	0.024	0.15	4.624	0
Enablers	0.119	0.032	0.144	3.729	0
Trainings	0.093	0.036	0.108	2.574	0.01

Interpretation

As the regression table number 5.16 shows, the value of R square is 0.679. It means that 67.9% of samples are closely fitted to the regression line. The table 5.17 generated also shows a significant probability value (p = 0.000) and signifies that all the tenDrivers significantly impact the KM implementation in POSOCO.Further, analysis reveals that Strategy (Beta = 0.199) accounts for the maximum significant impact on KM implementation in POSOCO, followed by Deterrents (Beta = 0.186), Culture (Beta = 0.184), Assets (Beta = 0.18), Processes (Beta =0.174), Incentives (Beta = 0.15), Structures (Beta = 0.147), Enablers (Beta =0.144), Technology (Beta =0.138), and Trainings (Beta = 0.108).

The Regression equation model can be drawn up as:-

Y=a+b1x1+ b2x2 + b3x3

Y is dependent variable

X1, x2, x3... are independent variables or predictors

KME = -.507 + 0.144*Strategy+ 0.122*Deterrents + 0.169*Culture + 0.124*Assets 0.119*Processes + 0.112*Incentives + 0.116*Structures + 0.119*Enablers + 0.093*Technology + 0.093*Trainings.

This sets the predictive relationship between the Drivers aka factors impacting the KM implementation in POSOCO.

5.7 RELATIONSHIP OF THE DRIVERS OF KM AND THE OVERALL EFFECTIVENESS OF KM IMPLEMENTATION ACROSS THE DEMOGRAPHIC VARIABLES

This section is related to examining the relationship between the demographic variables and the overall effectiveness of KM implementation in POSOCO. The in-depth study has been done in order to find out as to how the demographics (gender, age group, levels of education, levels of hierarchy, no. of years of experience) perceive the relative variance among the KM Drivers impacting the KM implementation in POSOCO. Thus, multiple regression analysis has been used. Accordingly, the following hypotheses were proposed as:-

H2: There is a relationship between KM Drivers and overall effectiveness of KM implementation across Genders.

Table 5.19: Relationship between KM Drivers and overall effectiveness of KM implementation across Genders

H2a: There is a relationship between Structures and overall effectiveness of KM implementation across Genders
H2b: There is a relationship between Assets and overall effectiveness of KM implementation across Genders
H2c: There is a relationship between Processes and overall effectiveness of KM implementation across Genders
H2d: There is a relationship between Culture and overall effectiveness of KM implementation across Genders
H2e: There is a relationship between Technology and overall effectiveness of KM implementation across Genders
H2f: There is a relationship between Strategy and overall effectiveness of KM implementation across Genders

Table 5.19: Continue

H2g: There is a relationship between Deterrents and overall effectiveness of KM implementation across Genders
H2h: There is a relationship between Incentives and overall effectiveness of KM implementation across Genders
H2i: There is a relationship between Enablers and overall effectiveness of KM implementation across Genders
H2j: There is a relationship between Training and overall effectiveness of KM implementation across Genders

H3: There is a relationship between KM Drivers and overall effectiveness of KM implementation across Age Groups.

Table 5.20: Relationship between KM Drivers and overall effectiveness of KM implementation across Age Groups

H3a: There is a relationship between Structures and overall effectiveness of KM implementation across Age Groups
H3b: There is a relationship between Assets and overall effectiveness of KM implementation across Age Groups
H3c: There is a relationship between Processes and overall effectiveness of KM implementation across Age Groups
H3d: There is a relationship between Culture and overall effectiveness of KM implementation across Age Groups
H3e: There is a relationship between Technology and overall effectiveness of KM implementation across Age Groups
H3f: There is a relationship between Strategy and overall effectiveness of KM implementation across Age Groups
H3g: There is a relationship between Deterrents and overall effectiveness of KM implementation across Age Groups
H3h: There is a relationship between Incentives and overall effectiveness of KM implementation across Age Groups
H3i: There is a relationship between Enablers and overall effectiveness of KM implementation across Age Groups
H3j: There is a relationship between Training and overall effectiveness of KM implementation across Age Groups

H4: There is a relationship between KM Drivers and overall effectiveness of KM implementation across varied levels of Education.

Table 5.21: Relationship between KM Drivers and overall effectiveness of KM implementation across varied levels of Education
H4a: There is a relationship between Structures and overall effectiveness of KM implementation across varied levels of Education
H4b: There is a relationship between Assets and overall effectiveness of KM implementation across varied levels of Education
H4c: There is a relationship between Processes and overall effectiveness of KM implementation across varied levels of Education
H4d: There is a relationship between Culture and overall effectiveness of KM implementation across varied levels of Education
H4e: There is a relationship between Technology and overall effectiveness of KM implementation across varied levels of Education
H4f: There is a relationship between Strategy and overall effectiveness of KM implementation across varied levels of Education
H4g: There is a relationship between Deterrents and overall effectiveness of KM implementation across varied levels of Education
H4h: There is a relationship between Incentives and overall effectiveness of KM implementation across varied levels of Education
H4i: There is a relationship between Enablers and overall effectiveness of KM implementation across varied levels of Education
H4j: There is a relationship between Training and overall effectiveness of KM implementation across varied levels of Education

H5: There is a relationship between KM Drivers and overall effectiveness of KM implementation across Levels of Hierarchy.

Table 5.22: Relationship between KM Drivers and overall effectiveness of KM implementation across Levels of Hierarchy
H5a: There is a relationship between Structures and overall effectiveness of KM implementation across Levels of Hierarchy
H5b: There is a relationship between Assets and overall effectiveness of KM implementation across Levels of Hierarchy

Table 5.22: Continue

H5c: There is a relationship between Processes and overall effectiveness of KM implementation across Levels of Hierarchy
H5d: There is a relationship between Culture and overall effectiveness of KM implementation across Levels of Hierarchy
H5e: There is a relationship between Technology and overall effectiveness of KM implementation across Levels of Hierarchy
H5f: There is a relationship between Strategy and overall effectiveness of KM implementation across Levels of Hierarchy
H5g: There is a relationship between Deterrents and overall effectiveness of KM implementation across Levels of Hierarchy
H5h: There is a relationship between Incentives and overall effectiveness of KM implementation across Levels of Hierarchy
H5i: There is a relationship between Enablers and overall effectiveness of KM implementation across Levels of Hierarchy
H5j: There is a relationship between Training and overall effectiveness of KM implementation across Levels of Hierarchy

H6: There is a relationship between KM Drivers and overall effectiveness of KM implementation across number of years of Experience.

Table 5.23: Relationship between KM Drivers and overall effectiveness of KM implementation across number of years of Experience

H6a: There is a relationship between Structures and overall effectiveness of KM implementation across number of years of Experience
H6b: There is a relationship between Assets and overall effectiveness of KM implementation across number of years of Experience
H6c: There is a relationship between Processes and overall effectiveness of KM implementation across number of years of Experience
H6d: There is a relationship between Culture and overall effectiveness of KM implementation across number of years of Experience
H6e: There is a relationship between Technology and overall effectiveness of KM implementation across number of years of Experience
H6f: There is a relationship between Strategy and overall effectiveness of KM implementation across number of years of Experience

Table 5.23: Continue

H6g: There is a relationship between Deterrents and overall effectiveness of KM implementation across number of years of Experience
H6h: There is a relationship between Incentives and overall effectiveness of KM implementation across number of years of Experience
H6i: There is a relationship between Enablers and overall effectiveness of KM implementation across number of years of Experience
H6j: There is a relationship between Training and overall effectiveness of KM implementation across number of years of Experience

The results of the Multiple Regression is presented in the tables below-

5.7.1 Gender

Table 5.24 Model Summary of Gender

Model: Gender	R	R Square	Adjusted R Square	Std. Error of the Estimate	F	Significance
Male	0.832	0.692	0.683	0.33455	74.591	0
Female	0.785	0.616	0.538	0.33254	7.867	0

Table 5.25: Coefficients and Significance of Determinants - Male

Model	Unstandardized Coefficients		Standardized Coefficients		
Male	B	Std. Erroi	Beta	t	Sig.
(Constant)	-0.512	0.168		-3.055	0.002
Structures	0.106	0.037	0.133	2.852	0.005
Assets	0.122	0.023	0.174	5.299	0
Processes	0.125	0.023	0.183	5.377	0
Culture	0.169	0.039	0.187	4.308	0
Technology	0.096	0.022	0.137	4.256	0
Strategy	0.132	0.023	0.178	5.656	0
Deterrents	0.125	0.022	0.183	5.784	0
Incentives	0.101	0.026	0.136	3.852	0
Enablers	0.136	0.034	0.164	3.949	0
Trainings	0.1	0.039	0.116	2.581	0.01

Interpretation

As the regression table shows, the value of R^2 is 0.692 in case of Males and 0.616 in case of females. It means that 69.2% of the sample is closely fitted to the regression line in Males as compared to females where the R^2 fits 61.6% (Table 5.18). The table 5.19 generated also shows a significant probability value (p = 0.000) and signifies that all the ten Drivers significantly impact the KM implementation in POSOCO as per the male respondents.

In case of male respondents, further analysis reveals that Culture (Beta = 0.187, t-value = 4.308, $p<0.05$) accounts for the maximum significant impact on KM implementation in POSOCO, followed by Processes (Beta = 0.183, t-value =5.377, $p<0.05$), Deterrents (Beta = 0.183, t-value = 5.377, t-value = 5.784 $p<0.05$)and, Strategy (Beta = 0.178, t-value = 5.656, $p<0.05$), Assets (Beta = 0.174, t-value = 5.299, $p<0.05$), Enablers (Beta =0.164, t-value = 3.949, $p<0.05$), Structures (Beta = 0.133, t-value = 2.852, $p<0.05$), Technology (Beta =0.137, t-value = 4.256, $p<0.05$), Incentives (Beta = 0.136, t-value = 3.852, $p<0.05$), and Trainings (Beta = 0.116, t-value = 2.581, $p<0.05$).

On similar lines, the coefficients table as per the female respondents is as:-

Table 5.26: Coefficients and Significance of Determinants - Female

Model	Unstandardized Coefficients		Standardized Coefficients		
Female	**B**	**Std. Error**	**Beta**	**t**	**Sig.**
(Constant)	-0.581	0.555		-1.047	0.3
Structures	0.15	0.092	0.201	1.631	0.109
Assets	0.12	0.061	0.201	1.988	0.052
Processes	0.053	0.077	0.066	0.68	0.5
Culture	0.225	0.141	0.208	1.596	0.117
Technology	0.114	0.057	0.203	2.001	0.051
Strategy	0.219	0.056	0.355	3.912	0
Deterrents	0.086	0.051	0.163	1.702	0.095
Incentives	0.19	0.07	0.253	2.719	0.009
Enablers	-0.002	0.103	-0.003	-0.023	0.981
Trainings	0.09	0.118	0.105	0.765	0.448

The table 5.20 generated shows a significant probability value (p = 0.000) and signifies that only two Drivers - Strategy and Incentives are significantly impacting the KM implementation in POSOCO in females. Further, analysis reveals that Strategy (Beta = 0.355, t-value = 3.912, $p<0.05$) accounts for the maximum significant impact on KM implementation in POSOCO, followed by Incentives (Beta = 0.253, t-value = 2.719, $p<0.05$).

5.7.2 Age

The results of the multiple regression for the age groups for its relationship with the KM Drivers impacting the KM implementation in POSOCO (dependent variable) is discussed as:-

Table 5.27: Model Summary of Age

Model : Age	R	R Square	Adjustec R Square	Std. Error ol the Estimate	F	Significance
23-30 years	0.819	0.671	0.651	0.3297	33.208	0
31-38 Years	0.897	0.805	0.782	0.30562	35.517	0
39-46 Years	0.762	0.581	0.481	0.37053	5.827	0
47-54 Years	0.861	0.741	0.648	0.34489	8.002	0
55 and Above Years	0.792	0.628	0.5	0.38165	4.894	0

The overall models across different age groups are significant at $p<0.05$ with good values of R^2 more than 0.5 across all age groups.

Table 5.28: Constructs Coefficients and their Significance across Age group 23-30 years

Model	Unstandardized Coefficients		Standardized Coefficients		
23-30 years	B	Std. Error	Beta	t	Sig.
(Constant)	-0.579	0.258		-2.239	0.027
Structures	0.119	0.05	0.157	2.392	0.018
Assets	0.101	0.034	0.148	3.001	0.003
Processes	0.138	0.035	0.21	3.925	0
Culture	0.169	0.056	0.185	2.996	0.003
Technology	0.107	0.031	0.169	3.406	0.001

Table 5.28: Continue

Model	Unstandardized Coefficients		Standardized Coefficients		
23-30 years	B	Std. Error	Beta	t	Sig.
Strategy	0.137	0.034	0.189	4.048	0
Deterrents	0.125	0.03	0.199	4.11	0
Incentives	0.135	0.037	0.189	3.648	0
Enablers	0.129	0.043	0.168	3.03	0.003
Trainings	0.07	0.053	0.08	1.327	0.186

Interpretation

It can be interpreted from the above table that here was a significant impact ($p<0.05$) of nine KM Drivers, on the implementation of KM in the age group of 23-30 years, except for the Training Driver. So, surprisingly enough, Training was not pointed out as a significant Driver for KM implementation among young executives. It may be because of the fact that young executives are Digital Natives unlike the older executives who are Digital Immigrants. Amongst the significant Drivers are Processes (Beta = 0.21, t = 3.925, $p<0.05$), followed by Deterrents (Beta = 0.199, t = 4.11, $p<0.05$), Strategy (Beta = 0.189, t = 4.048, $p<0.05$) and Incentives (Beta = 0.189, t = 3.648, $p<0.05$). The other significant Drivers were Culture (Beta =0.185, t = 2.996, $p<0.05$), Technology (Beta =0.169, t = 3.406, $p<0.05$), Enablers (Beta =0.168, t =3.03, $p<0.05$), Structures (Beta =0.157, t =2.392, $p<0.05$), and Assets (Beta =0.148, t =3.001, $p<0.05$).

Table 5.29: Constructs Coefficients and their Significance Across Age group 31-38 Years

Model	Unstandardized Coefficients		Standardized Coefficien's		
31-38 Years	B	Std. Error	Beta	t	Sig.
(Constant)	-0.575	0.263		-2.191	0.031
Structures	0.145	0.067	0.173	2.157	0.034
Assets	0.218	0.046	0.29	4.696	0
Processes	0.103	0.043	0.138	2.365	0.02
Culture	0.162	0.074	0.184	2.195	0.031
Technology	0.076	0.042	0.091	1.809	0.074
Strategy	0.128	0.041	0.16	3.156	0.002

Table 5.29: Continue

Model	Unstandardized Coefficients		Standardized Coefficien's		
31-38 Years	**B**	**Std. Error**	**Beta**	**t**	**Sig.**
Deterrents	0.156	0.037	0.209	4.23	0
Incentives	0.075	0.045	0.102	1.665	0.1
Enablers	0.11	0.084	0.115	1.311	0.193
Trainings	0.068	0.077	0.083	0.879	0.382

Interpretation

This table shows that in the age group of 31-38 years, except Technology, Incentives, Enablers and Training all other Drivers significantly ($p<0.05$) impact KM implementation. Amongst the significant Drivers, Assets is the most important (Beta = 0.29, t = 4.696, $p<0.05$) Driver in the effectiveness of the KM implementation followed by Deterrents (Beta = 0.209, t = 4.23, $p<0.05$). The other significant Drivers in the order of importance are Culture (Beta = 0.184, t = 2.195, $p<0.05$), Structures (Beta = 0.173, t = 2.157, $p<0.05$), Strategy (Beta = 0.16, t = 3.156, $p<0.05$), Processes (Beta = 0.138, t = 2.365, $p<0.05$).

Table 5.30: Constructs Coefficients and their Significance across Age group 39-46 Years

Model	Unstandardized Coefficients		Standardized Coefficients		
39-46 Years	**B**	**Std. Error**	**Beta**	**t**	**Sig.**
(Constant)	-0.053	0.598		-0.089	0.929
Structures	-0.002	0.12	-0.002	-0.014	0.989
Assets	0.032	0.07	0.049	0.458	0.65
Processes	-0.05	0.079	-0.067	-0.634	0.53
Culture	0.314	0.128	0.334	2.451	0.019
Technology	0.187	0.068	0.322	2.741	0.009
Strategy	0.094	0.068	0.146	1.371	0.178
Deterrents	0.1	0.061	0.193	1.648	0.107
Incentives	0.127	0.1	0.159	1.27	0.211
Enablers	0.031	0.1	0.043	0.311	0.757
Trainings	0.231	0.131	0.267	1.769	0.084

Interpretation

In the age group of 39-46 years, this set of respondents perceived that Culture (Beta = 0.334, t = 2.451, p<0.05) and Technology (Beta = 0.322, t = 2.741, p<0.05) is significantly important in the effective implementation of KM. All other Drivers do not significantly influence KM implementation.

Table 5.31: Constructs Coefficients and their Significance across Age group 47-54 Years

Model	Unstandardized Coefficients		Standardized Coefficients		
47-54 Years	B	Std. Erroi	Beta	t	Sig.
(Constant)	0.068	0.565		0.121	0.905
Structures	0.053	0.14	0.076	0.383	0.705
Assets	0.163	0.099	0.235	1.64	0.112
Processes	0.097	0.075	0.164	1.296	0.206
Culture	-0.054	0.128	-0.059	-0.423	0.676
Technology	0.071	0.084	0.094	0.841	0.407
Strategy	0.1	0.081	0.144	1.239	0.226
Deterrents	0.083	0.075	0.118	1.112	0.276
Incentives	0.007	0.098	0.009	0.072	0.943
Enablers	0.092	0.188	0.097	0.49	0.628
Trainings	0.41	0.18	0.437	2.272	0.031

Interpretation

The table 5.25 shows that in the age group of 47-54 years, the only KM Driver 'Training' significantly (Beta = 0.437, t = 2.272, p<0.05) impacts KM implementation. All other Drivers do not significantly influence KM implementation.

Table 5.32: Constructs Coefficients and their Significance Across Age group 55 and Above Years

Model	Unstandardized Coefficients		Standardized Coefficients		
55 and Above Years	B	Std. Error	Beta	t	Sig.
(Constant)	-0.765	0.956		-0.801	0.43
Structures	0.125	0.152	0.139	0.822	0.418
Assets	0.121	0.079	0.208	1.537	0.135

Table 5.32: Continue

Model	Unstandardized Coefficients		Standardized Coefficients		
55 and Above Years	**B**	**Std. Error**	**Beta**	**t**	**Sig.**
Processes	0.121	0.099	0.174	1.23	0.229
Culture	0.223	0.209	0.184	1.067	0.295
Technology	0.064	0.086	0.102	0.742	0.464
Strategy	0.219	0.079	0.347	2.773	0.01
Deterrents	0.071	0.099	0.087	0.713	0.481
Incentives	0.115	0.124	0.13	0.934	0.358
Enablers	0.238	0.13	0.281	1.832	0.077
Trainings	-0.017	0.133	-0.02	-0.131	0.897

Interpretation

Significantly the senior group perceives the "Strategy" can influence (Beta = 0.347, t = 2.773, $p<0.05$) the KM implementation in the age group of 55 years and above. All other Drivers do not significantly influence KM implementation.

Concluding, the younger age groups perceive almost all the Drivers can impact the KM implementation as compared to seniors. As top officials pay importance to strategy and training.

5.7.3 Education

The results of the multiple regression for the education groups for its relationship with the KM Drivers impacting the effectiveness of KM implementation in POSOCO (dependent variable) are discussed as-

The results of the Multiple Regression are presented in the tables from 5.27-5.29 below:-

Table 5.33: Model Summary of Education

Model: Education	R	R Square	Adjustet R Square	Std. Error of the Estimate	F	Significance
Graduation	0.797	0.635	0.62	0.34189	43.438	0
Post Graduation	0.872	0.76	0.742	0.31532	41.216	0
Doctorate	Negligible					

Table 5.34: Constructs Coefficients and their Significance across Graduates

Model	Unstandardized Coefficients		Standardized Coefficients		
Graduation	B	Std. Error	Beta	t	Sig.
(Constant)	-0.305	0.213		-1.433	0.153
Structures	0.146	0.044	0.187	3.301	0.001
Assets	0.115	0.028	0.171	4.169	0
Processes	0.121	0.029	0.176	4.166	0
Culture	0.121	0.047	0.131	2.568	0.011
Technology	0.099	0.027	0.158	3.726	0
Strategy	0.117	0.027	0.172	4.38	0
Deterrents	0.107	0.025	0.171	4.257	0
Incentives	0.096	0.032	0.129	3.042	0.003
Enablers	0.115	0.04	0.145	2.863	0.005
Trainings	0.115	0.048	0.134	2.375	0.018

Interpretation

It can be interpreted, from the above table, that there $p<0.05$ a significant impact of all the ten KM Drivers on the effective implementation of KM ($p<0.05$) in the graduation education group. (t-value =>1.99, $p<0.05$). Structures, Assets, Strategy, Processes and Deterrents are impacting KM implementation most prominently.

Table 5.35: Constructs Coefficients and their Significance across PostGraduates

Model	Unstandardized Coefficients		Standardized Coefficients		
Post Graduation	B	Std. Erroi	Beta	t	Sig.
(Constant)	-0.842	0.236		-3.565	0.001
Structures	0.063	0.054	0.078	1.158	0.249
Assets	0.132	0.035	0.185	3.775	0
Processes	0.117	0.034	0.167	3.396	0.001
Culture	0.269	0.064	0.294	4.236	0
Technology	0.093	0.034	0.119	2.707	0.008

Table 5.35: Continue

Model	Unstandardized Coefficients		Standardized Coefficients		
Post Graduation	B	Std. Erroi	Beta	t	Sig.
Strategy	0.203	0.036	0.255	5.671	0
Deterrents	0.125	0.033	0.177	3.826	0
Incentives	0.131	0.039	0.171	3.338	0.001
Enablers	0.119	0.054	0.135	2.205	0.029
Trainings	0.06	0.059	0.069	1.015	0.312

Interpretation

This table [5.2.9] shows that amongst the Post Graduates, except Structures and Training, all other Drivers are significantly (p<0.05) impacting KM implementation. Amongst the significant Drivers, Culture is the most important (Beta = 0.294, t = 4.236, p<0.05) Driver in the effectiveness of the KM implementation followed by Strategy (Beta = 0.255, t = 5.671, p<0.05). The other KM Drivers in the order of their importance are Assets (Beta = 0.185, t = 3.775, p<0.05), Deterrents (Beta = 0.177, t = 3.826, p<0.05), Incentives (Beta = 0.171, t = 3.338, p<0.05), Processes (Beta = 0.167, t = 3.396, p<0.05), Enablers (Beta = 0.135, t = 2.205, p<0.05) and Technology (Beta = 0.119, t = 2.707, p<0.05).

5.7.4 Level of Hierarchy

The results of the multiple regression for the nine levels have been clubbed to make four levels for its relationship with the KM Drivers impacting the effectiveness of KM implementation in POSOCO (dependent variable) is discussed below:-

Table 5.36: Model Summary of Level

Model: Level	R	R Square	Adjustet R Square	Std. Error of the Estimate	F	Significance
Level E1-E3	0.828	0.686	0.66	0.32185	27.04	0
Level E4-E5	0.871	0.758	0.739	0.31339	40.054	0
Level E6-E7A	0.824	0.678	0.632	0.34857	14.562	0
Level E8 & above	0.778	0.606	0.502	0.39093	5.839	0

Table 5.37: Constructs Coefficients and their Significance across Level E1-E3

Model	Unstandardized Coefficients		Standardized Coefficients		
Level E1-E3	B	Std. Error	Beta	t	Sig.
(Constant)	-0.619	0.293		-2.11	0.037
Structures	0.034	0.062	0.041	0.55	0.583
Assets	0.137	0.037	0.209	3.686	0
Processes	0.119	0.044	0.163	2.697	0.008
Culture	0.153	0.067	0.171	2.284	0.024
Technology	0.111	0.036	0.174	3.118	0.002
Strategy	0.098	0.041	0.126	2.393	0.018
Deterrents	0.094	0.032	0.156	2.919	0.004
Incentives	0.149	0.041	0.204	3.646	0
Enablers	0.147	0.073	0.155	2.009	0.047
Trainings	0.178	0.066	0.214	2.7	0.008

Interpretation

It can be interpreted, from the above table, that there is a significant impact of nine KM Drivers on the effective implementation of KM ($p<.005$) in the level E1-E3 except in the Driver Structure (t-value = 0.55 which is less than 1.99, $p<0.05$).

Table 5.38: Constructs Coefficients and their Significance across Level E4-E5

Model	Unstandardized Coefficients		Standardized Coefficients		
Level E4-E5	B	Std. Error	Beta	t	Sig.
(Constant)	-0.51	0.243		-2.097	0.038
Structures	0.222	0.053	0.271	4.208	0
Assets	0.095	0.036	0.125	2.618	0.01
Processes	0.135	0.037	0.192	3.62	0
Culture	0.211	0.062	0.215	3.415	0.001
Technology	0.083	0.034	0.111	2.457	0.015
Strategy	0.197	0.035	0.26	5.679	0
Deterrents	0.152	0.033	0.211	4.551	0

Table 5.38: Continue

Model	Unstandardized Coefficients		Standardized Coefficients		
Level E4-E5	**B**	**Std. Error**	**Beta**	**t**	**Sig.**
Incentives	0.105	0.038	0.14	2.758	0.007
Enablers	0.096	0.042	0.125	2.309	0.023
Trainings	-0.049	0.052	-0.057	-0.937	0.351

Amongst the respondents at the Level E4-E5, the results show that nine factors significantly impact KM implementation ($p<0.05$). Surprisingly, however, in the case of this Level of Hierarchy, it is found that the Training does not come out to be significant (t-value = -0.937 which is less than 1.99, $p<0.05$). The reason might be because of the factor that this level is in middle management where the executives are still having the impinging habit of taking decisions but not fully groomed to make decisions.

Table 5.39: Constructs Coefficients and their Significance across Level E6-E7A

Model	Unstandardized Coefficients		Standardized Coefficients		
Level E6-E7A	**B**	**Std.Error**	**Beta**	**t**	**Sig.**
(Constant)	-0.247	0.373		-0.663	0.51
Structures	0.02	0.092	0.028	0.218	0.828
Assets	0.15	0.055	0.213	2.744	0.008
Processes	0.038	0.05	0.06	0.761	0.449
Culture	0.09	0.08	0.111	1.128	0.263
Technology	0.166	0.057	0.26	2.898	0.005
Strategy	0.097	0.047	0.15	2.047	0.044
Deterrents	0.078	0.047	0.131	1.677	0.098
Incentives	-0.012	0.07	-0.017	-0.177	0.86
Enablers	0.195	0.087	0.239	2.248	0.028
Trainings	0.285	0.107	0.308	2.655	0.01

The results show that in the case of Level E6-E7A, the Drivers of Assets, Technology, Strategy, Enablers and Trainings are significantly impacting the KM implementation. ($p<0.05$).

Table 5.40: Constructs Coefficients and their Significance across Level E8 and Above

Model	Unstandardized Coefficients		Standardized Coefficients		
Level E8 & above	**B**	**Std. Error**	**Beta**	**t**	**Sig.**
(Constant)	-0.769	0.751		-1.023	0.313
Structures	0.079	0.141	0.099	0.559	0.579
Assets	0.12	0.067	0.204	1.783	0.083
Processes	0.124	0.067	0.206	1.854	0.072
Culture	0.117	0.169	0.104	0.693	0.492
Technology	0.112	0.078	0.168	1.444	0.157
Strategy	0.188	0.077	0.288	2.444	0.019
Deterrents	0.097	0.089	0.124	1.098	0.279
Incentives	0.099	0.105	0.113	0.95	0.348
Enablers	0.173	0.133	0.202	1.301	0.201
Trainings	0.17	0.147	0.179	1.16	0.253

It can be interpreted in case of respondents at the level E8 and above that, only one Driver i. e. Strategy is significant ($B= 0.288$, $t=2.444$, $p<0.05$). And all other Drivers are not significant. This is highest level below the Board [owners] and E-9 level executives are the top level so far as the functional head is concerned.

5.7.5 Experience

The results of the multiple regression for five experience groups for its relationship with the KM Drivers are impacting the effectiveness of KM implementation in POSOCO (dependent variable) as discussed thus far.

The results of the Multiple Regression are presented in the tables from 5.35-5.40 below:-

Table 5.41: Model Summary of Experience

Model Experience	R	R Square	Adjusted R Square	Std. Error of the Estimate	F	Significance
0-7 years	0.836	0.7	0.683	0.32905	41.438	0
8-14 years	0.891	0.793	0.771	0.28751	34.95	0
15-21 years	0.764	0.583	0.385	0.3931	2.942	0.018
22-28 years	0.855	0.732	0.574	0.32737	4.633	0.003
29 years and above	0.834	0.696	0.622	0.36052	9.391	0

The overall models across different experience groups are significant at $p<0.05$ with good values of R^2being more than 0.5 across all experience groups. Since 'p' value is lesser than 0. 05 at 95% Confidence Level, Experience in the range of 0-7 Years becomes significant.

This is in consonance with the robust data apropos the understanding of this participant researcher. It also brings the 'true' factor of null hypothesis. The nature (factor) of this model experience is not only significant but consistent also.

Table 5.42: Constructs Coefficients and their Significance across Experience 0-7 years

Model	Unstandardized Coefficients		Standardized Coefficients		
0-7 years	B	Std. Error	Beta	t	Sig.
(Constant)	-0.685	0.233		-2.94	0.004
Structures	0.093	0.047	0.12	1.98	0.049
Assets	0.12	0.03	0.175	3.958	0
Processes	0.151	0.034	0.219	4.428	0
Culture	0.179	0.053	0.201	3.361	0.001
Technology	0.098	0.03	0.146	3.286	0.001
Strategy	0.135	0.033	0.174	4.051	0
Deterrents	0.129	0.028	0.199	4.552	0
Incentives	0.125	0.035	0.172	3.551	0
Enablers	0.148	0.043	0.182	3.448	0.001
Trainings	0.077	0.049	0.092	1.578	0.116

Interpretation

It can be interpreted, from the above table, that there is a significant impact of nine KM Drivers on the effective implementation of KM ($p<.005$) in the respondents having experience of 0-7 years. Surprisingly, however, in the case of this group of respondents, it is found that the training is not coming out to be significant (t-value = 1.578 which is less than 1.99, $p<0.05$). The reason might be the fact that the executives at this level function as 'faculty' for trainees and other function- focused training programs.

Table 5.43: Constructs Coefficients and their Significance Across Experience 8-14 years

Model	Unstandardized Coefficients		Standardized Coefficients		
8-14 years	B	Std. Error	Beta	t	Sig.
(Constant)	-0.284	0.245		-1.161	0.249
Structures	0.268	0.067	0.332	4.019	0
Assets	0.193	0.047	0.252	4.072	0
Processes	0.069	0.039	0.097	1.794	0.076
Culture	0.26	0.073	0.267	3.567	0.001
Technology	0.052	0.037	0.073	1.397	0.166
Strategy	0.177	0.037	0.238	4.812	0
Deterrents	0.106	0.034	0.157	3.101	0.003
Incentives	0.117	0.045	0.162	2.594	0.011
Enablers	-0.028	0.058	-0.034	-0.475	0.636
Trainings	-0.044	0.073	-0.053	-0.611	0.542

Interpretation

This table shows that in the experience group of 8-14 years, except Processes, Technology, Enablers and Training all other Drivers significantly ($p<0.05$) impact KM implementation. Amongst the significant Drivers, Structure is the most important (Beta = 0.332, t = 4.019, $p<0.05$) followed by Culture (Beta = 0.267, t = 3.567, $p<0.05$), Assets (Beta = 0.252, t = 4.072, $p<0.05$). The other significant Drivers in the order of importance are Strategy (Beta = 0. 238, t = 4.812, $p<0.05$), incentives (Beta = 0.162, t = 2.594, $p<0.05$), and Deterrents (Beta = 0.157, t = 3.101, $p<0.05$).

Table 5.44: Constructs Coefficients and their Significance across Experience 15- 21years

Model	Unstandardized Coefficients		Standardized Coefficients		
15-21 years	**B**	**Std. Error**	**Beta**	**t**	**Sig.**
(Constant)	-0.362	0.97		-0.373	0.713
Structures	-0.118	0.205	-0.141	-0.575	0.571
Assets	0.126	0.107	0.192	1.177	0.252
Processes	-0.045	0.116	-0.066	-0.392	0.699
Culture	0.083	0.143	0.108	0.578	0.569
Technology	0.203	0.098	0.355	2.075	0.051
Strategy	0.036	0.093	0.067	0.387	0.702
Deterrents	0.015	0.098	0.03	0.156	0.878
Incentives	0.184	0.143	0.203	1.283	0.214
Enablers	0.148	0.191	0.176	0.774	0.447
Trainings	0.475	0.192	0.443	2.473	0.022

Interpretation

In this set of respondents, having experience of 15-21 years; training is the only significant Driver (Beta = 0.443, t = 2.473, $p<0.05$) impacting the effective implementation of KM. All other Drivers do not significantly influence KM implementation.

Table 5.45: Constructs Coefficients and their Significance across Experience 2228 years

Model	Unstandardized Coefficients		Standardized Coefficients		
22-28 years	**B**	**Std. Error**	**Beta**	**t**	**Sig.**
(Constant)	-1.029	0.997		-1.031	0.317
Structures	-0.009	0.185	-0.014	-0.049	0.962
Assets	-0.007	0.107	-0.012	-0.065	0.949
Processes	0.135	0.101	0.225	1.337	0.199
Culture	-0.004	0.132	-0.005	-0.029	0.978
Technology	0.091	0.104	0.132	0.877	0.393
Strategy	0.315	0.104	0.503	3.039	0.007

Table 5.45: Continue

Model	Unstandardized Coefficients		Standardized Coefficients		
22-28 years	**B**	**Std. Error**	**Beta**	**t**	**Sig.**
Deterrents	0.302	0.094	0.417	3.211	0.005
Incentives	-0.06	0.125	-0.079	-0.476	0.64
Enablers	0.382	0.227	0.418	1.678	0.112
Trainings	0.314	0.187	0.365	1.685	0.11

For the respondents having experience of 22-28 years, strategy (Beta = 0.503, t = 3.039, $p<0.05$) and Deterrents (Beta = 0.417, t = 3.211, $p<0.05$) are the most significant Drivers impacting effective KM implementation. The reason being the fact that executives at this level feel that the so called 'top management' is, in fact; middle management as POSOCO is a PSU. The 'deterrents' are providing 'negative' motivation in the age group where they are possessing the work experience of 22-28 years and this paved the way of 'creating challenges'. The challenges 'drive' this group to find out the mitigations for these, which in turn; provide the intrinsic sense of being 'winners' since they could be enjoying the very process of withstanding the impediments.

Table 5.46: Constructs Coefficients and their Significance Across Experience 29 years and above

Model	Unstandardized Coefficients		Standardized Coefficients		
29 years and above	**B**	**Std. Error**	**Beta**	**t**	**Sig.**
(Constant)	-0.404	0.577		-0.699	0.488
Structures	0.087	0.119	0.104	0.732	0.468
Assets	0.134	0.064	0.21	2.086	0.043
Processes	0.128	0.071	0.197	1.809	0.078
Culture	0.222	0.165	0.187	1.349	0.185
Technology	0.07	0.068	0.102	1.026	0.311
Strategy	0.162	0.063	0.243	2.586	0.013
Deterrents	0.046	0.07	0.062	0.66	0.513
Incentives	0.055	0.088	0.065	0.622	0.537
Enablers	0.233	0.114	0.26	2.048	0.047
Trainings	0.007	0.117	0.008	0.06	0.952

For the respondents having experience of 29 years and above Assets (Beta = 0.21, $t = 2.086$, $p<0.05$), Strategy (Beta = 0.243, $t = 2.586$, $p<0.05$) and Enablers (Beta = 0.26, $t = 2.048$, $p<0.05$) are the most significant Drivers impacting effective KM implementation. This factor is based on the perception at this level that their knowledge contribution does establish as an asset to POSOCO and strategizing is a part of the responsibility.

5.8 CONCLUSION

To sum up, the main KM Drivers which significantly impact the implementation of the KM in POSOCO are Strategy, Deterrents, Culture, Assets, Process, Incentives, Structures, Enablers, Technology, and Training.

The next chapter links this thread to present the Conclusions & Recommendations based upon the analysis presented in the foregoing pages.

CHAPTER 6

FINDINGS, RECOMMENDATIONS AND CONCLUSIONS

6.1 INTRODUCTION

This chapter presents the ' Findings, Recommendations and Conclusions' of the study describing the main KM Drivers affecting the KM implementation in POSOCO. In the first place, the literature surrounding KM was explored to identify the Drivers of KM and then qualitative (NVivo v.12) and quantitative statistical analyses were conducted. The data thus collected was analyzed. Additionally, the quantitative analysis was done on the responses obtained from 403 executives in POSOCO. The qualitative instruments for data collection results in the fructification as envisaged by triangular methodology. The analysis of qualitative data buttressed the findings of the analysis of quantitative data. For this, the statistical techniques using the Exploratory Factor Analysis (EFA) and the Confirmatory Factor Analysis (CFA) were administered to establish the factor validity. Then Multiple Regression was run to derive the relationship between the KM Drivers and the effective KM implementation using SPSS 26 and AMOS 26 software. NVivo of QSR International operated on Microsoft Windows software was used for analyzing the qualitative data. It facilitated "to organize, analyze and find insights" for penning this dissertation. Both quantitative and qualitative data were primary data; though the secondary data was also used extensively. The demographic relationship with these constructs amongst themselves was also examined in the study. The secondary sources of data were also looked into to buttress the study. The major conclusions of this study are presented in the following sections.

6.2 FINDINGS

6.2.1 Synthesis of Qualitative & Quantitative results

In the first place, it is pertinent to decipher the synthesis of the results derived from qualitative and quantitative research as they both complement each other to achieve the objectives of the study. This also provides a holistic view of Knowledge Management

Drivers to enable 'theory building' on the Knowledge Management implementation that can be extended to organizations similar to POSOCO. Infact, this synthesis is one of the interpretative inferences relying on both deductive and inductive logic, wherein the qualitative information pertained to determine 'what was actually said' and 'what it meant', whereas the quantitative information leads to determining of 'where to look' and 'how to assess the causal relationships'.

From the results of the qualitative analysis through NVivo Result for thematic value, word frequency and word frequency layout; it can be concluded that several themes which were extracted in the transcripts of the focus interviews, in-depth interviews and elite interview and participant-observation revolved around various aspects of KM Drivers. The outcome may be enumerated as- Training on Knowledge Management, its Structure and Culture besides Knowledge Management Policy. The other tools used in the Implementation of Knowledge Management were through Policy, Knowledge depository coupled with the availability of the subject matter experts. Knowledge dissemination and information sharing practices, Knowledge Maps and Matrices prepared and published, Knowledge portals, and Rewards and incentives were also traced. This means that, in POSOCO; information sharing systems, Training, Processes and Culture are conducive for adoption of 'Knowledge Management' in true spirit. Thus, POSOCO tends to be a knowledge based entity. The same themes were captured in the survey instrument which was administered to the executives of POSOCO to determine 'quantitatively'; the extent to which these KM Drivers impacted the KM implementation in POSOCO.

The quantitative results make a significant contribution in understanding the role and influence of KM Drivers in the effective implementation of Knowledge Management in POSOCO. All the ten factors- i.e. Structures, Assets, Processes, Culture, Technology, Strategy, Deterrent, Incentives, Enablers, and Training- are found to be the KM Drivers in POSOCO. This is corroborated through the results of 'Exploratory Factor Analysis' (EFA) and subsequently confirmed and validated in the results of the 'Confirmatory Factor Analysis' (CFA), thereby establishing the prevalence of these ten KM Drivers in case of POSOCO. Further, it can be concluded from the results of regression that all the KM Drivers significantly impact the effective KM implementation in POSOCO. The main KM Drivers in the order of their strength were found to be Strategy, Deterrents, Culture, Assets, Processes, Incentives, Structures, Enablers, Technology, and Trainings.

Overall, it can be concluded from the results of qualitative and quantitative research analyses that the management of POSOCO has got proper mechanisms in place and has succeeded in implementing Knowledge Management. KM is at the core in POSOCO as facilitated through its Systems, Structure and Culture, not necessarily through Technology and Training. So, it can be corroborated that Knowledge Management has been implemented in POSOCO in the right perspective and taking clues from this similar framework and variables the same can be extended to the organizations in the Power Sector and even to the firms with diverse departments. Further, as per the quantitative research analysis; many important conclusions can be drawn. The conclusions that came to the fore are presented in the following paragraphs.

6.2.2 Demographic Profile

First, the demographic distribution of the respondents who participated in the survey was found out which brought the information to the fore about their - Gender, Age group, Education, Level of Hierarchy, Work Experience, Departments and association with KM.

It can be discerned from the descriptive analysis on these demographic variables that the majority of the respondents were male and there were relatively very few female respondents in the population. As per their age group, it can be concluded that the majority of the respondents belonged to 23-30 years, followed by 31-38 years and 39-46 years. There were very few respondents in senior age group viz. above 55 years though some of them happened to be in the 47-54 years age group. As per their Education, it can be concluded that most of them were well-educated namely graduates and even post-graduates. There is only one respondent who possessed a Ph.D. Majority of the respondents belonged to levels of E1-E3 followed by E4-E5, E6-E7, and E8 and above. Department wise, the respondents were spread across mainly System Operation. Few were in SCADA/IT, Market Operation, Finance and HR. There were hardly any from the Materials or Law department. Further, it can be concluded that most of the respondents had a work experience of less than 7 years, followed by 8-14 years of work experience. Of these, most of the respondents did not have any prior work experience in a public sector organization while the rest had worked in the Public Sector organizations.

6.2.3 Drivers of KM

It can be crystalized from the Exploratory Factor Analysis results that there are ten main Drivers that could be christened as the Drivers of KM in POSOCO.

These ten Drivers are - Structure, Assets, Processes, Culture, Technology, Strategy, Deterrents, Incentives, Enablers and Training. These ten Drivers explain a total of 64.13% of the variance for the entire set of variables. This was also validated through the results of CFA that confirmed the KM Drivers. The reliability, convergent and discriminant validity hold good for all these Drivers in the CFA model. This finding is consistent with the results of many extant studies in the literature which have also drawn upon these Drivers as the precursors of KM in organizations worldwide (Almeida (2008), Anderson (2009), Armstrong (2012), Bates (1998), Brauner & Becker (2006), Burg, et.al (2008), Chen et.al (2012), Conway & Sligar (2002), Fullan (2011), Grant (2001), Hasnali (2005), Jones & George (2011), Klein (1998), Man et.al. (2008), Pandey (2016), Pasher & Ronen (2011), Peachey (2006), Shih & Chiang (2005), Swanson (2005), Teece (2001), Tryon Jr. (2012), Upadhyay (2011), Wood (2005)).

6.2.4 Relationship of KM Drivers with overall Effective Implementation of KM

It can be deduced from the results of Multiple Regression that all the ten KM Drivers significantly impact the KM implementation in POSOCO. The summary Table no. 6.1 presents the relative assessment of all the ten KM Drivers impacting the overall KM implementation apropos H1 as follows:-

H1: There is a relationship between KM Drivers and overall effectiveness of KM implementation.

Table 6.1: Summary of the KM Drivers and its effective KM implementation and KME

S. No.	Hypothesis	Outcome
1	H1a: There is a relationship between Structures and overall effectiveness of KM implementation.	Supported
2	H1b: There is a relationship between Assets and overall effectiveness of KM implementation.	Supported
3	H1c: There is a relationship between Processes and overall effectiveness of KM implementation.	Supported
4	H1d: There is a relationship between Culture and overall effectiveness of KM implementation.	Supported

Table 6.1: Continue

S. No.	Hypothesis	Outcome
5	H1e: There is a relationship between Technology and overall effectiveness of KM implementation.	Supported
6	H1f: There is a relationship between Strategy and overall effectiveness of KM implementation.	Supported
7	H1g: There is a relationship between Deterrents and overall effectiveness of KM implementation.	Supported
8	H1h: There is a relationship between Incentives and overall effectiveness of KM implementation.	Supported
9	H1i: There is a relationship between Enablers and overall effectiveness of KM implementation.	Supported
10	H1j: There is a relationship between Training and overall effectiveness of KM implementation.	Supported

It can be concluded from the results that all the ten KM Drivers significantly impact the overall implementation of the KM in POSOCO. It can also be concluded that relatively the more important KM Drivers happen to be - Strategy, Deterrents, Culture, Assets, Process, Enablers and Structures. This implies that in POSOCO, the Strategy, Culture, Assets, Deterrents, Process, Enablers and Structure are important and are in place which is contributing to the effective implementation of the KM in POSOCO. However, Technology, Incentives, and Training need to be properly aligned and augmented further for the effective implementation of KM therein.

The findings of this study are consistent with the outcomes and findings of several other studies. Organization structure as a facilitating construct has been reported by other researchers also in their finding (Gonzalez and Martins, 2014; Makani & Marche, 2012; Hendriks, 2006; Du, 2005; Ulrich & Brockbank, 2005). Du (2005) indicated that Knowledge Management could provide useful information, innovative ideas, and even non-structured knowledge to support the decision. For this, a Team based structure is recommended herein which can integrate various knowledge nuggets in a cohesive unit. The role of Process as an important Driver of KM was confirmed in the studies of Desouza & Paquette (2011); Chait(1999). As per Chait (1999) "Effective Knowledge Management system must coordinate four areas: content, culture, procedure, and infrastructure." Alongside, the role of Strategy was confirmed through findings of the study of Zack (1999). According to him, "The strategy of Knowledge Management would lead the operation of Knowledge Management, especially; resource allocation of Knowledge Management, application of Knowledge Management, and ways of Knowledge Management" The role of Enablers and Deterrents is in line with these components reported in the studies of (Pandey, 2016; Ten, 2005; Liao, 2002; Lin, 2001) with the findings. According to these scholars, there are five enablers in the organization, including the strategy of Knowledge Management, organizational culture, organizational framework, hardware environment, norm and human resources policy. The role of Culture as an important Driver of KM was confirmed in the studies of other scholars also Pandey, 2016; Abbar, 2016; Jurisicaet. al., 2004; Liebowitz and Chen, 2001; Arthur Andersen and APQC (1996). Yu,et. al. (2004) demonstrated the importance of Organizational Culture and indicated that learning attitude, communication, an intention to share knowledge, and the flexibility of organizational framework would influence Knowledge Management performance positively. Reward and encouragement are also asserted as the significant Drivers for 31-38 years as pointed out in the findings of the study by scholars namely, Amayah, 2013; Yu et al., 2004; Wu, 2008. Yu et al. (2004) who indicated that the reward of Knowledge Management would influence the performance of Knowledge Management positively. Wu (2008) specifically stated that if the enterprises could timely encourage staff to share knowledge and relate the contribution of sharing knowledge with performance assessment, then better outcome of knowledge sharing would be obtained for sure. Most importantly, it is the "Personnel who are at the core of creating organization knowledge and the source of creating and sharing knowledge, so how to encourage the personnel willing to create and share knowledge is very important" (Lee and Choi, 2003).

6.2.5 Relationship of Drivers of KM and the overall effectiveness of KM implementation across the demographic variables

As per the relationship between the demographic variables and the overall effectiveness of KM implementation in POSOCO, it can be concluded that with respect to Gender, the male respondents asserted that all the ten Drivers were significant in impacting the overall implementation of KM in POSOCO. This is in line with the results of Factor Analysis also. Since the females constitute a miniscule portion of the sample, so it can be overlooked but they highlighted the importance of Strategy as s a dominant Driver of KM.

As per the Age group, it can be concluded that there was a significant impact of nine KM Drivers, on the effective implementation of KM in the age group of 23-30 years. So, surprisingly enough, Training was not pointed out as a significant Driver for KM implementation by young executives. It can be concluded that for 31-38 years, except Technology, Incentives, Enablers and Training, all other Drivers significantly impacted KM implementation. Amongst the significant Drivers, were Assets followed by Deterrents, Culture, Strategy and Processes. It can be established safely that the respondents in the age group of 39-46 years perceived that Culture and Technology as significantly important tools in the effective implementation of KM while other Drivers were not significant in the KM implementation. Similarly, for the group of personnel in 47-54 years, the only KM Driver, was Training which significantly impacted KM implementation. The senior executives in the age group of 55 years and above confirmed the Strategy as significant for the KM implementation.

So, conclusively, the younger age groups perceive almost all the Drivers as significantly impacting the KM implementation as compared to senior executives. On the other hand, the older age group of executives perceive only a few factors as significantly impacting factors in the KM implementation, i.e. Culture, Technology, Training and Strategy. This may be due to the fact that they are quite likely to encounter difficulties in Technology usage and Training improves effectiveness when it comes to KM. So more emphasis should be given on these Drivers to leverage the KM implementation. At this juncture, it is not out of place to provide the snapshot of the analysis that popped up apropos the ten constructs playing a critically important role in KM implementation in POSOCO, the same is depicted in Table 6.2.

Table 6.2: Summary of KM Drivers impacting KM implementation across Age

	Hypothesis	Age in years	Outcome
Structure	There is a relationship between Structure and overall effectiveness of KM implementation across Age	23-30 years	Supported
		31-38 Years	Supported
		39-46 Years	Not Supported
		47-54 Years	Not Supported
		55 and Above Years	Not Supported
Assets	There is a relationship between Assets and	23-30 years	Supported
		31-38 Years	Supported
	overall effectiveness of KM implementation across Age	39-46 Years	Not Supported
		47-54 Years	Not Supported
		55 and Above Years	Not Supported
Processes	There is a relationship between Processes and overall effectiveness of KM implementation across Age	23-30 years	Supported
		31-38 Years	Supported
		39-46 Years	Not Supported
		47-54 Years	Not Supported
		55 and Above Years	Not Supported

Table 6.2: Continue

	Hypothesis	Age in years	Outcome
Culture	There is a relationship between Culture and overall effectiveness of KM implementation across Age	23-30 years	Supported
		31-38 Years	Supported
		39-46 Years	Supported
		47-54 Years	Not Supported
		55 and Above Years	Not Supported
Technology	There is a relationship between Technology and overall effectiveness of KM implementation across Age	23-30 years	Supported
		31-38 Years	Not Supported
		39-46 Years	Supported
		47-54 Years	Not Supported
		55 and Above Years	Not Supported
Strategy	There is a relationship between Strategy and overall effectiveness of KM implementation across Age	23-30 years	Supported
		31-38 Years	Supported
		39-46 Years	Not Supported
		47-54 Years	Not Supported
		55 and Above Years	Supported
Deterrents	There is a relationship between Deterrents and overall effectiveness of KM implementation across Age	23-30 years	Supported
		31-38 Years	Supported
		39-46 Years	Not Supported
		47-54 Years	Not Supported
		55 and Above Years	Not Supported
Incentives	There is a relationship between Incentives and overall effectiveness of KM implementation across Age	23-30 years	Supported
		31-38 Years	Not Supported
		39-46 Years	Not Supported
		47-54 Years	Not Supported
		55 and Above Years	Not Supported

Table 6.2: Continue

	Hypothesis	Age in years	Outcome
Enablers	There is a relationship between Enablers and overall effectiveness of KM implementation across Age	23-30 years	Supported
		31-38 Years	Not Supported
		39-46 Years	Not Supported
		47-54 Years	Not Supported
		55 and Above Years	Not Supported
Trainings	There is a relationship between Trainings and overall effectiveness of KM implementation across Age	23-30 years	Not Supported
		31-38 Years	Not Supported
		39-46 Years	Not Supported
		47-54 Years	Supported
		55 and Above Years	Not Supported

As far as levels of Education are concerned, it can be pinpointed effectively that the graduates perceived all the ten KM Drivers which are significantly impacting the implementation of KM, especially; Structures, Assets, Strategy, Processes and Deterrents. For the Post Graduates, except Structures and Training, all other Drivers were significant, impacting KM implementation. Amongst the significant Drivers, which have been perceived as important happen to be Culture and Strategy. These Drivers are in pivotal position for the effectiveness of the KM implementation. So, it can be concluded that Structures and Training must be reinforced for the effective KM implementation. It is pertinent here to trace the impact of Education on KM drivers in POSOCO.

Table 6.3: Summary of KM Drivers impacting KM implementation across Education

	Hypothesis	Education	Outcome
Structure	There is a relationship between Structure and overall effectiveness of KM implementation across varied levels of Education	Graduation	Supported
		Post Graduation	Not Supported
Assets	There is a relationship between Assets and overall effectiveness of KM implementation across varied levels of Education	Graduation	Supported
		Post Graduation	Supported

Table 6.3: Continue

	Hypothesis	Education	Outcome
Processes	There is a relationship between Processes and overall effectiveness of KM implementation across varied levels of Education	Graduation	Supported
		Post Graduation	Supported
Culture	There is a relationship between Culture and overall effectiveness of KM implementation across varied levels of Education	Graduation	Supported
		Post Graduation	Supported
Technology	There is a relationship between Technology and overall effectiveness of KM implementation across varied levels of Education	Graduation	Supported
		Post Graduation	Supported
Strategy	There is a relationship between Strategy and overall effectiveness of KM implementation across varied levels of Education	Graduation	Supported
		Post Graduation	Supported
Deterrents	There is a relationship between Deterrents and overall effectiveness of KM implementation across varied levels of Education	Graduation	Supported
		Post Graduation	Supported
Incentives	There is a relationship between Incentives and overall effectiveness of KM implementation across varied levels of Education	Graduation	Supported
		Post Graduation	Supported
Enablers	There is a relationship between Enablers and overall effectiveness of KM implementation across varied levels of Education	Graduation	Supported
		Post Graduation	Supported
Trainings	There is a relationship between Trainings and overall effectiveness of KM implementation across varied levels of Education	Graduation	Supported
		Post Graduation	Not Supported

As for the Levels of Hierarchy, it can be concluded that E1-E3 executives perceived all the nine Drivers, except Structure as significant in the KM implementation. Further, the executives at the Level of E4-E5, asserted the significance of all the nine Drivers, except Training. In the case of Level E6-E7A, the Drivers Assets, Technology, Strategy, Enablers were significantly impacting the KM implementation while executives at level E8 and above, cited Strategy as the only one significant Driver impacting KM implementation. So, it can be concluded that Structures and Training again are the grey areas that need improvement in the effective KM implementation in POSOCO. The prioritizing of the factors manifesting themselves have been varied in POSOCO and the same are described in Table 6.4.

Table 6.4: Summary of KM Drivers impacting KM implementation across Levels of Hierarchy

	Hypothesis	Levels of Hierarchy	Outcome
Structure	There is a relationship between Structure and overall effectiveness of KM implementation across Levels of Hierarchy	E1-E3	Not Supported
		E4-E5	Supported
		E6-E7A	Not Supported
		E8 & above	Not Supported
Assets	There is a relationship between Assets and overall effectiveness of KM implementation across Levels of Hierarchy	E1-E3	Supported
		E4-E5	Supported
		E6-E7A	Supported
		E8 & above	Not Supported
Processes	There is a relationship between Processes and overall effectiveness of KM implementation across Levels of Hierarchy	E1-E3	Supported
		E4-E5	Supported
		E6-E7A	Not Supported
		E8 & above	Not Supported
Culture	There is a relationship between Culture and overall effectiveness of KM implementation across Levels of Hierarchy	E1-E3	Supported
		E4-E5	Supported
		E6-E7A	Not Supported
		E8 & above	Not Supported
Technology	There is a relationship between Technology and overall effectiveness of KM implementation across Levels of Hierarchy	E1-E3	Supported
		E4-E5	Supported
		E6-E7A	Supported
		E8 & above	Not Supported

Table 6.4: Continue

	Hypothesis	Levels of Hierarchy	Outcome
Strategy	There is a relationship between Strategy and overall effectiveness of KM implementation across Levels of Hierarchy	E1-E3	Supported
		E4-E5	Supported
		E6-E7A	Supported
		E8 & above	Supported
Deterrents	There is a relationship between Deterrents and overall effectiveness of KM implementation across Levels of Hierarchy	E1-E3	Supported
		E4-E5	Supported
		E6-E7A	Not Supported
		E8 & above	Not Supported
Incentives	There is a relationship between Incentives and overall effectiveness of KM implementation across Levels of Hierarchy	E1-E3	Supported
		E4-E5	Supported
		E6-E7A	Not Supported
		E8 & above	Not Supported
Enablers	There is a relationship between Enablers and overall effectiveness of KM implementation across Levels of Hierarchy	E1-E3	Supported
		E4-E5	Supported
		E6-E7A	Supported
		E8 & above	Not Supported
Trainings	There is a relationship between Trainings and overall effectiveness of KM implementation across Levels of Hierarchy	E1-E3	Supported
		E4-E5	Not Supported
		E6-E7A	Supported
		E8 & above	Not Supported

As far as the number of years of Work Experience is concerned, it can be concluded that those with experience of 0-7 years perceive all the nine Drivers, except Training, as significantly impacting factor in the KM implementation. For those with 8-14 years, except Processes, Technology, Enablers and Training, all other Drivers are significantly impacting KM implementation. However, executives with greater work experience i.e. 15-21 years, Training was cited as the only significant Driver in KM implementation. Executives with 22-28 years of work experience cited Strategy and Deterrents as the significant Drivers, while executives of 29 years and above perceived Assets, Strategy and Enablers as significant in impacting the KM implementation. It is clearly emerging that the deterrents are motivating the executives at this level. So, it can be concluded that with respect to work experience, Processes and Technology need to be reinforced to buttress and effectuate KM implementation. It is to be noted that those with maximum work experience stated Training as an important Driver which was not seen in responses of others. At this juncture, the role played by Training is to be studied and to be pinpointed as it entails the component of 'continuous learning'.

Table 6.5: Summary of KM Drivers impacting KM implementation across No. of Years of Experience

	Hypothesis	**No. of Years of Experience**	**Outcome**
Structure	There is a relationship between Structure and overall effectiveness of KM implementation across number of years of Experience	0-7 years	Supported
		8-14 years	Supported
		15-21 years	Not Supported
		22-28 years	Not Supported
		29 years and above	Not Supported
Assets	There is a relationship between Assets and overall effectiveness of KM implementation across number of years of Experience	0-7 years	Supported
		8-14 years	Supported
		15-21 years	Not Supported
		22-28 years	Not Supported
		29 years and above	Supported
Processes	There is a relationship between Processes and overall effectiveness of KM implementation across number of years of Experience	0-7 years	Supported
		8-14 years	Not Supported
		15-21 years	Not Supported
		22-28 years	Not Supported
		29 years and above	Not Supported
Culture	There is a relationship between Culture and overall effectiveness of KM implementation across number of years of Experience	0-7 years	Supported
		8-14 years	Supported
		15-21 years	Not Supported
		22-28 years	Not Supported
		29 years and above	Not Supported

Table 6.5: Continue

	Hypothesis	No. of Years of Experience	Outcome
Technology	There is a relationship between Technology and overall effectiveness of KM implementation across number of years of Experience	0-7 years	Supported
		8-14 years	Not Supported
		15-21 years	Not Supported
		22-28 years	Not Supported
		29 years and above	Not Supported
Strategy	There is a relationship between Strategy and overall effectiveness of KM implementation across number of years of Experience	0-7 years	Supported
		8-14 years	Supported
		15-21 years	Not Supported
		22-28 years	Supported
		29 years and above	Supported
Deterrents	There is a relationship between Deterrents and overall effectiveness of KM implementation across number of years of Experience	0-7 years	Supported
		8-14 years	Supported
		15-21 years	Not Supported
		22-28 years	Supported
		29 years and above	Not Supported
Incentives	There is a relationship between Incentives and overall effectiveness of KM implementation across number of years of Experience	0-7 years	Supported
		8-14 years	Supported
		15-21 years	Not Supported
		22-28 years	Not Supported
		29 years and above	Not Supported
Enablers	There is a relationship between Enablers and overall effectiveness of KM implementation across number of years of Experience	0-7 years	Supported
		8-14 years	Not Supported
		15-21 years	Not Supported
		22-28 years	Not Supported
		29 years and above	Not Supported
Trainings	There is a relationship between Trainings and overall effectiveness of KM implementation across number of years of Experience	0-7 years	Not Supported
		8-14 years	Not Supported
		15-21 years	Supported
		22-28 years	Not Supported
		29 years and above	Not Supported

It can be concluded that with respect to demographic variables, the KM Drivers of Structures, Processes, Training and Technology need to be reinforced for the effective KM implementation in POSOCO. The other Drivers, namely; Strategy, Assets and Enablers are critically impacting the KM implementation therein.

6.3 EMERGED TAM MODEL AND ITS USE

TAM model is the outcome of reification process resulting in visual form. This has helped inference of the concept in totality which is in consonance with the amalgamation of the quantitative results by providing the interrelatedness of various variables and their interplay in a pictorial manner so that the entire gamut of the dynamics of KM implementation could be perceived in totality at the same time. This becomes more and more relevant to provide the bidimensional view of the cues required by the processes of KM implementation in POSOCO.

6.4 RECOMMENDATIONS

It can be inferred from findings of the study that all the ten Drivers are significantly impacting the KM implementation in POSOCO. However, a relative assessment of these in relationship with the demographic variables revealed that some Drivers are more important than the other Drivers in effectuating KM implementation. So, the implications drawn from this are that the top management in POSOCO needs to consolidate the important KM Drivers and closely monitor some Drivers of KM to strengthen it further. The invigoration through the strengthening processes should lead to the systemic routine for day-to-day tasks. Overall, the strong KM Drivers were - Strategy, Deterrents, Culture, Assets, Process, and Structure. This implies that in POSOCO, the Strategy, Culture, Assets, Deterrents, Process, and Structure are important and are in place to an extent that they contribute to the effective implementation of the KM in POSOCO. However, Technology, Incentives, Enablers and Training need to be more aligned for the effective implementation of KM in POSOCO. Based on the dissection of each sub-item/variables of all the ten KM Drivers individually, it can be recommended that in POSOCO, the management needs to pay focused attention to critical areas and improve upon it. The continuous education and value addition to the knowledge, repertoire and personality of the executives in the light of the above.

1. So far as 'Strategy' is concerned, it can be recommended that management should consolidate its vision and ensure that this is shared across the workforce enabling to reinforce KM implementation. This is supported by collegial, team based, open door policy in POSOCO. In POSCO, the KM implementation is facilitated through encouraging learning from mistakes and through

utilization of multiple reports and documents building the KM repository. It can be recommended that there should be continuous assessment of existing knowledge forces, and engagement of the knowledge workforce in mapping the future needs creatively with the given resources.

2. It can also be recommended that, in the case of 'Deterrents', it needs to focus upon the conspicuous aspects, like availability of subject matter experts in the department, reducing the time wasted in accessing the documents in the department. There should be more interaction between those who need specific knowledge with the subject matter experts to widen the knowledge base of the employees leading to capitalization. Moreover, it is recommended that employees should be encouraged for knowledge acquisition and its application in novel and innovative ways to solve complex problems and participate in major decisions affecting them like transfers, promotions, career advancement, etc. They should be held accountable for the decisions that they make or take as required by POSOCO.

3. As far as the 'Culture' is concerned, it is seen that the POSOCO's organizational culture is constrained in the sense that an informal and collaborative work environment does not prevail and the employees lack clarity apropos the mission of KM. There is no system of special awards to prod the employees for KM. Despite this there is strong advocacy and support for KM from the top management with the prevalence of 'power portal' made accessible to all the employees for knowledge sharing. The best part is that executives opined that aesthetically oriented culture for Knowledge Management is prevalent in POSOCO which is very encouraging for KM implementation. So, it can be recommended that 'value orientation' among employees is required to be inculcated so that they share insights and expertise with each other. They should understand the vision of the organization. An environment of trust and cooperation should be enforced in the organization.

4. In POSOCO, the KM implementation is effectively managed through its 'Assets' wherein knowledge is treated as an object in the department. Besides, there are best practices which are assets to POSOCO like daily transfer of knowledge which are creating innovation and adding to the value addition of KM. POSOCO has good physical infrastructure like Meeting/Conference rooms available for Team meetings and discussions. Notice boards are kept at various vantage points in this organization besides electronic bill boards which play an important role in informing the personnel of various news and events pertaining to the accomplishment of tasks in consonance with the responsibilities assigned to them by POSOCO. Encouragement for periodically

curating and updating the documents produced in the form of technical reports, papers for journals, etc. are to be ensured to continue unabated.

5. In the domain of 'Process', POSOCO does well through informal discussions and interactions. So, it can be recommended that there should be more dashboard meetings and impromptu interaction with subject matter experts (SME) to critically review the performance being done to bolster KM. POSOCO needs to augment e-communications and Communities of Practice (CoP) to facilitate KM implementation.
6. POSOCO has good practices of 'Incentives' for employee participation and feedback, to motivate users to learn and use Knowledge, Reward and recognition for new ideas and culture of experimentation in Knowledge Management are traced as pivotal tools. These are the incentives which are helping in effective KM implementation. So, it is to be continued so that these can be augmented by giving recognition, titles, certificates and commendation letters. Performance Management is a crucial area, especially; when the reward of Knowledge Management would influence the performance of knowledge workers positively. So, it is recommended that POSOCO should encourage employees to share knowledge and use it to optimize the use of resources and improve upon things that matter. This should be linked with appraisal system and employees should be rewarded accordingly.
7. In POSOCO, 'Structure' is well defined in terms of departmental structure, coordination, span of control, reporting relationships but emphasis should be directed towards POSOCO in building it as a 'knowledge-intensive organization (KIOS)'. It is also recommended that there are certain areas which must be augmented to build better KM structure in POSOCO such as hierarchy and the flow of communication, better centralized repository, accessibility to requisite documents pertaining to the outcome of past research programs, display of information about accessibility to project reports, research facilities and equipment.
8. POSOCO has 'Enablers', like Chief Knowledge Officer' (or equivalent) who is responsible for managing the knowledge-related activities, periodic team meetings to review the progress and discuss issues pertaining to work, use of knowledge maps and matrices for knowledge requirements, employees can download any document they want from the Intranet website/portal. Information regarding the steps, stages of process-description can be uploaded in the organization's Knowledge Bank at Power Portal, the intranet of the company. With this in view, it is recommended that the point for augmentation in the Enablers is to work by dedicated staff for 'knowledge capture' and

acquisition, sharing of personal best practice and management of KM related issues.

9. Further, it can be recommended that the 'Technology' should be upgraded forthwith in POSOCO; it should always be the latest state of the Art. Due to short shelf life the procurement of the requisite technology can be converted into a continuous process. It may be kept updated always since it is the foundation of this company to be able to provide 'real time service.' The driving force for KM implementation lies in providing intranet/website, Experts Database, blogging platforms wherein the personnel can share their experiences through blogs and Online Discussion Forum. POSOCO can work more on TeleConferencing and can provide all documents in the digital format. The shift of digital immigrant to digital natives is of paramount importance in POSOCO.
10. 'Training' as a Driver needs to be reinforced in POSOCO. The Training Need Analysis of POSOCO is of course being done to match the organizational training needs with the employee training needs. The equilibrium of training needs between the organization and employees needs refinement. Though POSOCO conducts regular seminars/ lectures by external experts on a periodic basis but it requires 'continuous education' all the more. All the employees in all the departments are willing to share their knowledge with others which is a very healthy sign. However, it is not cited as a strong area in KM implementation. So, it is recommended that Knowledge Management related training should be identified as the part of the organizational training; right from the individualized need assessment and to feedback sharing mechanism with the trainees so that training may become more meaningful. The organization should encourage employees to participate in international/ national conferences and seminars to expand the knowledge base in the current scenario. The rising trend of paid webinars and other media of virtual learning should also be taken benefit from. Frequent colloquiums 'on the bottom line' of a firm is the zenith of service provider and the same may be adopted by POSOCO. Employees may be encouraged to pursue 'crash courses, reorientation and refresher courses' on commercial "online institutions" such as Coursera, Khan Academy.

To sum up, the above discussion; relative assessment indicating the current status of KM Drivers in POSOCO can be represented through the following figure:

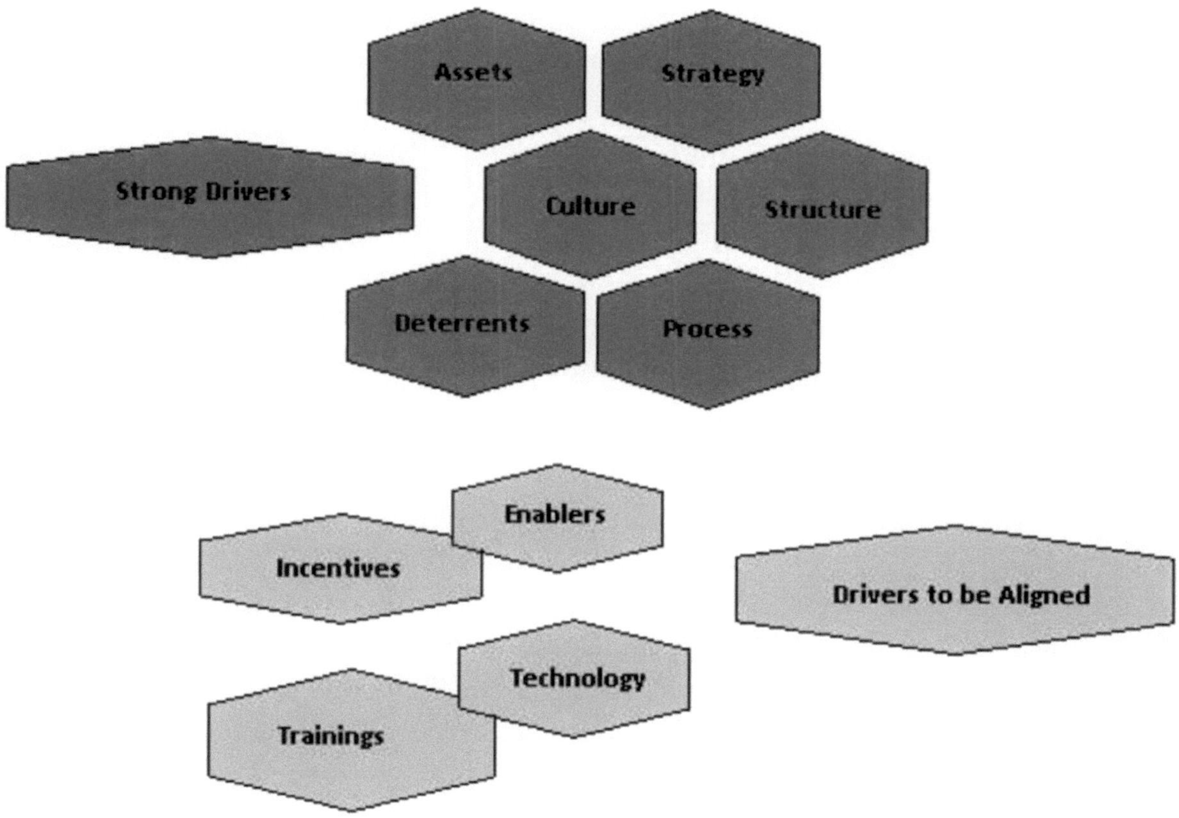

Figure 6.1: Status of KM Drivers in POSOCO

6.5 LIMITATIONS OF THE STUDY

Like all research studies, this study has some constraining elements that form the limitations of the study. These are primarily attributable to location and time constraints which limit the widespread generalizability of this study to other sectors or regions. The other limitations of this study are as follows:-

First, limitation is the response bias i.e. due to generation of responses from limited participants, and inability to curtail the prevalence of intervening variables.

Second, the employees might have given subjective or socially desirable and biased responses under the given circumstances as this researcher is a C-suite executive in POSOCO. This can be overcome by conducting a longitudinal study including an analysis; spread out at different time periods. However, the present study is limited by the time constraint which did not facilitate to take up longitudinal analysis.

Third, the study is also constrained by sampling error which arises from estimating a population characteristic by looking at only one part of the population rather than the entire population. Due to resource and time limitations, the study couldn't take a wider population for investigation. However, a sufficiently and adequately large sample size has minimized the sampling error as demonstrated in the result of Kaiser-Meyer-Olkin Test as Table 5.10 in this study.

Fourth, the 'linguistic chauvinism' could not be taken care of because the use of English in creating the tools for this research such as, Focus Group, In-Depth Interview and Elite Interview in qualitative and Survey Instrument, popularly known as the questionnaire, in quantitative methods were taken recourse to.

Fifth, non-executive employees could not form the part of the 'population' as they were not adept in the use of English and the services of an interpreter being very costly proposition.

Last but not the least; the data collection was confined only to the POSOCO executives. So, this limited the generalizability of the study's findings in other industries that must be taken into account besides the contextual background and the unique organizational culture that would affect the results therein. However, the study has tried to minimize response error through reliability and validity tests

6.6 SCOPE OF APPLICABILITY OF THE STUDY

The study has chiefly undertaken the most emergent and eminent areas of Knowledge Management. This leads to several related studies that can be conducted in the other sectors with vital implications for improving their competitive sustainable advantage.

First, the scope of this study extends to other related studies in the domain of Knowledge Management that could be carried out at inter-organizational level for firms in the Energy and Power Sector.

Besides this, other studies can be conducted taking up each of the significant Drivers individually to examine its impact on KM implementation across departments and even across different industries in other sectors. The applicability of the findings of study can be tried out in the case of Small and Micro Enterprises also besides the service sector enterprises with contextual sensitivity and understanding.

The scope of this study extends to examining the inter-linkages between the KM Drivers to suggest a structural model which can form the theoretical base model to be implemented across related enterprises.

At the macro level, the study may be extended to other studies linking the relationship between the KM and firm performance, sustainability and competitiveness. This would provide a rich insight for effectively implementing KM in diverse organizations.

6.7 SUGGESTIONS FOR FUTURE RESEARCH

The emerging areas of artificial intelligence and machine learning and their interfaces with KM may be explored to create a balance between 'man and machine' synchronization. Another area which is gaining momentum is that of Natural Language Processing. The research in this area may be facilitated by KM as it is an interdisciplinary endeavour of researchers. KM can be used in creating ideal ergonomic condition and better environment for personnel in 'telecommuting'; and 'work from home', especially, in the aftermath of Covid-19 pandemic. The world is a living laboratory which is the source of exploration, creation and inspiration. Accordingly, it may be used as a testing ground for exploration, creation and inspiration. The three types of knowledge i.e. tacit, explicit and implicit may be used as the genres for future researches to devise new mechanism and sort out the problems of 'machine learning' by digital immigrants.

It can also be used to overcome the slack and procrastination in the domain of learning and pave the way for data-enabled learning. The virtualization of learning process has created a paradigm shift. Earlier the learning was institution centric because it was the era of lack of information. In this context the professor, the libraries and the classmates were of paramount importance. The availability of data and information at the touch of a button is a reality resulting in 'the era of over information' which has created 'the learner centric continuous education'. At this juncture, KM can be used for remaining rooted in the higher education and the wants of millions of individuals for learning may be converted into their needs. However, KM tools may help the e-learning but these tools will have to be validated beforehand. The researchers may explore this to create a win-win situation for both, the learners and the enablers including the humans and technologies emanating from the Information and Communication *per se.*

REFERENCES

1. *Abbas, K.D. (2016) Knowledge Management Strategies and Practices in Nigerian Agricultural Research Institutes, ukzn-dspace.utzn.ac.za*
2. Audretsch, D.B.; et. al. (2020), Knowledge Management and Entrepreneurship; *International Entreprenuership and Management Journal*: 1-13
3. Abdelwhab Ali, A., Panneerselvam, D., Paris, L. and Gunasekaran, A. (2019), "Key factors influencing knowledge sharing practices and its relationship with organizational performance within the oil and gas industry", *Journal of Knowledge Management,* 23 (9) 1806-1837. https://doi.org/10.1108/JKM-06-2018-0394
4. Abhilasha Singh and EbrahimSoltani.(2010). Knowledge Management Practices in Indian Information Technology Companies. *Total Quality Management,* 21 (2), 145-157.
5. Abu-Shanab, E. and Shehabat, I. (2018), "The influence of Knowledge Management practices on e-government success: A proposed framework tested", *Transforming Government: People, Process and Policy,* 12 (%) 286- 308. https://doi.org/10.1108/TG-02-2018-0016
6. Ahmed, S., Fiaz, M. & Shoaib, M. (2015). Impact of Knowledge Management Practices on Organizational Performance: An Empirical Study of Banking Sector in Pakistan. *FWU Journal of Social Sciences,* 9(2), 147-167.
7. Alavi, M., Kayworth, T. & Leidner, D. (2005). An Empirical Examination of the Influence of Organizational Culture on Knowledge Management Practices. *Journal ofManagement.*
8. Alavi, M. & Liender, D.E. (2002), Knowledge Management Systems; Issues, challenges and benefits in Barnes, S. (ed) *Knowledge Management System: Theory and Practice;* Thomson Asia Pvt. Ltd. Singapore.
9. Alavi, M. and Leidner D. (2001). Review: Knowledge Management and Knowledge Management Systems.-Conceptual Foundations and Research Issues. *MIS Quarterly* 25(1),107-136.
10. Alavi, M. & Leidner, D. (1999) Knowledge Management Systems: Issues, Challenges, and Benefits; *Communications of the Association for Information Systems;* (1), 7, 1999
11. Amayah, A.T. (2013) Determinants of Knowledge Sharing in a Public Sector Organization; *Journal of Knowledge Management;* emerald.com

12. Almeida, P. (2008), "Localization of Knowledge and the Mobility of Engineers" in Regional Networks" in Kogut, B (Eds.) *Knowledge, Options and Institutions,* Oxford University Press, Britain.

13. American Productivity and Quality Center: *APQC,* http://www.apqc.org, Access date: July 11, 2020.

14. Anderson; Arthur/APQC (1996) The American Productivity and Quality Center: *The Knowledge Management Assessment Tool: External Benchmarking Version,* APQC, Chicago.

15. Anderson, K.K. (2009), *Organizational Capabilities as Predictors of Effective Knowledge Management: An Empirical Examination,* Ph.D. Thesis of H. Wayne Huizenga School of Business and Entrepreneurship, Nova Southern University.

16. Andries,P. and Wastyn, A.(2012). Disentangling value-enhancing and cost-increasing effects of Knowledge Management. *Journal of Knowledge Management,* 16 (3), 387-399.

17. Antonio Mini Ramirez, Victor Jesus Garcia Morales and Rodrigo Martin Rojas, (2011).'Knowledge Creation, Organizational Learning and their effects on Organizational Performance' *Journal of Engineering Economics, Work* Humanism,22(3),309-318.

18. Argote Linda and Paul Ingram (2000). Knowledge Transfer: A Basis for Competitive Advantage In Firms', *Organizational Behavior and Human Decision Processes.* 82(l), 150-169.

19. Armstrong, M. (2012), *"Armstrong's Handbook of Human Resource Management Practice*[1]*"*, 12th Edition, Kogan Page Ltd., London

20. Arumugam Rathinavelu and Mahalingam.(2005).The design of the Knowledge Management System for higher education. *Proceedings of the Conference on Recent Advances in Information Technology.* Pg 190-196

21. Bagozzi, R.P. and Yi, Y (1988) On the Evaluation of Structural Equation Models; *Journal of the Academy of Marketing Science,* Springer

22. *Bates, W.R.J. (1998), Organizational Learning and Knowledge Technologies in a Dynamic Environment. Kluwer Academic Publishers, Boston.*

23. Becerra-Fernandez, Irma, R.S. (2001). Organizational Knowledge Management: A Contingency Perspective.' *Journal of Management Information Systems,* 18(1), 23 - 55.

24. Bhatti, K. K. & Qureshi, T. M. (2007). Impact of Employee Participation on Job Satisfaction, Employee Commitment and Employee Productivity. *International Review of Business Research Papers,* 3(2), 54-68.

25. Brauner, E. & Becker, A. (2006), "Knowledge Management in Interaction: Transactive Knowledge Systems and the Management of Knowledge" in Renzl. B, Matzler, K.

26. Brelade, S. & Harman, C. (2006) *A Practical Guide to Knowledge Management,* Viva Books Private Limited, New Delhi, p.5.

27. Brown, C.P. (2020) *Export Controls: America a Es Other National Security Threat,* Perarson Institute for International Economics; Working Paper

28. Bueren, A., Schierholz, R., Kolbe, L. & Brenner, W. (2005). Improving Performance of Customer-Processes with Knowledge Management. *Business Process Management,* 11(5), 2005

29. Bukowitz, W.R. & William, R. L. (1999), *"The Knowledge Management Fieldbook',* Pearson Education Ltd. Great Britain.

30. Bures, V. (2009), "Methodology of Knowledge Management Implementation", Paper presented in *International Conference on Multimedia and ICT in Education,* 22-24, April, 2009, Lisbon, Portugal.

31. Burkholder, G.J. and Burbank, P.M. (2019) Philosophical Foundations and the Role of Theory in Research; *Research Design and Methods: An Applied Guide for the Scholar Practitioner* 13, 2019

32. Burg, E.V., Berends H. & Raaji E.V. and Raaji (2008), "Organizing knowledge sharing in networks: the theory", in Man, A.P.D. (Eds.) *Knowledge Management and Innovation in Networks* Edward Elgar, Cheltenham, UK.

33. Byukusenge, E., Munene, J. & Orobia, L. (2017). Knowledge Management and Business Performance: Mediating Effect of Innovation. *Journal of Business and Management Sciences,* 4(4), 82-92.

34. Byukusenge Eugenie and John C. Munene (2017). *Knowledge Management and business performance: Does innovation matter*? Available at https: / / doi.org / 10.10 80 / 23311975.2017.1368434

35. *Canongia, C., Santos, D., Santos, M. & Zackiewicz, M. (2004) Foresight, Competitive Intelligence and Knowledge Management as Innovation Management Tools. Gestao e Produ^cao, 11(2), 231-238.*

36. Captureanu, S. And Captureanu, E. (2010), "Knowledge Creation / Conversion Process", *Review of International Comparative Management,* 11(1), 150.

37. Carley. K (1992). Organizational learning and personnel turnover. *Journal of Organizational Science,* 3(1), 20-46.

38. Cascio, W.F. & Nambudiri, R (2010) *Managing Human Resources: Productivity, Quality and Work Life, Profit,* Tata Mc Gran Hill Education Pvt. Ltd., New Delhi

39. CEA website www. cea.nic.in

40. CERC order in Petition No. 167 / Suo-Moto / 2012 dated 22.2.2014

41. CERC Regulations dated 05.05.2019 on Fees and Charges of Regional Load Dispatch Centre and other related matters
42. CERC (Open Access in Inter-State Transmission) Regulations 2008.
43. CERC Regulations dated 15.06.2010 on Sharing of Inter-State Transmission Charges and Losses.
44. CERC Regulations dated 04.06.2010 on the Power System Development Fund Regulations.
45. CERC (Regulation of Power Supply) Regulations, 2010.
46. CERC Regulations dated 22.12.2009 on Measures to relieve congestion in real time operation.
47. CERC website www.cercind.gov.in
48. Chait LP (1999). Creating a Successful Knowledge Management System. *Journal of Business Strategy,* 20(2): 23-26.
49. Chalard Chantarasombat and Rungthip Singporn (2008) Developing A Knowledge Management Model for Educational Quality Assurance in Faculty Of Education, Mahasarakham University. *Educational Journal of Thailand,* 2 (1),
50. Chang, C. L.-h. & Lin, T.-C. (2015).The Role of Organizational Culture in the Knowledge Management Process. *Journal of Knowledge Management,* 19(3), 433455.
51. Chen, Y. Y.; Yeh, S.P. and Huang, H.L. (2012), "Does Knowledge Management "fit" matter to business performance?", *Journal of Knowledge Management,* 16, (5), 671-687.
52. Choo, C.W. (2000). Working with Knowledge: How information professionals help organizations manage what they know'. *Library Management.* 21(8), 395-403.
53. Ciborra, C. and R. Andreu (2001). Sharing knowledge across boundaries. *Journal of Information Technology,* 16, 73-81.
54. Concept of Rubik Cube KM Method, created by Andreas Maratheft is during a three month project and applied to a client organization, The Pan Cyprian Company of Bakers, based in Cyprus.
55. Conway, S. & Sligar, C. (2002) *Unlocking Knowledge Assets: Solutions from Microsoft,* Prentice-Hall of India Pvt. Ltd., New Delhi - 110 001. P.1.
56. Cooper, D.R. and Schindler, P.S. (2006) *Marketing Research,* McGraw-Hill/Irwin
57. *Costello, G.(1996).Knowledge Management in Strategic Alliances: the role of Information Technology. Templeton College. Oxford, University of Oxford.*
58. Cramton, C.D. (2001) The Mutual Knowledge Problem, and Its Consequences for Dispersed Collaboration; *Organization Science;* pubsonline.informs.org

59. Cummings, J.N (2004). Work Groups, Structural Diversity and Knowledge Sharing in a Global Organization. *Journal, Management Science.* 50(3), 352-364.

60. Dahiya, D., Gupta, M. & Jain, P. (2012). Enterprise Knowledge Management System: A Multi Agent Perspective. *Information Systems, Technology and Management,* 285(4), 271-281.

61. Dan Holtshouse (2009) *'The future of Knowledge Workers, Part* 1'. Available online at: http://www.kmworld.com

62. Davenport, T. H. & Prusak, L. (1998), *Working Knowledge, How Organizations, Manage What They Know,* Harvard Business School Press, Boston, Massachusetts.

63. Davenport.T.H and J. Glaser (2002). Just-in-time delivery comes to Knowledge Management'. *Harvard Business Review.* 80(7), 107-111.

64. Deepak Chawla and Himanshu Joshi, (2010). Knowledge Management Practices in Indian Industries — A comparative study. *Journal of Knowledge Management,* 14(5), 708 - 725.

65. Department of Public Enterprises (DPE) website www.dpe.gov.in

66. Desouza, K.C. & Paquette, S. (2011), *Knowledge Management: An Introduction,* Facet Publishing, London, p99.

67. Dessler, G. (2003), *Human Resource Management,* Prentice-Hall of India Pvt. Ltd., New Delhi.

68. Dhamdhere, S.N. (2015) Importance of Knowledge Management in the Higher Educational Institutes, *Turkish Online Journal of Distance Education,* 16(1) 162-183

69. Dickel, D. G. & Moura, G. L. d. (2016) Organizational Performance Evaluation in Intangible Criteria: A Model Based on Knowledge Management and Innovation Management. *RAI Journal of Technology Management and Innovation,* 13(3), 211-220.

70. Ding, X.H.; Liu, H. and Song, Y. (2013). Are internal knowledge transfer strategies double edged swords?' *Journal of Knowledge Management,* 17 (1), 81.

71. Disaster Management: As per Ministry of Power letter dated 27th May 2009,

72. Drucker, P.F. (2002), *Managing in the Next Society,* Butterworth Heinemann, Oxford.

73. Du P. M. (2005), Drivers of Knowledge Management in the corporate environment. *International Journal of Informational Management,* 25 (3): 193-202.

74. Durmusoglu, S, Jacobs M. Nayir, D.Z., Khilji S. and Wang, X. (2014), "The Quasi- moderating role of organizational culture in the relationship between rewards and knowledge shared and gained", *Journal of Knowledge Management,* 18, (1), 19.37.

75. *Dyer, J.H and NobeokaK. (2000). Creating and Managing a High-Performance Knowledge-Sharing Network: The Toyota Case.' Harvard School University Press, 345-367.*

76. ERLDC website(https://erldc.in/)

77. Felix F Wu; K.Moslehi; A. Bose (2005)..*Proceedings of IEEE 2005-* ieeexplore.ieee.org

78. Fierro, J. C., Florin, J., Perez, L. & Whitelock, J. (2011). Inter-firm Market Orientation as Antecedent of Knowledge Transfer, Innovation and Value Creation in Networks. *Management Decision,* 49(3), 444-467.

79. *Fishbein, M., & Ajzen, I. (1975). Belief, attitude, intention and behavior: An introduction to theory and research. Reading, MA: Addison-Wesley*

80. Fong, P. S. W. & Choi, S. K. Y. (2009). The Processes of Knowledge Management in Professional Service Firms in the Construction Industry: A Critical Assessment of Both Theory and Practice. *Journal of Knowledge Management,* 13(2), 110-126.

81. F orum of Regulators CABIL Report.

82. Frunham, A. & Barrie, G. (1993), *Corporate Assessment: Auditing a Company's Personality,* Routledge, New York.

83. Fullan, M. (2011), *Change Leader: Learning to Do What Matters Most,* Jossey-Bass, A Wiley Imprint, San-Francisco, CA.

84. Games, D. and Rendi, R.P. (2019). The effects of Knowledge Management and risk taking on SME financial performance in creative industries in an emerging market: the mediating effect of innovation outcomes. *J. Glob Entreprises9* (44) Available at. https://doi.org/10.1186/s40497-019-0167-1

85. Garcia Muina, Fernando Enrique, Martin de Castro, Greegorio and Lopez Saez, Pedro

86. (2010) *Knowledge-Creation Process: A Critical Examination of the SECI Model, Available* at: \vmv.warwick,ac.uk /fac /soc/wbs/conf/olkc/arcln\-e/04elc3/ papers /idl 51.pdf.

87. Geisler, E. & Whickramasinghe, N. (2009) *Principles of Knowledge Management: Theory Practice and Cases,* M.E. Sharpe, Armonk, New York, pp.44-45.

88. Girish, G P & Joseph, Dennis & Roy, Souvik & Raju, Amar. (2015). Factors influencing Adoption of Knowledge Management Systems in India from a Micro, Small and Medium Enterprise's Perspective. *International Review of Management and Marketing*. 5. 135-140.

89. Gold, A., Malhotra, A. & Segars, A. (2001). Knowledge Management: An Organizational Capabilities Perspective. *Journal of Management Information Systems*, 18(1), 185-214.

90. Gonalez, R.V.D. and Martius M.F. (2014), Knowledge Management: An Analysis from the Organizational Development; *Journal of Technology Management & Innovation*, I (1), 131-147, 2014

91. Gottschalk, P. (2007), *Knowledge Management System*, Idea Group Publishing, Hershey, London.

92. Grant, R.M. (2001), "Knowledge and Organization" in Nonaka, I. and Teece, D.J. (eds.), *Management of Industrial Knowledge: Creation, Transfer and Utilization* SAGE Publications, London.

93. Greiner, M., Bohmann, T. & Krcmar, H. (2007). A Strategy for Knowledge Management. *Journal of Knowledge Management*, 11(6), 3-15.

94. Griffith, T., Sawyer, J. & Neale, M. (2003).Virtualness and Knowledge in Teams: Managing the Love Triangle of Organizations, Individuals, and Information Technology. *MIS Quarterly*, 27(2), 265-287.

95. Grover, V. Y Davenport, T.H. (2001) General Perspectives on Knowledge Management: Fostering & Research Agenda, *Journal of Management Information Systems*, 18(1) pp. 5-21.

96. Guchait, P., Namasivayam, K. & Lei, P.-W. (2011). Knowledge Management in Service Encounters: Impact on Customers' Satisfaction Evaluations. *Journal of Knowledge Management*, 15(3), 513-527.

97. Gumus, M. (2007), The Effect of Communication on Knowledge Sharing in Organizations; *Journal of Knowledge Management Practice*; 8(2),15-26, 2007

98. Guidelines issued by Department of Public Enterprises regarding MoU. (https://dpe.gov.in/)

99. Han, K.H. & Park, J.W. (2009) Process-Centerd Knowledge Model and Enterprise ontology for the development of Knowledge Management system in *Expert Systems with Applications* 36 (2009) 7441-7447 accessed on 15.06.2020 at www.el sevi er.com/locate/ e & wa

100. Handzic, M. and Ozlen, K. (2013). Knowledge Management Success in Clinical Service Environments. *Journal of Information and Knowledge Management*, 12 (2), 135.

101. Hansen, M. T, Nohria N. and Tiemey T. (1999), What's your strategy for managing Knowledge. *Harvard Business Review.* 77(2), 106-116.

102. Hasnali, F. (2005), "Building a Knowledge-sharing Network: Plan, Design, Execute.... Reap?" in Manmohan Rao (Eds), *Knowledge Management Tools and Techniques.* Elsevier, New York.

103. Hawryszkiewycz, I. (2010), *Knowledge Management: Organising Knowledge Based Enterprises,* Palgrave Mcmillan, Hampshire, U.K. pp-72-73

104. Hendriks, P.H.J. (2006), "Organizational Structure" in Schwarts, D.G. (ed), *Encyclopedia of Knowledge Management,* Idea Group Reference, Hershey, London.

105. *Hislop, DC (2013) Knowledge Management in organizations: A critical Introduction, Oxford University Press, Oxford*

106. Hooff, B. V. D. & Huysman, M. (2009). Managing Knowledge Sharing: Emergent and Engineering Approaches. *Information & Management,* 46(1), 1-8.

107. Holsapple, C.W. & Wu J. (2008) In Search of a Missing Link, *Knowledge Management Research & Practice,* 6(1) 31-40

108. Holtzman, S. and Leich, C.M. (2014) Wittgenstein: to follow a Rule; (Vol. 4) Rontledge

109. IEX website www.iexindia.com

110. Indian Electricity Act, 2003 (www.cercind.gov.in)

111. Indian Meteorological Department Website (https://mausam.imd.gov.in)

112. Ipe, M. (2003). Knowledge Sharing in Organizations: A Conceptual Framework. *Human Resource Development Review,* 2(4), 337-359.

113. Janz, B.D. & Prasaruphanich, P. (2003), Understanding the Antecedents of Effective Knowledge Management: The Importance of Knowledge Centerd Culture", *Decision Science,* 34(2), 351-384.

114. Jelenic, D. (2011). The Importance of Knowledge Management in Organizations - With Emphasis on the Balanced Scorecard Learning and Growth Perspective. Celje, Slovenia, *International School for Social and Business Studies.*

115. Johnsen, Maria (2020) Knowledge Management Available at http://www.mana- johnsen.com/Knowledge-management/ accessed on 25.05.2020

116. Jones, J. S. & Linderman, K. (2014) Process Management, Innovation and Efficiency Performance. *Business Process Management,* 20(2), 335-358.

117. Jones, R.G. & George, J.M. (2011), *Contemporary Management* 7th Edition, McGraw Hill Irvin, New York.

118. Jurisica, I, Mylopoulos, J.;Yu, E. (2004); Ontologies for Knowledge Management: An Information Systems Perspective; Knowledge and Information Systems, Springer

119. Kahn, R. and Cannell, C. (1957) The Dynamics of Interviewing, John Wiley, New York

120. Kankanhalli, A., Tan, B. & Wei, K.-K. (2005). Contributing Knowledge to Electronic Knowledge Repositories: An Empirical Investigation. *MIS Quarterly,* 29(1), 113-143.

121. Kayworth, T. & Leidner, D. (2003). *Organizational Culture as a Knowledge Resource.* 1st ed. Heidilberg: Springer-Verlag.

122. Keng-Goon Goi (2009). 'TQM and Knowledge Management: Literature review and proposed framework'. *African Journal of Business Management,* 3 (11), 633-643.

123. 723.Kiesling, R. (2011) *In memory of Man* :2.0 Good Reads, Accessed on August 11, 2020 on the Platform, Originally published in 2010 in the *Journal of Knowledge Management Practice.*

124. Kjaergaard, A. & Kautz, K. (2006) A Process Model of establishing Knowledge Management: Insights from a longitudinal field study in *Science Direct/ omega 36 (2008)* 282-297 accessed on 15.06.2020 at www.elsevier.com/locate/omega.

125. *Klein, D.A. (1998), The Strategic Management of Intellectual Capital: An Introduction Butterworth-Heinemann, Boston.*

126. Kothari, C.R. (2004) Research Methodology: Methods and Techniques, New Age International Publishers, Delhi.

127. Kulkarni, V. (2016) Expectations of Indian B-Schools based on KM Systems, *International Journal of Research and Analytical Reviews,* Vol. 17, 2016.

128. Lee, M. R. & Lan, Y. C. (2011). Toward a Unified Knowledge Management Model for SMEs. *Expert Systems with Applications,* 38(1), 729-735.

129. Lee H, & Choi B (2003). Knowledge Management Enablers, Processes, and Organizational Performance: an Integrative View and Empirical Examination. *Journal of Management & Informational System,* 20(1): 179-228.

130. Leidner, D., Alavi, M. & Kayworth, T. (2006). The Role of Culture in Knowledge Management: A Case Study of Two Global Firms. *International Journal of Collaboration,* 2(1), 17-40

131. Levin, D. Z and R. Cross (2004). The Strength of Weak Ties You Can Trust: The Mediating Role of Trust in Effective Knowledge Transfer. *Management Science.* 50 (11), 1477-1490.

132. Liana, R., Kathrin, Kirchener & Pia N. (2016). What Factors Influence Knowledge Sharing in Organizations?: A Social Dilemma Perspective of Social Media Communication. / In: *Journal of Knowledge Management,* 20(6), DOI: http://dx.doi.org/10.1108/JKM-03-2016-0112

133. Liao, S. (2002) Problem Solving and Knowledge Inertia, Expert Systems with Applications; 22 (1) 21-31, 2002

134. Liebowitz, J.; Chen, Y. (2001) *Developing Knowledge* Sharing Proficiencies; *Knowledge Management Review*; 3, 12-15, Melcrum Publishing

135. Lin WW (2001). *The study of enabling factors of Knowledge Management inside organizations.* Institute of Human Resource Management of the Sun Yat-sen University, Master's Thesis.

136. Liu, S. & Deng, Z. (2015). Understanding Knowledge Management Capability in Business Process Outsourcing: A Cluster Analysis. *Management Decision,* 53(1), 124-138.

137. Lopes, I.T. (2008), Towards an Electronic Knowledge Management Culture; *ICFAI Journal of Knowledge Management,* 6(4); 7-24, 2008

138. Lopez, V.W.B and Esteves, J. (2013). Acquiring external knowledge to avoid reinvention. *Journal of Knowledge Management,* 17(1), 89.

139. Losey, M.; Meisigner, S. and Ulrich, D. (2005), *The Future of Human Resource Management,* Society for Human Resource Management, Alexandrina, Virginia, U.S. A., Indian Reprint by Wiley India, New Delhi.

140. Loureiro, M. G., Alonso, M. V. & Schiuma, G. (2015). Knowledge and Sustained Competitive Advantage: How Do Services Firms Compete?. *Investigaciones Europeas de Direcciony Economia de la Empresa,* 21(2), 55-57.

141. Luders, C. (2004), "Field Observations and Ethnoraphy" in Flick, U. Kardroff, K.V. and Stienke, I. (Eds) *A Companion to Qualitative Research;* Sage Publications Ltd. London

142. Lytras, M., Pouloudi, A. & Poulymenakou, A. (2002). Knowledge Management Convergence - Expanding Learning Frontiers. *Journal of Knowledge Management,* 6(1), 40-51.

143. M. Alavi and D.Leidner.(1999). Knowledge Management and Knowledge Management Systems; Conceptual Foundations and Research Issues. Working Paper in the *INSEAD Working Paper Series. INSEAD,* Fountainebleau,France.

144. *Maclver, J.P. and Carmines (1981) Unidimensional Sacling: Quantitative Applications in the Social Sciences, Sage: Beverly Hills, CA, USA*

145. Maier, D.J., & Moseley, J.J. (2003). The Knowledge Management assessment tool (KMAT). ANNUAL-SAN DIEGO-PFEIFFER AND COMPANY- 1, 169-184.

146. Makani, J. and Marche, S. (2012) "Classifying Organisations by Knowledge Intensity - Necessary Next Steps", *Journal of Knowledge Management,* 16(2), 243266.

147. Mamta Bhusry and Jayanti Rajan (2011). Knowledge collaboration in higher educational Institutions in India: charting a Knowledge Management solution. *International Journal of Computer Science,* 8 (5), 332-341.

148. Man, A.P.D.,Berends, H, Lammers, I, Raaij, E.V.and Weele, A.V.(2008), "Knowledge and innovation in networks: a conceptual framework", in Man, A.P.D. (Eds.) *Knowledge Management and Innovation in Networks* Edward Elgar, Cheltenham, UK.

149. Manish Kumar, Souren Paul and Suresh Tadisina (2005). Knowledge Management Practices in Indian Software development Companies: Findings from an exploratory study. *Asian Academy of Management Journal.* 10(1), 59-78.

150. Mansoor Ezzati Jivan and Maryam Zarandi (2012). Factors Effecting on Knowledge Management in Service -Oriented Organizations (Senior Managers Opinion Using Analytical Hierarchy Process (AHP). *International Journal of Business and Management,* 7(5), Available online at URL: http://dx.doi.org /10.5539 /ijbm.v7n5pl50.

151. Markus M. Lynne, Ann Majchrzak, Les Gasser (2002). A Design Theory for Systems That Support Emergent Knowledge Processes. *MIS Quarterly,* 26(3), 179-212.

152. Markus, Lynne M. (2001). Toward a Theory of Knowledge Reuse Situations and Factors in Reuse Success. *Journal of Management Information Systems,* 18(1), 57-93.

153. Marques, D. P. & Simon, F. J. G. (2006). The Effect of Knowledge Management Practices on Firm Performance. *Journal of Knowledge Management,* 10(3), 143-156.

154. Marrewijk, M. Tinmers, J. (2003), "Human Capital Management: New Possibilities in People Management", *Journal of Business Ethics,* 44, 171-184.

155. *Martinez-Canas, R. et.al. (2012), Knowledge Acquisition Mediation of Social Capital-firm Innovation, Journal of Knowledge Management, 16, (1).*

156. Marshall, C. and Rossman, B. (2006) Designing Qualitative Research, Sage Publications, Thousand Oaks, London, New Delhi.

157. Massey, A. & Montoya-Weiss, M. (2006). Unraveling the Temporal Fabric of Knowledge Conversion: A Model of Media Selection and Use. *MIS Quarterly,* 30(1), 99-114.

158. Mathew, Viju and Mary,Kavitha (2008). The Critical Knowledge transfer in an Organization: Approaches. *The ICFAI University Journal of Knowledge Management,* 6(4), 25-39.

159. Mathi Kavindra (2004). Key success factors for Knowledge Management'. MBA: *International Business Management & Consulting,* Lindau, University of Applied Sciences, Germany.

160. McCarthy, A. F. (2006). Knowledge Management: evaluating strategies and processes used in higher education (Ph.D.). Retrieved March 28, 2012, from *Digital Dissertation Consortium (3221289).*

161. Mc Kibbon, K.A. & Lokker, C.: http://whatiskt.wikispace.com/knowledge + dissemination(2012) Accessed on 3rd May 2020 accessed on 20/05/2020 at http://whatiskt.wikispace.com/knowledge + dissemination.

162. Mello, J. A. (2001), *Strategic Human Resource Management,* Wadsworth, Cengage Learning, New Delhi.

163. Miikka Lehtonen, 'Nonaka's Knowledge Creation Theory Revisited: A Semiotic Analysis of Communicating Knowledge in a Geographically Dispersed Team'. International Business Communication, Master *Thesis,* 23"* March 2009. Available at h ttps://aaltodoc.aalto.fi/bitstream/handle/.../hse_ethesis_1 2 048.pdJ?... 1

164. Ministry of Earth Science website www.moes.gov.in

165. Ministry of Power, vide OM dated 2nd March, 2005

166. Ministry of Power, vide OM dated 27thSeptember, 2010

167. Ministry of Power, vide OM dated 25th March, 2015

168. Ministry of Power Gazette notification dated 19th December, 2016

169. Ministry of Power letter dated 27th May 2009

170. Ministry of Power, vide OM dated 04th July 2008

171. Ministry of Power vide order dated 05.01.2016assigned the responsibility of Registry of ESCerts trading to the POSOCO.

172. Ministry of Power website (https://powermin.nic.in/)

173. MIT 90's Framework for Critical Success Factors: Internal Factors & External Factors Towards Actionable Insights {Adapted from Mishart Scolt Morton, 1991} Management Science Letters 8(7) 725-736 [Publisher-Growing Science] Accessed on July 20, 2018

174. Narayan, Tarun (2005) The Knowledge Edge, The Journal of All India Management Association

175. National Electricity Policy, 2005

176. Nawaz, M. S., Hassan, M. & Shaukat, S. (2014). Impact of Knowledge Management Practices on Firm Performance: Testing the Mediation Role of Innovation in the Manufacturing Sector of Pakistan. *Pakistan Journal of Commerce and Social Science,* 8(1), 99-111.

177. Newell, S., Tansley, C. & Huang, J. (2004) Social Capital and Knowledge Integration in an ERP Project Team: The Importance of Bridging and Bonding. *British Journal of Management,* 15(1), 43-57.

178. Newman, B.D and Conrad, K.W (2000). A Framework/or characterizing Knowledge Management Methods, Practices And Technologies'. *Proceedings of the Third International Conference on Practical Aspects of Knowledge Management (PAKM2000),* Basel, Switzerland.

179. Nissen, M.E. (2002), An Extended Model of Knowledge-Flow, Dynamics in Communications of the Association for Information System 8, pp.251-266.

180. *Nonaka I and Takeuchi H. (1995). 'The Knowledge Creating Company: How Japanese Companies Create the Dynamics of Innovation', Oxford University Press, New York.*

181. Nonaka, I. (1994) A Dyanmic Theory of Organizational Knowledge Creation, Organization Science, pubsonline.informs.org

182. O'Dell, C. *(2004),The Executive's Role In Knowledge Management,* Tata McGraw-Hill Publishing Company Ltd. New Delhi.

183. Orlikowski, W.J. (2002) Knowing in Practice: Enacting a Collective Capability in Distributed Organising; Organization Science, pubsonline.informs.org

184. Pandey, K.N. (2016) *Paradigms of Knowledge Management: With Systems Modelling Case Studies,* Vol 60 in Studies in Systems, Decision and Control, Springer Nature p5

185. Pasher, E. & Ronnen T.; (2011) "The Complete Guide to Knowledge Management: A Strategic Plan to Leverage your company's Intellectual Capital", John Wiley & Sons Inc. Hoboken, New Jersey p.188.

186. Pathak Deepti (2009). Managing Knowledge Worker across different stages of employment'. *HRMReview,* 9(10).

187. Pawlowski, J. & Bick, M. (2012). The Global Knowledge Management Framework: Towards a Theory for Knowledge Management in Globally Distributed Settings. Electronic, *Journal of Knowledge Management,* 10(1), 92-108.

188. Peachey, T.A. (2006), "An Examination of the Effects of Cultural, Climatic, Structural and Technological Factors on Knowledge Management Effectiveness", Ph.D. Thesis; Asburn, Alabama.

189. Pee L.G. and Kankanhalli A. (2016) Interactions among Factors Influencing Knowledge Management in Public-Sector Organizations: A Resource-Based View, *Government Information Quarterly,* 33 (1), pp. 188-199

190. Pension, K., Nyasha, M., Sheiller, M. & Vhuramai, C. (2013). Impact of Knowledge Management on Organizational Performance: A Case Study of Grain Marketing Board (GMB). *Greener Journal of Business and Management Studies,* 3(6), 270278.

191. Pfeffer, J. & Sutton, R.I (2000)The *Knowing Doing Gap: How Smart Companies Turn Knowledge into Action,* Harvard Business School Press, Boston, MS

192. Po-Ying Chu, Li-Chieh Chen, Wan-Li Wei.(2007). A study on the effect of using a Knowledge Management system on design education. *International Journal of Information Management.*

193. POSOCO Annual Reports - (2018-19 and 2019-20)

194. POSOCO website www.posoco.in

195. POSOCO departmental files - POSOCO Internal Documents.

196. POSOCO Knowledge Management Policy- POSOCO Internal Documents

197. POSOCO CSR- (https://POSOCO.in/useful-links/csr/).

198. POSOCO Website (https://POSOCO.in/wpcontent/uploads/2020/02/POSOCO_SCED_Pilot_Detailed_F eedback_Report_Jan_2020.pdf

199. POWERGRID websitewww.powergridindia.com

200. POWERGRID Knowledge Management Policy is available on POWERGRID Intranet portal.

201. Prat, Nicolas (2006), A Hierarchical Model for Knowledge Management in Schwartz, *D.G. (Ed) Encyclopedia of Knowledge Management Idea Group Reference,* Hershey, London, Melbourne, Singapore. Pp 211-212, 213-217.

202. Probert K Stephen, (2003). A Critical Analysis of the Knowledge Creation Process' *AJIS,* 11(1). Available online at:http://dl.acs.org.au/index.php/ajis/article/view/li6/116.

203. Probst, G. et.al (2002), *Managing Knowledge Building Blocks for Success,* Wiley, West Sussex, England.

204. PXIL website www.powerexindia.com

205. Rahimli, A. (2012). Knowledge Management and Competitive Advantage. *Information and Knowledge Management,* 2(7), 37-43.

206. Ram Shukla, and Rohtak, C. (2012). Knowledge Management in higher education. International *Journal of Reviews, Surveys, and Research (IJRSR)* Available at http://www.ijrsr.com/index.php/volume-1-issue-1september-2012

207. Rasula, J., Vuksic, V. B. & Stemberger, M. I. (2012). The Impact of Knowledge Management on Organizational Performance. *Economic and Business Review,* 14(2), 147-168.

208. Research Design- http://researchdesignmethod.com/wpcontent/uploads/2013/10/

209. Rodriguez, E. & Edwards, J. (2010). People, Technology, Processes and Risk Knowledge Sharing. *Electronic Journal of Knowledge Management,* 8(1), 139-150.

210. Saleh, N.M. et al. (2010), Intellectual Capital Disclosure Quality: Lessons from selected Scandinavian Countries, *IUP Journal of Knowledge Management,8* (u) 39, 2010

211. Sanghani Parag (2008). 'Does Organization Size Matter for Starting a Knowledge Management Program?'. *The ICFAI University Journal of Knowledge Management,* 6(5), 7-19.

212. Sasmita Palo, S. Charles L. (2015). Investigating Factors Affecting Knowledge Sharing Intention of Salespeople, Management Labour40 (3), 302-324

213. Schultze, U. & Leidner, D. (2002). Studying Knowledge Management in Information Systems Research: Discourses and Theoretical Assumptions. *MIS Quarterly,* 26(3), 213-242.

214. Scoblic, J.P. (2020) Learning from the future, *Harvard Business Review,* July-August Issue

215. Sekaran, U and Bougie, R. (2010) Research Methods for Business: A Skill Building Approach, 5th Edition, Wiley India, New Delhi

216. Shih, H.A. and Chiang, Y.H. (2005), "Strategy alignment between HRM, KM and corporate development", *International Journal of Manpower,* 26(6), 582-606.

217. Shrafat, F. (2018), "Examining the factors influencing Knowledge Management system (KMS) adoption in small and medium enterprises SMEs", *Business Process Management Journal,* 24 (1), 234-265.https://doi.org/10.1108/BPMJ-10-2016-0221

218. Shukla, A. & Srinivasan, R. (2002), *Knowledge Management Architecture: How to Implement Successful Knowledge Management Programme,* Response Books, A Division of Sage Publication, New Delhi, Thousand Oaks, London.

219. Singh, J. and Agarwal A.K. (2005). Collaborative Networks as Determinants of Knowledge Diffusion Patterns. *Journal of Management Science.* 51(5), 756-770.

220. Singh, Sanjay Kumar (2008). Managing Knowledge in Software Company-Role of people's Biographical profiles'. *Udyog Pragati, The Journal for Practicing Manager.* 32 (4).

221. Soliman, F. & Spooner, K. (2000), "Strategies for Implementing Knowledge Management: Role of Human Resource Management", *Journal of Knowledge Management,* 4(4), 337-345.

222. Sourav Mukherji (2005). Knowledge Management Strategy in Software Services Organization: Straddling Codification and Personalization", *IIMB Management Review,* 17(3), 33-39. Also available online at: http://tejas- iimb. org/interviews/20.php.

223. Stone, R. D. (2011). The Real Value of Training, Tata McGraw Hill Education P. LTD, New Delhi.

224. Storck, J. & Hill, P. (2000). Knowledge Diffusion through Strategic Communities. *Sloan Management Review,* 41(2), 63-74.

225. Sung Chul Park. (2007). The Comparison of Knowledge Management Practices between Public and Private Organizations: An Exploratory Study. The Pennsylvania State University, 2007 Ph.D. Thesis.

226. Suresh, A. (2012). An Empirical Evaluation of Critical Success Factors of Knowledge Management for Organizational Sustainability. *Astitva International Journal of Commerce Management and Social Sciences,* 1(1), 1-12.

227. *Swanson, T.C. (2005). Knowledge Management: An Analysis of Knowledge Integrator Effectiveness in Managing Organizational Knowledge, Ph.D. Thesis ofCapella University.*

228. Tanriverdi, Huseyin (2005). Information Technology Relatedness, Knowledge Management Capability and Performance of Multi-business Firms', *MIS Quarterly,* 29(2).

229. *Teece, J.D. (2001), Strategies for Management of Knowledge Asset: the Role of Firm Structure and Industrial Context in Nonaka, I and Teece, D.J. (eds.), Management of Industrial Knowledge: Creation, Transfer and Utilization SAGE Publications, London.*

230. Ten WK (2005).A *Study of Knowledge Management Enablers, Processes and Organizational Performance.* The department of Business Administration at Chung Yuan Christian University. Master's Thesis

231. Thite, M. (2004) Managing People with New Economy: Targetted HR Practices that Persuade People to Unlock their Knowledge Power, Response Books, New Delhi.

232. *Tryon, Jr. C.A. (2012), Managing Organisational Knowledge" 3rd Generation Knowledge Management.... And Beyond CRC Press Taylor & Francis Group, London.*

233. Turner, J. R., Zimmerman, T. & Allen, J. (2012). Teams as a Sub-Process for Knowledge Management. *Journal of Knowledge Management,* 16(6), 963-977.

234. Types of Research Design (https://assets.pubpub.org/tv5qu5gn/01521405490221.pdf)

235. Ulrich, D. and Brockbank, W. (2005), The HR Value Proposition, Harvard Business School Press, Boston, Massachusetts.

236. Union Cabinet Committee, Minutes of Meeting on 10.12.2014

237. *Upadhyay, G. (2011), HR Interventions in the Age of Competitiveness: Analysis of HR-Based Change Interventions Introduced in Large Manufacturing Organizations, Reem Publications Pvt. Ltd. New Delhi.*

238. Vasudevan, Hari & Chawan, Anup. (2014). Demystifying Knowledge Management in Indian Manufacturing SMEs. *Procedia Engineering.* Available at 97. 10.1016/j.proeng.2014.12.324.

239. Vedpuriswar, A.V. (2009) Knowledge Management from A to Z: Concepts, Principles and Contemporary Practice; Vision Books, New Delhi, Mumbai, Hyderabad.

240. Viale, R. (2010) The Capitalisation of Knowledge Edward Elgan, UK.

241. Walliman, N. (2005). *Your Research Project,* Sage London.

242. Webster Dictionary.

243. Wickramasinghe, N. (2006), "Knowledge Creation in Schwartz, D.G. (ed) *Encyclopedia of Knowledge Management,* Idea Group Reference, Hershey, London.

244. *Wood, C. (2005), Ph.D. dissertation titled An empirical Examination of factors influencing work - unit Knowledge Management effectiveness in organizations, University of Texas at Arlington, USA.*

245. Woody, Clifford (1961) Research Method, Webster's New International Dictionary [As adapted from OJI University of Michigan]

246. Wu, I. L. & Chen, J. L. (2014). Knowledge Management Driven Firm Performance: The Roles of Business Process Capabilities and Organizational Learning. *Journal of Knowledge Management,* 18(6), 1141-1164.

247. Wu K.M. (2008). The Synergistic Effect of Market Orientation and Learning Orientation on Organizational Innovation and Organizational Performance: An Integration and Empirical Study

248. Yin, R.K. (2014) *Case Study Research Design and Methods,* Sage Publication, Thousand Oak, CA, USA

249. *Yu S.H.,et. al. (2004),Linking organizational Knowledge Management Drivers to Knowledge Management performance: an exploratory study. Proceeding of the 37th Hawaii International Conference on System Sciences, pp. 1-10.*

250. Zack, M.H. (1999) Developing a Knowledge Strategy, Califormia Management Review, 41 (3) 125-145

251. Zaim, H. (2006). Knowledge Management Implementation in IZGAZ. *Journal of Economic and social Research,* 8(2), 1-25.

APPENDIX A

Focus Group Discussion with Nodal officers of Knowledge Management:

Moderator:

Meenakshi Davar (Director HR)

Purpose:

The purpose of the Focus Group Discussion was to get an insight into the role played by HR in the implementation of Knowledge Management practices in POSOCO. The discussion proved very fruitful because the HR representative of the RLDC was also the earmarked nodal officer under the Knowledge Management policy.

- Brief Background provided to the participants of Focus Group:
- POSOCO is a PSU under the Ministry of Power and has a hierarchical structure. As a normal practice policies and guidelines flow from the top to the bottom. The Knowledge Management Policy was accordingly approved by the Board of Directors before its implementation.
- As a model case the Knowledge Management Policy was first implemented in SRLDC. It was found that it did not suffice certain issues in Finance Department. So the policy was modified and implemented through all the RLDCs in 2010.
- The Head of HR was the designated Nodal officer under the policy. He would ensure that the Policy when implemented covered all the 5 Department of the company i.e. System Operator, Market Operation, Finance & Accounts, Human Resource Management and Technology & Innovation.
- The responsibility assigned to the Nodal officer included:
  - ✓ To design Knowledge map for the RLDC that took into consideration the knowledge needs, the resources available and their categorization and the knowledge users.
  - ✓ To ensure that awareness was created in the RLDC about the Knowledge Management policy and about the Knowledge Management maps.
  - ✓ To conduct Knowledge sharing sessions and to identify and groom knowledge agents.

- With the involvement of coordinators from the other Department the Knowledge maps and matrices were finalized. These took into consideration the tacit and explicit knowledge available in the RLDC.

Conclusion of Focus Group Discussion:

- During this exercise certain knowledge gaps were identified. Subject matter experts were sought from within the organization and outside. Another exercise was to create the Corporate Yellow pages to declare the expert in every field. These Yellow pages were then circulated. This shows that HR aspects such as Processes are deeply related to driving Knowledge Management practices.
- It emerged from the Focus Group Discussions that while explicit Knowledge could be shared by the processes that had been envisaged in the Knowledge Management policy and through circulars, memos, letters, mails and the Knowledge portals; the challenge was to share the tacit Knowledge.
- It further emerged that sharing tacit Knowledge was dependent upon the 'culture' of the organization. This is where HR had a very important role to play along with the role of all other senior officers.
- Further it emerged that 'training' was one of the most important activity that helped in the implementation of Knowledge Management. Whether it was training about the Knowledge Management policy or importance of Knowledge sharing or training about the subject or training in the area of knowledge sharing skills or training in improving the attitude of the person.
- The Nodal Officers i.e. Heads of HR were of the unanimous opinion and correctly so, that the One year in-house, residential training given to the new entrants brought about a spirit of camaraderie that helped in the lifelong knowledge sharing training.
- 'Job rotation' in different areas and rotation to different RLDCs was considered a very important HR factor in Knowledge Management and sharing. This hinted to the Diversity and years of experience as KM Drivers.
- Overall, it emerged HR aspects such as processes and structures of Knowledge Management were extremely critical and crucial in the implementation of Knowledge Management.

APPENDIX B

In-depth Interview of EDs of RLDCs

Researcher	**Why do we need a Knowledge Management policy in POSOCO?**
ED (NLDC)	POSOCO is a knowledge based organization. The only assets we have are our people; and the knowledge and data that they have. All this Knowledge and information helps in the real time grid operation.
Researcher	**What do you think are the objectives of the Knowledge Management policy?**
ED (NERLDC)	The objectives are primarily to: - Leverage the expertise of our personnel across the organization. - Managing the intellectual assets of the company. - Improving knowledge exchange amongst employees. - Facilitating Organizational learning and innovation. - Enhancing employee motivation by facilitating resources for learning. - Harnessing the potential of Information Technology. - Improving POSOCO's efficiency and performance. - All leading to the smooth and secure functioning of the Indian Power Grid.
Researcher	**What process was followed by your RLDC to implement the policy and encourage the objectives of the policy?**
ED (SRLDC)	- The nodal officers were identified which were the Heads of HR in the RLDC. - They interacted with the identified executives across various Departments- System Operation, Market Operation, Finance, HR, Information and Technology. The Knowledge domains were identified i.e. the knowledge was captured. - Subsequently a knowledge base was made which helped classifying and codifying the knowledge collected.

	- Sharing of knowledge is done on a regular basis. This is done through meetings, knowledge portal, briefings, seminars, informal interactions. In fact it has become a way of life. - HR department has played a major role in as far as training and information sharing is concerned. As an ED of the RLDC I have enabled creation of friendly culture. We celebrate Birthdays and other such occasions. On every such get together we discuss one issue.
Researcher	**How did you harness the Explicit & Tacit knowledge?**
ED (WRLDC)	Explicit knowledge was captured by the representative of the concerned department. It was circulated either by mail or uploaded on the Intranet. Views, opinions and suggestions were also asked. Tacit Knowledge was again made easy by the HR practices and interventions. Any employee could post his knowledge, findings, problems, issues observations on the knowledge portal. This was open for reviews. Once a week we were conducting sessions in which people would share their experiences. This would then he documented and sent to other regions for comments. The owner of the information/ topic would be rewarded by appreciation and recognition.
Researcher	**As an ED of the RLDC what concrete steps did you take to ensure all the above could take place?**
ED (ERLDC)	- We ensured that the following were in place. - Establishment of Knowledge Portal. - Finalization of Corporate Yellow Pages. - Availability of Training Material: presentations, notes, articles, online courses. - Library- with relevant books, articles, papers. - Discussion forums and WhatsApp groups. - External Resources included links to sites, rules and regulations, practices and policies followed by other organization; seminars and discussions with external agencies. - Records of meetings, Discussion of the meetings with the Forum of Load Dispatchers and the meetings of the Regional Power Committees. - Once the knowledge maps, matrices and Yellow pages were made available we could take care of almost all the explicit knowledge and most of the tacit knowledge.

Researcher	**I am interested in the sharing of Tacit knowledge. How did you ensure that?**
ED (NRLDC)	As other RLDCs have told you the knowledge matrices and maps as well as the corporate yellow pages took care of most of the tacit information objectively. All employees were encouraged to describe their area of expertise and specialization. Informal discussions were first had with them so that they could feel comfortable; these discussions were formalized documents and papers which were uploaded on the POSOCO group. Opinions and views sought. Then we entired loaded on the portal.
Researcher	**What support did you get from the senior management?**
ED (NRLDC)	We have the whole hearted support of our CMD and our Directors. Their role in making POSOCO learning organization where human capital is the biggest asset is commendable. The organizational culture of caring (for the work) and sharing (of information) is primarily because of encouragement from the top leadership.
Researcher	**How do you see the role of HR Department towards the implementation of Knowledge Management?**
ED (WRLDC)	HR Department is the pivot of Knowledge Management. Right from framing of the policy, to its implementation the HR department has contributed in letter and spirit.
ED (ERLDC)	They started by conducting awareness programs about the policy. Trained employees in communication skills. Verbal and written. Brought about an attitude of sharing and contributing.
ED (SRLDC)	HR was sensitive to the needs of the people. When the pilot project was first implemented in SRLDC- some resistance and inertia was seen in the management and employees but the HR department managed to make the KM efforts sail through all difficulties.
Researcher	**Do you feel the current technology is adequate to take care of Knowledge Management?**
ED (NLDC)	Initially the technology was not as per requirement but over a period of time the technical experts and the IT department have ensured that the technology is well ahead and caters to all over requirements.
ED (WRLDC)	Yes, technology follows because there is a will created by the top management and the HR and we are all aware of the importance of Knowledge Management in POSOCO.

Researcher	**How do you measure the process of implementation of Knowledge Management?**
ED (NLDC)	This is measured by the number of participants that attend the Knowledge Management program. - Number of responses that we get when we circulate a paper. - The number of questions asked to the subject matter experts. - The number of hits on our knowledge portal. - Also informal sharing & discussions.
ED (SRLDC)	Even the number of people who visit the library.
ED (WRLDC)	By the number of papers published in every RLDC.
ED (ERLDC)	Sometimes by the number of employees who request for getting associated with external specialists.
Researcher	**Do you associate external experts in your Knowledge Management implementation process?**
ED (NLDC)	Yes, we send our employees to other SLDC's to learn and teach them we send our employees to neighboring and other countries to understand their issues and learn from them.
Researcher	**How do you plan to get the best from Knowledge Management in the future?**
ED (WRLDC)	As far as explicit and tacit knowledge is concerned we are quite happy and our efforts have borne fruits. As far as implicit knowledge is concerned we are planning to get it from our employees who have superannuated and those who are nearing superannuation by inviting them for meetings.

APPENDIX C

Elite Interview of Shri KVS Baba CMD POSOCO

Researcher	**Thank you so much for giving me some time. This is regarding my Study on HR Aspects of Knowledge Management in POSOCO.**
Sh.KVS Baba	I'm sure this study will be really useful for POSOCO. You don't have to thank me. This is the time we are together investing for the betterment and progress of the company.
Researcher	**What is your vision of Knowledge Management in POSOCO?**
Sh.KVS Baba	We have vast resources in terms of Human Capital and ours is a knowledge based company. The important thing is to manage these resources, build on them, use them, reuse them & capitalize the knowledge we have.
Researcher	**What would be your strategy towards Knowledge Management?**
Sh.KVS Baba	The Knowledge Management strategy is a part of the overall strategy of the company. India has the largest single Powergrid in the world running on one frequency. The RLDCs in conjunction with the SLDCs are responsible for monitoring the real time operation of the grid & dispatch of electricity. The Knowledge Management strategy enables information to flow enabling close monitoring of system parameters, such as frequency, voltages, line loading while facilitating inter-state & interregional power exchange.
Researcher	**How does the strategy translate into practice?**
Sh.KVS Baba	We have the Knowledge Management policy in line with the overall organization strategy. At the RLDC level I have my nodal officers who are responsible for the Knowledge matrices & knowledge maps which they make after interacting with communities of practice under various Departments. Dedicated teams are there at various RLDCs to acquire, create, share and use knowledge.
Researcher	**Do they have adequate resources to handle this task?**

Sh.KVS Baba	They have enough and also get whatever they require in terms of training, manpower, time & financial resources.
Researcher	**How do you see the Culture of the organization as a Driver for Knowledge Management?**
Sh.KVS Baba	Culture is one of the most important Driver in knowledge sharing. Right from the Chairman to the Liftman we all have no barriers to communication. Any policy, any practice and procedure, any problem is first shared on the intranet and everyone involved gives his suggestions/opinions. This we do as a matter of routine. Any kind of knowledge sharing is rewarded by way of recognition to the concerned employee. In this way, we encourage a knowledge sharing culture.
Researcher	**As a part of the Board of Directors how to do ensure knowledge sharing?**
Sh.KVS Baba	We have encouraged our employees to feel secure in their jobs. So knowledge is not treated as power to be kept within them. It is treated as an asset which when shared reaps multiple benefits to the employees. We encourage our employees to write papers & publish them; attend conferences & seminars. POSOCO is the coordinator of the FOLD (Forum of Load Dispatcher). We conduct meetings every quarter with the members of FOLD. These interactions help in sharing information knowledge, practices, procedures.
Researcher	**What kind of Competitive Advantage do you get by treating knowledge as an asset?**
Sh.KVS Baba	Sustained growth in the Power Sector is a key parameter to drive economic development. As an impartial grid operator POSOCO has no financial interest in any market segment. POSOCO ensures that diverse resources have equal access to the transmission network to ensure that load is balanced at all times. Our assets are Human Resources, SCADA (Supervisory Control and Data Acquisition), and Energy Management Systems along with software tools. We ensure that every day we improve ourselves. So, basically the competitive advantage is with respect to ourselves being better than what we are one day before.
Researcher	**How do you see Learning as an activity especially in the context of Knowledge Management?**

Sh.KVS Baba	POSOCO is a learning organization. The highest importance is given to learning and sharing. Whether it is classroom learning or experience sharing or conferences, or seminars, or meetings all employees are encouraged to participate.
Researcher	**How do you visualize the future of Knowledge Management in POSOCO?**
Sh.KVS Baba	My vision of Knowledge Management is, POSOCO being a knowledge provider to the State Load Dispatch Centers. To take up consultancy assignments at national and international level. To provide expertise and encourage writing of papers on how to manage grid disturbances, solar eclipses and integration of renewable energy in the grid.

APPENDIX D

QUESTIONNAIRE SURVEY OF KNOWLEDGE MANAGEMENT IN POSOCO

Dear Sir / Madam,

Greetings to you.

As a working professional and expert in your field of responsibility in POSOCO, you would be aware much more importance is given to the management of knowledge. I am pursuing my research study, "Human Resource Aspects of Human Knowledge Management: A Case Study of Power System Operation Corporation Limited". Knowledge Management (KM) is an umbrella term which refers to any deliberate effort to manage the knowledge of an organization's workforce, which can be achieved via a wide range of methods through the use of particular types of Information and Communication Technology. KM deals as much with people and how they acquire classify and disseminate knowledge through information technology. As part of this research, I need to assess the affairs of Knowledge Management in POSOCO from envisioning up to the evaluation of Knowledge Management in our Company.

A questionnaire dealing with various aspects of Knowledge Management is enclosed. Most of the questions pertain to the work areas of POSOCO and its business. You are ideally suitable to respond to this survey from your perspective of Knowledge Management in areas under your control and influence or the one in which you are working.

I assure you that your response will be used for the purpose of research and will remain confidential. Thank you very much for your participation.

(Meenakshi Davar)

PERSONAL INFORMATIONS

(Please put (√) mark in the box of your choice)

1. Name (optional):
2. Gender: Male □ Female □
3. Age:
   a) 23-30 years □
   b) 31-38 years □
   c) 39-46 years □
   d) 47-54 years □
   e) 55 years & above □
4. Please mention your highest educational qualification:
   a) Graduation □
   b) Post-Graduation □
   c) Doctorate □
5. Your current level in POSOCO:
   a) E1-E3 □
   b) E4-E5 □
   c) E6-E7A □
   d) E8 & above □
6. Department ______________
7. Total industry/work experience:
   a) 0-7 years □
   b) 8-14 years □
   c) 15-21 years □
   d) 22-28 years □
   e) 29 years & above □

8. Have you worked in any other public sector organization previously?

   Yes □ No □

9. Year ofjoining POSOCO ____________

10. Are you associated with Knowledge Management work?

    Yes □ No □

QUESTIONNAIRE SURVEY OF KNOWLEDGE MANAGEMENT IN POSOCO

Scale: SD (Strongly Disagree), D (Disagree), NA/DA (Neither Agree nor Disagree) A (Agree), SA (Strongly Agree)

Please put a (V) mark in the box of your choice.

		Your Response				
	Question			**NA/DA**		
	Knowledge Management has taken place in POSOCO					
	Most of the time I find that it is pretty time consuming to access any document in my department					
	In my department, Knowledge Management activities are taking place satisfactorily					
	There are lots of documents/reports lying unutilized in my department					
	I have come across situations in work where the same mistake done by someone in the past is being repeated					
	In my opinion, there are very few Subject Matter Experts available in my department					
	Employees in POSOCO are having informal, open-					
	minded and collaborative working					
	Knowledge is treated as an object in my department					
	There are appropriate values and mind set towards Knowledge Management amongst employees of my Company					
	The personnel in POSOCO are oriented towards Knowledge Management very positively					

	Knowledge Management is being used constantly as a business strategy					
	Aesthetically oriented culture for Knowledge Management is a way of life in POSOCO					
	Information regarding relevant topics are readily available to the employees in my Company					
	Knowledge is treated as a resource/asset in POSOCO					
	'Personal best practices can be shared with other employees easily' can be said as a part of job in POSOCO					
	Knowledge is used as an important and critical resource in my department					
	POSOCO has got a vision in Knowledge Management which properly articulates its knowledge needs					
	Reward and recognition for suggestion of Best Practices, have been incorporated in POSOCO's annual plan					
	Transfer of Knowledge and Best Practices are taking place in day-to-day working of employees					
	Innovation and Knowledge Creation are a way of life in my Company					
	Information about the outcome of implementing Best					
	Practices is translated in practice in my department / company					
	Dedicated staff for Knowledge capture and acquisition are earmarked in my department					
	Information regarding process description can be uploaded in the Organization's Knowledge Bank at Power Portal, the intranet of Company					
	The organization has enabling structures in terms of hierarchy and communication flows that facilitates knowledge sharing					
	A cohesive and powerful vision of the organization is shared across the workforce to promote need for strategic thinking at all levels					

	My organization has an Experts Database that can be used by Employees to locate experts within the organization					
	I use Knowledge maps and matrices of my Company for knowledge requirements					
	The organization provides incentives to motivate users to learn from experiences and use the Knowledge Management System of POSOCO					
	The organization continuously strives for Knowledge acquisition, dissemination and capture for its employees					
	Employees are provided 'instant messenger' or 'chat' - video conferencing facilities through which they can have conversations with their colleagues					
	The Intranet site provides an Online Discussion Forum in which employees can share information and post their doubts					
	Employees are provided the 'blogging' platform wherein they can share their experiences through blogs					
	Employees can upload their documents or reports to Power Portal					
	Employees can download any document they want from the Intranet site/portal					
	My organization has a 'Chief Knowledge Officer' (or equivalent) who is responsible for managing the knowledge-related activities					
	I visit Power Portal for my knowledge needs					
	All programs have periodic team meetings to review the progress and discuss issues pertaining to the work					
	I contact subject matter experts by using my Corporate Yellow Pages					
	Our Company has got collegial, flat, team based, open door policy					
	We strive to have matrix form of structure of Company					

	Brick-and-mortar model (dealing with the customer face-to-face) structure is followed in our Company					
	Every employee is imparted training required by him for his job					
	Knowledge Management related training is identified as part of organizational training need assessment					
	My organization has a central repository / library where all the necessary documents/reports are stored					
	All important documents in my organization are available in the electronic format					
	Documents pertaining to past research programs are					
	arranged in such a manner that they can be easily accessed and used as and when necessary					
	There are enough Meeting/Conference rooms available for Team meetings and discussions					
	Employees/Teams can discuss work through TeleConferencing (i.e. through telephones, VOIP, Mobile, etc.)					
	Notice boards kept at various vantage points in my organization plays an important role in informing me of various news and events					
	In my department/organization, every program has a closure meeting to critically review the performance					
	Within the team/department, employees share their knowledge in an informal manner					
	There is very good interaction between departments/ groups in my organization					
	My organization's newsletter/bulletin will inform me about the latest happenings in your organization and outside					
	My organization's intranet/website plays a vital role in disseminating information to the employees					

	All important communications in my organization are sent to me through circulars or memos in electronic environment					
	In my organization, every employee is encouraged to periodically produce *documents* in the form of technical reports, journal papers, presentations, articles, etc.					
	Information about locations of project reports, research facilities and equipment available are displayed prominently in my organization					
	A Communities of Practice exists in POSOCO.					
	Company has got proper facility for Research & Development					
	Acquisition of knowledge is a regular practice in our Company					
	Use of knowledge is a way of work life in every employees' job					
	There is Knowledge Management Cell in POSOCO which collects knowledge nuggets and disseminates it through Power Portal					
	My organization sponsors trips for employees to international/national conferences and seminars					
	I have free access to any information I want irrespective of where it resides in my organization					
	In my organization, it is mandatory for every employee to document insights *(in the form of best practices, lessons learnt etc.)* from the work/project					
	My organization has a directory of personnel containing information of names of people, their designation, division, program, phone number, email, etc.					
	My organization arranges seminars/ lectures by external experts on a periodic basis					
	The mission and objectives of Knowledge Management are clearly understood by employees propagated throughout POSOCO					

	Recognition in form of titles, certificates & commendation letters are periodically awarded to the contributors of knowledge					
	All employees in my department are willing to share their knowledge with others					
	My superiors fully endorse my way of handling Knowledge Management related issues					
	I feel that I have got support from Management for Knowledge Management					
	My organization actively promotes a 'culture of experimentation' that encourages employees to try new ideas and take risks					
	My organization periodically gives special awards to employees who make significant contributions to the organization					
	My organization measures and manages its intellectual capital (IC) in a systematic way					
	POSOCO publishes regular intellectual achievements and reports it to its external stakeholders					
	The evaluation of work/projects that are completed successfully has been done in my organization from KM point of view.					

THANK YOU VERY MUCH FOR YOUR HELP & COOPERATION

APPENDIX E

Knowledge Map and Matrices of POSOCO

Analysis & Feedback

I. Knowledge Map

Strategy	To aim far continuous improvement in the functioning of various departments
Knowledge Requirement	**Analysis & Feedback to the concerned Depll./ Authorities/ Organizations/ ERCs** • Real Time Grid Operation • Marta t Operation • Regulatory Affairs • Operational Planning • Capacity Building « Logistics • HR
Knowledge Gap	• Capacity Building
Knowledge Asset	• Books / Terder Documents. Manuals • Different Websites • Training / Workshops etc. • Web Groups • Standards • Regulations / Order / EA'03 etc. • Presentations, Documents
Knowledge Domain	**Analysis & Feedback to the concerned Depll./ Authorities/ Organizations/ ERCs**

Analysis & Feedback

II. Knowledge Matrix

What knowledge is needed?	Who has it?	Who needs it?	Where is it?	Is it Tacit or Explicit?	Is it Routine or Non Routine?	What issue(s) does it address?
Operational constraints	Central Roam	All stakeholders	Control Roams/ Stakeholders	Explicit/ Tacit	Routine	Helps is GRID Management
Market Operations	NLDC	All stakeholders	NLDC	Explicit	Routine	Capacity Building
CERC Regulations & Orders	CERC	All stakeholders	Regulations/ Order	Explicit	Routine	Policy inputs/ Parliamentary Questions/ Smooth Operation of GRID
EA'03/NEP/ Tariff Policy etc	MOP	All stakeholders	Websites/ Books	Explicit	Routine	Policy inputs/ Parliamentary Questions/ Smooth Operation of GRID
Disaster Management	NLDC	All stakeholders	Websites/ Books	Explicit	Routine	Capacity Building
Capacity Building	HRD	Employees in all Departments	Need Analysis/ Websites/ Books/ Training/ Workshops etc.	Explicit/ Tacit	Routine	Capacity Building
SCADA/EMS	Employees in System Operation and Logistics	Control Roam	Manuals and Training Documents	Explicit/ Tacit	Routine	System Operations and maintenance of SCADA/ EMC system

Disaster Management

I. Knowledge Map

Strategy	• Prevention, Mitigation, Preparedness, Switch Response and Capacity Buildirg far Disaster Management in the Power Sector.
Knowledge Requirement	• Disaster Maragement • Importance of Disaster Management for Power Sector • Disaster Maragement Policy • Channels of Communication during Disaster • MOP Guidelines • Functions of NLDC/RLDC/SLDC/ Power station/ Sub Station during Disaster
Knowledge Gap	• Capacity Buildirg
Knowledge Asset	• Different Websites • Policy an Disaster Management • Web Groups • Crisis & Disaster Management Plan for Power Sector • MOP Guidelines
Knowledge Domain	Disaster Management

Disaster Management

II. Knowledge Matrix

What knowledge is needed?	Who has it?	Who reeds it?	Where is it?	Is it Tacit or Explicit?	Is it Routine or Non Routine?	What issue(s) does it address?
MOP Guidelines	All Stakeholders	All Stakeholders	Books/ Campendiums	Explicit	Routine	Capacity Building quick Response for Disaster Maragement
Functions of All Stakeholders	All Stakeholders	All Stakeholders	Books/ Campendiums/ Websites	Explicit	Routine	Capacity Building for Disaster Maragement
Comunication Channels during Disaster	All Stakeholders	All Stakeholders	Books/ Campendiums/ Websites	Explicit	Routine	Capacity Building for Disaster Maragement
Black Start Procedures / Restoration Procedures	NLDC/ RLDCs/ SLDCs	All Stakeholders	Books/ Campendiums/ Websites	Explicit	Routine	Capacity Building for Disaster Maragement
Knowledge of Back-up System available	NLDC/ RLDCs/ SLDCs	All Stakeholders	Books/ Campendiums/ Websites	Explicit	Routine	Capacity Building for Disaster Maragement

Human Resource Department

I. Knowledge Map

Strategy	• To facilitate development of Human Capital in POSOCO as to enable Operation of Regional, national (and now international) Grids to facilitate transfer of electric power with reliability, Security ard Economy.
Knowledge Requirement	• Process Charts for Employee Benefits and Employee Facilities to ensure Standardization, streamlining and process efficiency. • Detailed information regarding various Learning and Development (LGD) conducted during the year. • Information regarding latest trends, practices and processes in Training, Employee Benefits, Leadership Development etc. • Capacity Building in Rajbhasha to facilitate more and more correspsndence/ information sharing in Rajbhasha. • Resource Centre for NLDC - Subscription to technical journals (online and otherwise), collection of refererce books etc.
Knowledge Gap	• Information regarding employee benefits (amount spent, number of employee availing etc.) could be further streamlined by making it centrally available. • Centralized Database regarding Module Structures for L&C programmes faculty information could be further organized. Analysis of Training Feedback (on trainer/ Modules etc. can be documented by employees and made available for further information sharing). • Tour Reports/ Training Logs for employees to record their key learnings and activities in capacity building workshops. L & D programmes for the purpsse of Streamling Training Programmes and Knowledge Sharing. • Processes for Administering various employees benefits, facilities etc. can be documented. • Capacity Building for HR on latest Trends, practices and Processes in Learning and Development, Employee Benefits, Facilitating Leadership Development.

Knowledge Asset	• HRIS • HR Policy Manuals / Online Formats and Policy Details • Employee Data • Learning and Development details: Employee nomination • Monthly 1E Reports • Monthly eNewsletter • Web Groups • POWERGRID HR Website • Professional Networkirg Websites (linkdln, NHRDM, SHRM etc.) • Online Rajbhasha websites (Shabdkosh etc.)
Knowledge Domain	• Procurement • Maintenance • Development • Separation of Human Resources

Human Resource Department

II. Knowledge Matrix

What knowledge is needed?	Who has it?	Who needs it?	Where is it?	Is it Tacit or Explicit?	Is it Routine or Mon Routine?	What issue(s) does it address?
Processes of Employee Benefits and Employee Facilities	HR	Stakeholders	Tacit, Explicit Repositories	Explicit	Routine	Streamlining Processes, Efficiency, Employee Communication
Detailed Information regarding various Learning find Development (L & D) conducted during the year	HR	Stakeholders	Partly with HR/ Partly Tacit	Explicit	Routine	Process, Policy Improvement in Learning and Development practices across the levels
Information regarding latest trends, practices and processes in Training, employee Benefits, Leadership Development etc	Subject Matter Experts (SMEs)	HR	Various Training organizations/ Online/Other Resources	Explicit	Nan-Routine	Capacity Buildirg for HR Professionals
Rajbhasha	Subject Matter Experts	All employees	Subject Matter Experts/ Online, Physical resource centers	Explicit / Tacit	Routine	Capacity Buildirg in Rajbhasha (Hindi)

Logistics Document

I. Knowledge Map

Strategy	Td operate Regional, National (and now international) Grids ta facilitate transfer of electric power with reliability, security and economy.
Knowledge Requirement	• Logistics • Administration • C & M • Finance and Accounts • FOLD • HR/HRD • MIS • Support & Services
Knowledge Gap	• Capacity Building
Knowledge Asset	• Books/Tenders Documents, manuals • Different Websites • Training/Workshops etc. • Web Groups • Accounting and Audit Standards
Knowledge Domain	• Logistics

Logistics Document

II. Knowledge Matrix

What knowledge is needed?	Who has it?	Who needs it?	Where is it?	Is it Tacit or Explicit?	Is it Routine or Non Routine?	What issue(s) does it address?
Civil/ Electrical maintenance	Employees in HR department	Employees in all departments	Manuals and booklets/ contract documents	Explicit/ Tacit	Routine	Support NLDC/ RLDCs in performance of its duties
HR (Admin)	Employees in HR department	Employees in all departments	Manuals and booklets and on web site	Explicit	Routine	Support NLDC/ RLDCs in performance of its duties
MIS	Employees in System Operation and Logistics	All Stakeholders	Employees in all departments	Explicit	Routine	Policy Inputs & smooth operation of the Grid
FOLD	FOLD secretariat	All Stakeholders	MOM/ Reports/ Regulations/ Orders	Explicit	Non-Routine	Policy Inputs & smooth operation of the Grid
Consultancy	Employees in all departments	Employees in all departments	Books/ Regulations/ Manuals/ Softwares/ Stakeholders/ websites	Explicit/ Tacit	Non-Routine	Earning and Capacity building in organization
Coordination with CERC / RLDCs/ MOP/ RPC/ CEA/ FOR	Employees in System Operation and Logistics	All Stakeholders	Books/ Regulations/ Manuals/ Softwares/ Stakeholders/ websites	Explicit	Routine	Policy Inputs & smooth operation of the Grid
IT Support	Employees in IT Department	Employees in all departments	Books / Manuals / Softwares / websites	Explicit/ Tacit	Routine	Support NLDC/ RLDCs in performance of its duties
Knowledge of DG set operation & maintenance	C & M group	Employees in all departments	Manuals & procedures	Explicit	Routine	Smooth operation of essential support services

Switchgear panel operation & Maintenance	C & M group	Employees in all departments	Manuals & procedures	Explicit	Routine	Smooth operation of essential support services
A/C plant maintenance	C & M group	Employees in all departments	Manuals & procedures	Explicit	Routine	Smooth operation of essential support services
Capability of handling support activities such as supervision of maintenance-contract, repair & trouble shooting of basic electrical & civil installation etc.	C & M group	Employees in all departments	Manuals, WPP. Files	Explicit	Routine	Smooth operation of essential support services
POWERGRID contractual procedures, General terns & condition of contract	C & M group	Employees in all departments	Manuals, documents, pc, files	Explicit	Routine	Procurement of goods ir right quality and quantity in time and at right price
WPP, DOP	C & M group	Employees in all departments	Respective manuals	Explicit	Routine	Procurement of goods ir right quality and quantity in time and at right price
Awareness of product specifications, vendors etc.	C & M and other group	Employees in all departments	Manuals, documents, pc, files, websites, advertisements	Explicit	Non-Routine	Procurement of goods in right quality and quantity in time and at right price

Market Operations

I. Knowledge Map

Strategy	To operate Regional, National (and now international) Grids to facilitate transfer of electric power with reliability, security and economy.
Knowledge Requirement	**Market Operation** • Calculation af ATG/TTC for Market Operations • Commercial aspects • CERC Regulations - Open access, Power Markets, IEGC 2010 • Open Access Regulations • Procedures for Collective Transactions • Procedures for Bilateral Transactions • Products Traded in Electricity markets in India
Knowledge Gap	• Capacity Building for shift operators
Knowledge Asset	• Different Websites • Exposure to State of the art Technologies through Training, Seminar etc. • Regulations / order/IEGC etc. • Technical hand books • Web Groups
Knowledge Domain	• Market Operation

Market Operations

II. Knowledge Matrix

What knowledge is needed?	Who has it?	Who needs it?	Where is it?	Is it Tacit or Explicit?	Is it Routine or Non Routine?	What issue(s) does it address?
Calculation of ATC/TTC for Market Operations	CERC	Stakeholders	Online/ Compendiums	Explicit/ Tacit	Routine	Capacity Building
Products Traded on Power Exchanges	CERC	Stakeholders	Regulations/ Orders	Explicit	Routine	Capacity Building
Open Access Regulations	CERC	Stakeholders	Online/ Compendiums	Explicit	Routine	Capacity Building
Commercial Aspects	CERC	Stakeholders	Online/ Compendiums	Explicit	Routine	Capacity Building
Various Regulations pertaining to Market Operations	CERC	Stakeholders	Online/ Compendiums	Explicit	Routine	Capacity Building
CERC Regulations- Open Access, Power Markets, IEGC 2010	CERC	Stakeholders	Online/ Compendiums	Explicit	Routine	Capacity Building
Procedures for Collective Transactions	CERC	Stakeholders	Online/ Compendiums	Explicit	Routine	Capacity Building
Procedures for Bilateral Transactions	CERC	Stakeholders	Online/ Compendiums	Explicit	Routine	Capacity Building
Impact and role of Markets in Power System	MO, OS, GM.	MO, GM, F & A	Books, Literatures	Explicit	Non-Routine	To facilitate the functioning of Market
Power Exchange concept, operational procedures	MO, OS, GM.	MO. GM	Regulatory orders, By laws for exchanges, procedures	Explicit	Non-Routine	To facilitate the functioning of Market

Knowledge on Open access participants, traders, byers-contact details etc.	MO, OS	MO, GM, F & A	CERC MMC reports, Application details	Explicit	Routine	To facilitate the functioning of Market
Calculation of UI	MO, OS	MO, GM, F & A	Regulations	Explicit	Routine	To facilitate the functioning of Market
Handling pool account	MO, OS	MO, F & A	Regulations & Procedures	Explicit	Routine	To facilitate the functioning of Market
Payment handling, lanes & duties	MO and F & A	MO, F & A	laws/acts on taxes and duties	Explicit	Routine	To facilitate the functioning of Market
Accounling strategies, book keeping	MO, F & A	MO, F & A	Documents and manuals	Explicit	Non-Routine	To facilitate the functioning of Market
List of SEM meter locations	MO	MO, OA, GM. SCADA	Documents and procedures	Explicit	Non-Routine	To facilitate the functioning of Market
Metering principle	MO	MO, OA, GM. SCADA	Documents & procedures	Explicit	Non-Routine	To facilitate the functioning of Market
Main meter, back-up meter, check meter concept	MO and OS	MO, OA, GM, SL	CEA Regulation on Meters	Explicit	Non-Routine	To facilitate the functioning of Market
SEM Data validation	MO	MO & GM, SL	Metering documents and procedures	Explicit	Routine	To facilitate the functioning of Market
Vendors of Meters	MO	MO	Files and other documents	Explicit	Non-Routine	To facilitate the functioning of Market

Features of Meters	MO, OA	MO, OA, GM, SL	GEA Regulations & Metering documents and procedures	Explicit	Non-Routine	To facilitate the functioning of Market
Processing meter data through metering softwares	MO	MO, OA, GM, SL	Metering documents and procedures	Explicit	Routine	To facilitate the functioning of Market
List of Generators/ IPPs	MO, OS, GM	MO, GM, SL	Operating procedures and MIS data base	Explicit	Routine	Empowering MO executives with current system status
Logic of Drawl/ Injection calculation	MO, OS, GM	MO, GM, SL	Operating procedures and MIS data base	Explicit	Non-Routine	Empowering MO executives with current system status
Report making/ uploading	MO, OA, GM	MO, OA, GM, SL(IT)	Operating procedures	Explicit	Routine	Information sharing
Database concept	MO(MB), sum	MO(MIS), GM, OA, SLflT)	Books Literatures and trading documents	Explicit	Non-Routine	Information sharing
Coordination with stakeholders, RPC Secretariat for OCC, Commercial, TCC, RPC meetings	MO, GM, SL	MO, GM, SL	Agendas, MOMs	Explicit/ Tacit	Routine	Coordination for transparent operation, dispute resolution & Image building

Real Time Grid Operation

I. Knowledge Map

Strategy	Td operate Regional, National (and now international) Grids to facilitate transfer of electric power with reliability, security and economy.
Knowledge Requirement	**Real Time Grid Operation** • Indian Electricity Grid code/Black Start Procedure • Load Forecasting • Ul Regulations • SCADA, IT and Telemetering • Scheduling and Despatch • System Security Aspects • Basics of Power Station Operation • Substation layout schemes • Communication Skills
Knowledge Gap	• Detailed Knowledge of Regional Grids • Detailed Knowledge of Generating Stations • Detailed Knowledge of Protection System
Knowledge Asset	• Exposure to State of the art Technologies through Trainirg, Seminar etc. • GRID Standards/IEGC • Restoration Procedure/ Ul Regulations/ Congestion Regulation • Technical hand books • Web Groups
Knowledge Domain	**Real Time Grid Operation**

Real Time Grid Operation

II. Knowledge Matrix

What knowledge is needed?	Who has it?	Who needs it?	Where is it?	Is it Tacit or Explicit?	Is it Routine or Non Routine?	What issue(s) does it address?
System Studies	Employees in Technical Services Departments	Emplsyees in all departments	Books/ Regulations/ Manuals/ Softwares/ Stakeholders/ websites	Explicit	Routine	Dealing with reliability issues
Reliability Coordination	Employees in Technical Services Departments	Emplsyees in all departments	Books/ Regulations/ Manuals/ Softwares/ Stakeholders/ websites	Explicit / Tacit	Routine	For smooth and Reliable operation of the GRID
Ancillary Services	Employees in Technical Services Departments	Emplsyees in all departments	Beaks/ Regulations/ Manuals/ Softwares/ Stakeholders/ websites	Explicit	Routine	For smooth and Reliable operation of the GRID
MIS Reports to MOP/ CERC/ POWERGRID	Employees of Grid Management Department	Stakeholders	Control Room	Explicit	Routine	Knowledge dissemination / Inputs to policy making
Statutory Functions of NLDC/ RLDCs	Employees of Grid Maragement Department	Emplsyees in all departments	Electricity Act/ Grid Cade/ Grid Standard	Explicit	Routine	Fulfills the statutory Requirement
Coordination with & Supervision of RLDCs/ SLDCs	Employees of Grid Maragement Department	GM/OS/MO	Electricity Act/ Grid Cade/ Grid Standard	Explicit / Tacit	Routine	For smooth and Reliable operation of the GRID
Approval and Scheduling of Collective Transactions	Employees of Grid Maragement Department	GM/OS/MO	Procedure af Collective Transactions	Explicit	Routine	Helps in Power Market Development

Dynamic/ transient Stability concepts	Employees of Grid Maragement Department	GM/OS/MO	PSSE hand book, Books, documents, journals, different papers, web groups	Explicit	Non - Routine	Capacity building of the Grid Operators
Generator Dynamics	Employees of Grid Maragement Department	GM/OS/MO	PSSE hand book, Books, documents, journals, different papers, web groups	Explicit	Non - Routine	Capacity building of the Grid Operators
Generator Capability curve	Employees of Grid Maragement Department	GM/OS/MO	PSSE hand book, Books, documents, journals, different papers, web groups	Explicit	Non - Routine	Capacity building of the Grid Operators
Details on Grid elements	Employees of Grid Maragement Department	GM/OS/MO	Operating procedures, Documents, reports, PC, files	Explicit	Routine	to Know the basics of Grid operation
Network up to at least 132KV level	Employees of Grid Maragement Department	GM/OS/MO	Operating procedures, Documents, reports, PC, files	Explicit	Routine	to Know the basics of Grid operation
Line length, type of conductors etc. of important lines	Employees of Grid Maragement Department	GM/OS/MO	Operating procedures, Documents, reports, PC, files	Explicit	Routine	to Know the basics af Grid operation
Availability of Reactors/ Transformers along with rating	Employecs of Grid Maragement Department	GM/OS/MO	Operating procedures, Documents, reports, PC, files	Explicit	Routine	to Know the basics of Grid operation
Transformer Tap positions	Employees of Grid Maragement Department	GM/OS/MO	Operating procedures, Documents, reports, PC, files	Explicit	Routine	to Know the basics of Grid operation

Generation details	Employees of Grid Maragement Department	GM/OS/MO	Operating procedures, Documents, reports, PC, files	Explicit	Routine	to Know the basics of Grid operation
Installed capacity, Effective capacity, Decalred capacity of each unit	Employees of Grid Maragement Department	GM/OS/MO	Operating procedures, Documents, reports, PC, files	Explicit	Routine	to Know the basics of Grid operation
Availability of TCSC, FSC, SVC etc. along with settings	Employees of Grid Maragement Department	GM/OS/MO	Operating procedures, Documents, reports, PC, files	Explicit	Routine	to Know the basics of Grid operation
Availability of HVDC stations	Employees of Grid Maragement Department	GM/OS/MO	Operating procedures, Documents, reports. PC, files	Explicit	Routine	to Know the basics of Grid operation
Ramp rates of HVDCs	Employees of Grid Maragement Department	GM/OS/MO	Operating procedures, Documents, reports, PC, files	Explicit	Routine	to Know the basics of Grid operation
Reactor/ capacitor Banks	Employees of Grid Maragement Department	GM/OS/MO	Operating procedures, Documents, reports, PC, files	Explicit	Routine	to Know the basics of Grid operation
characteristics of FACTS	Employees of Grid Maragement Department	GM/OS/MO	Operating procedures, Documents, reports, PC, files	Explicit	Routine	to Know the basics of Grid operation
characteristics of SVCs/ SCs	Employees of Grid Maragement Department	GM/OS/MO	Operating procedures, Documents, reports, PC, files	Explicit	Routine	to Know the basics of Grid operation
Knowledge of flow gates	Employees of Grid Maragement Department	GM/OS/MO	Operating procedures, Documents, reports, PC, files	Explicit	Routine	to Know the basics of Grid operation

Knowledge of daily as well as seasonal load patterns	Employees of Grid Maragement Department	GM/OS/MO	Operating procedures, Documents, reports, PC, files	Explicit	Routine	to Know the basics of Grid operation
Knowledge of power flow limit of various lines	Employees of Grid Maragement Department	GM/OS/MO	Operating procedures, Documents, reports, PC, files	Explicit	Routine	to Know the basics of Grid operation
Assessing state of the system	Experierced And Knowledgeable Executive	GM/OS/MO	EMC, Experience, skill set	Tacit	Routine	Capacity ro predict exigencies
ascertaining impact of outage	OS GROUP	GM/OS/MO	documents, reports, PC, files, SCADA	Explicit/ Tacit	Routine	–
Database management	GM GROUP	GM/OS/MO	documents, reports, files	explicit	Routine	tools for record keeping
OCC meeting requirements and handling	GM GROUP	GM/OS/MO	documents, reports, files	explicit	Routine	cahesive working with stakeholder
Incidence/ disturbance analysis	OS AND GM GROUP	GM/OS/MO	documents, reports, files	Explicit / Tacit	Non - Routine	Dealing with reliability issues
Scheduling procedure	OS, WO AND GM GROUP	GM/OS/MO	IEGC, Operating procedure	Explicit	Routine	Implementing regulatory directives
Knowledge of Grid Code	OS, MO AND GM GROUP	GM/OS/MO	IEGC, Operating procedure	Explicit	Routine	–
Accessing reports	OS AND GM GROUP	GM/OS/MO	Documents, reports, PC, files	Explicit	Routine	For maintaining records
uploading/ downloading files	OS AND GM GROUP	GM/OS/MO	Documents, reports, PC, files	Explicit	Routine	–
Shift Activiily Register update	GM GROUP	GM/OS/MO	Experience, discussion, operating procedure	Explicit	Routine	–
Real Time Outage Coordination	GM GROUP	GM/OS/MO	IEGC, Operating procedure	Explicit / Tacit	Routine	For managing exigency and restoration of grid incident

Black start	OS AND GM GROUP	GM/OS/MO	Black start procedure, experience	Explicit / Tacit	Non - Routine	–
Disturbance Handling	OS AND GM GROUP	GM/OS/MO	Black start procedure, experience	Tacit	Non - Routine	–
VIP visits Handling	All Departments	All Departments	Experience	Tacit	Non - Routine	Knowledge Dissemination / Image building exercise

REC Mechanism

I. Knowledge Map

Strategy	Operationalization at REC Mechanism as Central Agency
Knowledge Requirement	**Renewable Energy Certificate Mechanism** • Policies an Renewable energy • CERC/SERC Regulations ard orders • EA'03, National Electricity Policy • Concept of Renewable Erergy Certificate • Approved Procedure for REC Mechanism • Functioning of Pawer Excharge • Software & Hardware
Knowledge Gap	• Capacity Building for stakeholders of REC Mechanism • International Experience of REC • Related policies like PAT, CDM etc.
Knowledge Asset	• National Electricity Policy/IEGC/GRID cade • Relevant CERC/SERC Regulations & Orders • Tariff Regulations for Renewable by CIERC/SERC • Seminars/Workshops etc. • Web Groups • Different Websites • RPO Report by CRISIL
Knowledge Domain	Renewable Energy Certificate Mechanism

REC Mechanism

II. Knowledge Matrix

What knowledge is needed?	Who has it?	Who needs it?	Where is it?	Is it Tacit or Explicit?	Is it Routine or Non Routine?	What issue(s) does it address?
Procedure for issuance of REC	All the stakeholders	All the stakeholders	Online / Compendiums	Explicit	Routine	Provide institutional Mechanism for issuance of REC
Relevant Regulations/ orders by CERC/ SERCs	All fhe stakeholders	All the stakeholders	Online/ Compendiums	Explicit	Routine	Provide institutional Mechanism for issuance of REC
Hardware	NLDC	NLDC	Presently on NRLDC server to be shifted to NIC server	Explicit	Routine	Facilitates the process of issuance of REG
Software	NLDC	All Ihe stakeholders	Presently on NRLDC server to be shifted to NIC server	Explicit	Routine	Facilitates the process of issuance of REC
Functions of State Nodal Agency/ Central Agency/ SLDC etc	All the stakeholders	All the stakeholders	Online/ Compendiums	Explicit	Routine	Provide institutional Mechanism for issuance of REC

Regulatory Affairs

I. Knowledge Map

Strategy	To Operate Regional. National (and now international) Grids to facilitate transfer af electric power with Reliability, Security and Economy.
Knowledge Requirenents	**Regulatory Affairs** • Regulatory furctisns of RLDCs / NLDC • Functions of Regulatory Commissions (CERC / SERCs) • Knowledge of EA, various Regulations, Orders and Amendment there of. • Understanding of Electricity Act, 2003, National Electricity Plan, National electricity Policy. • Understanding different Regulations and Rules issued by CEA, CERC, APTEL and Courts.
Knowledge Gap	Catalog including snapshot of relevant passages, of regulations can be made available.
Knowledge Asset	• Capacity building workshops on Regulatory Affairs. • Different Websites. • Technical hand books. • Web groups. • Regulations / order / EA'03 etc. • Presentations, Documents.
Knowledge Domain	Regulatory affairs

Regulatory Affairs

II. Knowledge Matrix

Whst knowledge is needed?	Who has it?	Who needs it?	Where is it?	Is it Tacit or Explicit?	Is it Routine or Non-Routine?	What issue(s) does it address?
Regulatory functions of RLDCs/ NLDC	Available via Open Sources	Stakeholders	Online/ Compendiums	Explicit	Non-Routine	Implementation of regulatory & statutory functions
Functions of Regulatory Commissions (CERC / SERCs)	Available via Open Sources	Stakeholders	Online/ Compendiums	Explicit	Non-Routine	Implementation of regulatory & statutory functions
Electricity Act 2003, National Electricity Plan, National Electricity Policy	Available via Open Sources	Stakeholders	Online/ Compendiums	Explicit	Non-Routine	Implementation of regulatory & statutory functions
Different Regulations and Rules issued by CEA, CERC APTEL and Courts	Available via Open Sources	Stakeholders	Online/ Compendiums	Explicit	Non-Routine	Implementation of regulatory & statutory functions

SCADA/EMS Department

I. Knowledge Map

Strategy	Ta operate Regional, National (and now international) Grids to facilitate transfer of electric power with reliability, security and economy.
Knowledge Requirement	SCADA / EMS / IT • DBMS • IT Hardware and Software • New technofogies in SCADA/EMS • SCADA functions/ Real Time Network Applications • Vender specific SCADA online system • System Backup • Cyber Security • Latest Communication Profocols • WAMS Technology • CIM Structure
Knowledge Gap	Capacity Building in the fallowing areas: • Data Acquisition • Real Time Network Applications • Networking • Cyber Security
Knowledge Asset	• Different Websites • Technical hard books • Different standards • Exposure to State of the art Technologies through Training, Seminar etc. • Tender Documents, manuals regarding usage of SCADA and EMS functions etc. • Web Groups
Knowledge Domain	SCADA/EMS/IT

SCADA/EMS Department

II. Knowledge Matrix

What knowledge is needed?	Who has it?	Who needs it?	Where is it?	Is it Tacit or Explicit?	Is it Routine orNon - Routine?	What issue(s) does it address?
Knowledge of Regional Network	Employees in all departments	Employees in all departments	Manuals / booklets / web site / information provided by stakeholders	Explicit	Routine	knowing and updation af Regional Network
Installed Capacity of Generation On All India Basis	—	Employees in all departments	Manuals / booklets / web site / information provided by stakeholders	Explicit	Routine	Technical Issues of Generating Stations and installed capacity details
Knowledge of Transmission lines	Employees in System Operation ard Logistics Deptt.	Employees in System Operation and Logistics	Manuals / booklets / web site / information provided by stakeholders	Explicit	Routine	Technical issues of Transmission lines and configuration ard technical parameters
Knowledge on Substations	—	Employees in System Operation and Logistics	Manuals / booklets / web site / information provided by stakeholders	Explicit	Routine	Maintaining the quality of Supplier items and works
Knowledge of SCADA and EMS functions	—	Employees in System Operation and Logistics	Manuals and Training Documents	Explicit	Routine	System Operations and maintenance of SCADA / EMS system
IT Hard ware and Software (Computers, Routers, UNIX etc..)	—	Employees in System Operation and Logistics	Manuals and Training Documents	Explicit	Routine	System Operations and maintenance of SCADA / EMS system

Data communication and Protocols	—	Employees in System Operation and Logistics	Manuals and Training Documents	Explicit	Routine	Network updation
Updation of Database in SCADA System		Emplayees in System Operation and Logistics	Data-base updation dacLiments	Explicit/ Tacit	Routine	Network updatian
Power Flow Solution	System Study group	Employees in System Operation and Logistics	Engineering books, periodicals, journals, internet & web groups	Explicit	Non - Routine	Basic concept of Pawer system operation needed for understanding & troubleshooting
Stability concepts	-do-	Employees in System Operation and Logistics	Engineering books, periodicals, journals, internet & web groups	Explicit	Non - Routine	—
Dynamic/ transient	-do-	Employees in System Operation and Logistics	Engineering books, periodicals, journals, internet & web groups	Explicit	Non - Routine	—
Generator Dynamics	OS Group, Design Group, Engineering group Employees in System Operation and Logistics	Engineering books, periodicals, journals, internet & web groups	Explicit	—	Non - Routine	—
HVDC concepts	-do-	Employees in System Operation and Logistics	Engineering books, periodicals, journals, internet & web groups	Explicit	Non - Routine	—

Transformer concepts	-do-	Employees in System Operation and Logistics	Engineering books, periodicals, journals, internet & web groups	Explicit	Non - Routine	—
Knowledge of Grid elements	Grid Operation group, System Study group, MIS group	Employees in System Operation and Logistics	Operational database, various reports generated by grid operation & MIS group, Bus connectivity diagrams, information received from sites	Explicit	Non - Routine	Basic knowledge on regional as well as national power system network needed for ULDC system maintenance, updates, troubleshooting & analysis
Network up to at least 132 KV level	—	Employees in System Operation and Logistics	—	Explicit	Non - Routine	—
Line length, type of conductors etc. of inportanl lines	—	Employees in System Operation and Logistics	—	Explicit	Non - Routine	—
Availability of reactors along with rating	—	Employees in System Operation and Logistics	—	Explicit	Non - Routine	—
Availability of transformers along with rating	—	Employees in System Operation and Logistics	—	Explicit	Non - Routine	—
Installed capacity. Effective capacity, of each unit	—	Employees in System Operation and Logistics	—	Explicit	Non - Routine	—

Availability of TCSC, FSC, SVC etc. along with settings	—	Employees in System Operation and Logistics	—	Explicit	Non - Routine	—
Availability of HVDC stations	—	Employees in System Operation and Logistics	—	Explicit	Non - Routine	—
Knowledge of future connectivities / elements	—	Employees in System Operation and Logistics	—	Explicit	Non - Routine	—
Creating Database for new stations	System Lagistics Department	Employees in System Operation and Logistics	Operation, Maintenance & troubleshooting manuals provided by the vendors, Training materials, Help files	Tacit	Non - Routine	Detailed knowledge of Hardware and software under ULDG scheme needed for day-to-day routine activities, new integration. Monitoring maintenance activity conducted by the vendor, knowledge sharing among constituents
Modification of existing database	—	Employees in System Operation and Logistics		Tacit	Routine	
Database administration	—	Employees in System Operation and Logistics		Tacit	Routine	
RTU integration	—	Employees in System Operation and Logistics		Tacit	Non - Routine	
Establishment of communication link	—	Employees in System Operation and Logistics		Tacit	Non - Routine	
Trouble shooting regarding communication failures	—	Employees in System Operation and Logistics		Tacit	Routine	

RTU connectivity and communication link diagram	—	Employees in System Operation and Logistics		Tacit	Non - Routine	
Creating displays	—	Employees in System Operation and Logistics		Tacit	Routine	
Storing and restoring data through various methodologies such as HIM, HABDDE, HABACCESS etc.	—	Employees in System Operation and Logistics		Tacit	Routine	
Connecting through Exceed to VMS system	—	Employees in System Operation and Logistics		Tacit	Routine	
Database Finetuning	—	Employees in System Operation and Logistics	—	Tacit	Routine	
Running EMS, DTS	—	Employees in System Operation and Logistics	—	Tacit	Routine	
Concept of ICCP	LD & C group	Employees in System Operation and Logistics	—	Explicit	Non - Routine	
Concept of RTU		Employees in System Operation and Logistics	—	Explicit	Non - Routine	
Knowledge of various other communication protocols, data flow		Employees in System Operation and Logistics	—	Explicit	Non - Routine	

Knowledge of contractual procedures, WPP, DOR	C & M group	Approving authorities as well as executing officers	WPP Vol I & II, DOP documents	Explicit	Routine	All type of procurement and administrative requirements
Handling the User Interfaces of SCADA/EMS workstation / PC	System Logistics Department	Engineers working at SCADA group, Engineers working at IT group	O & M and troubleshooting manuals, IT books, journals, internet knowledge sites	Tacit	Routine	Detailed knowledge of various uses of the ULDC scheme, maintenance of supporting systems, auxiliaries, day- to-day activities using SCADA system
Day to day checks / maintenance activities	—	—	—	Tacit	Routine	—
Updating/ creating reports	IT professionals, MIS group, Grid Operation group	—	—	Tacit	Routine	V
File movement scripts	—	—	—	Tacit	Routine	—
Updating Scheduling s/w	—	—	—	Tacit	Routine	—
Report making uploading designs	—	—	—	Tacit	Routine	—
Activity Register	—	—	—	Tacit	Routine	—
Monitoring state of system	—	—	—	Tacit	Routine	—
Analysis of Failures	—	—	—	Tacit	Routine	—
FTP, Telnet etc.	—	—	—	Explicit	Routine	—
Troubleshooting of UPS system	OEM / Supplier ergineer		O & M and troubleshooting manuals	Tacit	Routine	—
Battery bank maintenance				Tacit	Routine	—

Networking concept, LAN, WAN	IT professionals, IT Institutions	Engineers working in IT group	Books, periodicals, journals, internet a web groups, Training materials of various IT institutions, OEM Help files	Tacit	Routine	Detailed knowledge of IT infrastructure establishment, maintenance & upgradations to enable maximum availability of the IT support system
Design & Establishment of LAN/ WAN	—	—	—	Tacit	Routine	—
Router configuration	—	—	—	Tacit	Non - Routine	—
Firewall configuration	—	—	—	Tacit	Non - Routine	—
Hardware maintenance of PC, Printer etc.	—	—	—	Tacit	Routine	—
Troubleshooting on network problems	—	—	—	Tacit	Routine	—
Updated information on vendors & products related to IT	—	—	—	Explicit	Non - Routine	—
Basic programming using scripting languages such as VB script, Java Script, C# etc.	—	—	—	Tacit	Routine	Advanced knowledge at RDBMS & scripting languages aiming to wards development of automation & structured data storage
Database concept, knowledge on DBMS	—	—	—	Explicit	Non - Routine	—

<table>
<tr><td>Web page development and upgradation using ASP. Net or similar development technology</td><td>—</td><td>—</td><td>—</td><td>Tacit</td><td>Routine</td><td>—</td></tr>
<tr><td>Basic knowledge on applications like MS Excel, MS Word, MS PowerPoint, IE etc.</td><td>—</td><td rowspan="2">All employees working in System Lugistics group</td><td rowspan="2">O & M and troubleshooting manuals</td><td>Tacit</td><td>Routine</td><td rowspan="2">Day-to-day office activities. Communication system, security system etc.</td></tr>
<tr><td>Operation and maintenance of ancillary systems viz. CCTV, Access Control, VOIP, VC etc.</td><td>Engineers of respective vendors I OEM</td><td>Tacit</td><td>Routine</td></tr>
</table>

APPENDIX F

CORPORATE YELLOW PAGES
(Subject Matter Expert)

Professional Area: RLDC

Emp. No.	Name (Sh.)	Designation	E-mail	Mobile No.
50033	A.B. Sengupta	Manager	anwayasen@POSOCO.in	9433041872

Area of Specialization: SCADA / IT

Type of Expertise: Planning, design, enginnering of IT infrastructure, Web based application development, VB Macro, RLDC Market operation, Substation O & M, ISO certification

Brief Description of experience/exposure/problems faced/solutions offered/tools and Drivers used:

- Testing & commissioning of switchyard equipment
- Development of web based application for office automation, ERLDC web site, Intranet Site
- ISO certification audit (internal) for ISO 9001, 14001, 18001, 27001
- RLDC Market Operation activity such as STOA, Metering

Notable experience/significant exposure (if any):

- KRA Co-ordination, CAPEX Planning, RLDC Fees & Charges billing & collection processes.
- Certified Lead auditor for ISO 14001, 18001 & 27001 certification.
- Preparation of feasibility report & technical specification for WAMS project of ER. Development of web based scheduling application.

Professional Area: Power Market – NLDC

Emp. No.	Name (Sh.)	Designation	E-mail	Mobile No.
50024	Subhendu Mukheijee Ch	Manager	subhendu@POSOCO.in	9433041874

Area of Specialization:

Power Market Development / Power Sector reforms

Type of Expertise:

Implementation of STOA / Power Exchanges / ABT, Transmission pricing

Brief Description of experience/exposure/problems faced/solutions offered/tools and Drivers used:

- Apportionment of losses for power exchange transaction without disturbing existing scheduling mechanism. point of connection tariff was proposed for px transaction.
- Smooth implementation of multi-exchange px transaction. Detailed procedures for electronic flow of information were developed.
- Development of operating procedures for STOA for dispute free implementation. Updation of procedure and timely feedback to regulator was provided for dispute free implementation.

Notable experience/significant exposure (if any):

- Convincing stakeholders that UI is not a penalty but a commercial mechanism to improve grid discipline and a win-win situation for all stakeholders.
- Smooth implementation of multiple power exchanges in India, unique experience
- Dispute free implementation of STOA

Professional Area: RLDC

Emp. No.	Name (Sh.)	Designation	E-mail	Mobile No.
10029	M Pradeep Reddy	Manager	Pradeep.reddy@ POSOCO.in	9148034595

Area of Specialization:

GRID MANAGEMENT

Type of Expertise:

GRID MANAGEMENT, SCHEDULING AND DISPATCH

Brief Description of experience/exposure/problems faced/solutions offered/tools and Drivers used:

- REAL TIME DAY TO DAY OPERATION OF SOUTHERN REGION AND INTEGRATED OPERATION NEW GRID
- CO-ORDINATION AND PLANNING FOR SHUT DOWN OF GENERATORS AND TRANSMISSION ELEMENTS
- PREPARATION OF GENERATOR AND DISPATCH SCHEDULE

Notable experience/significant exposure (if any):

- GRID MANAGEMENT

Professional Area: NLDC

Emp. No.	Name (Sh.)	Designation	E-mail	Mobile No.
10034	Phanisankar Chilukuri	Manager	pchilukuri@POSOCO.in	8527908282

Area of Specialization:

Power System Simulation

Type of Expertise:

Application of PSS/E software

Brief Description of experience/exposure/problems faced/solutions offered/tools and Drivers used:

- Calculation of ATC/TTC
- Design of new special protection scheme
- Dynamic simulation

Professional Area: RLDC

Emp. No.	Name (Sh.)	Designation	E-mail	Mobile No.
20036	Riza Naqvi	Manager	riza.naqvi@POSOCO.in	9650480505

Area of Specialization:

Power System Simulation

Type of Expertise:

Application of PSS/E software for carrying out system studies

Brief Description of experience/exposure/problems faced/solutions offered/tools and Drivers used:

- Regular Calculation of Inter Regional ATC/TTC
- Designing of logic for Special Protection Schemes (SPS)
- Dynamic simulation

Professional Area: SCADA & IT - NLDC

Emp. No.	Name (Sh.)	Designation	E-mail	Mobile No.
10030	Mohneesh Rastogi	Manager	mohneesh@POSOCO.in	7042892660

Area of Specialization:

SCADA system design

Type of Expertise:

Design and Operation & maintenance of SCADA/EMS system for Load dispatch centers

Brief Description of experience/exposure/problems faced/solutions offered/tools and Drivers used:

- Design of SCADA system for NLDC Substation automation.
- Operation, maintenance and upgradation of NR-complete SCADA-EMS system.
- Responsible for implementation of the state of art Unified Load Dispatch and communication scheme- an elaborate scheme involving SCADA and EMS system so far the most modern in world.
- System Study for system improvement, contingency analysis for the Grid operation.

Notable experience/significant exposure (if any):

- Implementation and Operation and maintenance of SCADA & EMS system of NLDC

Professional Area: MO, EASS – RLDC

Emp. No.	Name (Sh.)	Designation	E-mail	Mobile No.
50019	Nadim Ahmad	CM	nadim@POSOCO.in	9432351831

Area of Specialization:

Market Operation & Grid Management

Type of Expertise:

Energy Accounting and settlement system

Brief Description of experience/exposure/problems faced/solutions offered/tools and Drivers used:

- Co-ordination with regional constituents for smooth transaction of Special Energy Meter
- SEM data processing, validation, Regional loss Computation
- Preparation of Future requirements of meter
- Dispute Free UI disbursement, VAR Disbursement

Notable experience/significant exposure (if any):

- UI Reconciliation
- Internal Auditor for ISO 9001:2000, OHSAS 18001:2007, ISO 14001:2004, IMS

Professional Area: EASS - RLDC

Emp. No.	Name (Sh.)	Designation	E-mail	Mobile No.
20048	Prashant Garg Dy	Manager	prashant.garg@ POSOCO.in	8800557136

Area of Specialization:

Market Operation function e.g., Energy Accounting & Settlement System, Open Access etc.

Type of Expertise:

Grid Management, Market Operation function

Brief Description of experience/exposure/problems faced/solutions offered/tools and Drivers used:

- Energy Accounting & settlement System department. Efforts were made to automate the Metering System and Settlement system.
- Worked in Grid Management in RLDC.
- Worked in MIS Department. Archiving of data pertaining to system operation of RLDC.

Printed by Libri Plureos GmbH in Hamburg,
Germany

9 789390 011681